For Dia

Hai

Beautiful

Life!

CURSE OF THE FIRST BITE

1 August 2014

STAN

Cover and book design: Mr.Hales
Cover illustration: *Curse of the First Bite* by David LaBounty

Curse of the First Bite

An Epic Poem

by

Stanley Victor Paskavich

Oh, what a cold, bone-chilling night,

without any clouds and the moon in full sight.

Why is she out there, walking all alone?

She should be tucked warmly in her home,

with safety and security of all the four walls,

hidden behind the door where nobody calls.

There's something that's beckoning to her

deeply in her mind, but it seems as a blur.

Oh, the sensation that calls, so sweet,

touches emotions she keeps discreet.

Oh, the yearning she's feeling within

burns so deeply under her skin.

Each streetlight Anna passes, her emotions ignite,

going higher and higher on this mystical plight.

She thought, "What is this that's calling to me?"

Her mind says, "Stop," but her heart says, "Go see,"

pounding ever faster with each step she takes.

She pleads, "God, please don't let this be a mistake.

I'm wearing the best clothes I own,

going somewhere into the unknown.

My mind is racing to and fro,

yet my heart says 'You must go.'"

There's a woman ahead. She's walking Anna's way,

dressed in black with a scarf that looks gray.

Should she talk to her or just pass her by?

As she got closer, Anna believed she would try.

"Hello, miss, isn't it a cold night tonight?"

She said, "It's lovely. All the bats are in flight."

Anna thought to herself, "What a strange thing to say.

It's the nineteenth of December. All the bats are away."

As she passed, the woman hummed a tune,

instantly Anna felt sensations of doom.

She turned to run, and her ankle gave way,

there on the sidewalk in pain she did lay.

She tried not to yell out, but the pain was so bad,

she let out a scream and felt very sad.

As Anna lay sobbing she felt someone near,

and looked over her shoulder and shuddered in fear.

At first glance he seemed to be a foe,

but when he spoke her heart started to glow.

His voice was serene and removed all her pain,

although she still wondered what direction he came.

Anna stood up and her ankle felt fine.

she brushed off her dress and calmed her poor mind.

The gentleman asked, "Are you okay?"

She replied, "No, this is a strange day."

He said, "Isn't it late for you be out here alone?

If you need, ma'am, I'll walk you back home."

The calmness of his voice gave Anna security.

Anna said, "Sure, walking me home would be alright with me."

He held her hand. She felt his grip, it was cold and icy,

but inside of her heart was a warmth that ran free.

She didn't think anything of it because it was so cold,

and for her to trust a stranger was something quite bold.

But the tender words that he spoke as they walked along,

seemed to be melodies from a long-forgotten song.

They walked and talked about life and love with every step back to her door.

She opened it as he stood patiently near and put one foot on the floor.

He asked, "You want me to come in, don't you?"

Anna answered, "Yes," before she really knew.

"Oh, this is so strange," she thought deep within her mind.

He said, "I'll just stay a bit," as he looked at the time.

Anna went and made some coffee to take off the cold night chill,

and offered him a steaming cup. He said, "I don't believe I will."

He asked, "Is that your piano? Do you mind if I play?"

She said, "If you like. It's gathered dust since my mother went away."

He opened up the keys and gently tapped on them;

the music seemed like a long lost friend.

Anna started to dance inside, feeling a loving groove,

then her whole body shook and her feet began to move.

It was like a ballet that she had always known,

this man had brought life into a once-dismal home.

She thought, "Oh, can it be that us two strangers that have met, are connected in ways that two lovers never get?"

Once again her mind was overpowered by her heart.

The man stood up, then kissed Anna, and said, "I must depart."

All of a sudden her world crashed, and she asked, "Will I see you again?"

He said, "Yes, you may just call my name in the wind."

Then it occurred to her that they had never said their names,

all the walking and talking was like a cheerful, childish game.

She burst out, "My name is Ann, actually Anna Marie."

He said, "My name is Raphael," all so gingerly.

Raphael was a name she had seldom heard,

as it burned deep inside as an unspoken word.

He said, "Right now I must go, but we will meet soon again,

tomorrow night in the park where the tree creaks from within."

He bent and kissed her tenderly and gently bit her lip,

her breasts up-heaved with emotion burning down to the hips.

This was a sensation she hadn't felt in years,

as he walked out the door her eyes filled with tears.

She stood and thought, "Will I ever see him again?"

She jerked the door open, but he was gone like the wind.

He had disappeared as fast as he had appeared when they met, but that was no concern, loneliness is now what she regrets.

She thought, "Will this man ever come back to me again,

or will I be lonely forever, calling his name to the wind?"

It's been so long since she's had a date,

She sets her table with only one plate.

"Raphael, Raphael," Anna cried to the new dawn,

there was no reply and she began to yawn.

She closed the door and went to her bed,

laying there hearing the words he had said.

Trembling with passion, thinking of his kiss,

imagining things many would call bliss.

Oh, how he looked in his suit and his cape,

that vision is a thought she cannot escape.

Anna pulled the covers over her head wishing it was nightfall,

pretending to be in the park, and Raphael she did call.

As she uttered his name under the bedspread,

in the darkness all alone in her cold bed,

she envisioned the next time the two of them would meet,

and the deep-felt emotion from her head to her feet.

Anna could hear his tender voice and kind words he'd say

and, with this loving feeling, she drifted away.

She awoke to someone knocking at the front door.

Anna was still in her nice clothes from the night before.

She opened the door to hear a woman say, "Don't you have a date?

All of you silly mortals really do sleep so late."

Rubbing her eyes to get a good look at her,

all she saw was an outline, of a woman as a blur.

It shocked her so quickly she slammed the door and locked it.

The lady said, "Raphael's waiting, so don't you forget."

She thought to herself "Raphael, that name, so it wasn't a dream..."

Her thoughts were so jumbled she wanted to scream.

Walking back into the living room she did see,

The piano open with it's eighty-eight keys.

Remembering each note Raphael had played,

deep in her heart the sensations had stayed.

The clock in her mother's room chimed twelve A.M.

She changed her clothes and left like the wind.

Anna wondered why she had slept so long in bed.

Was it the love and compassionate words he had said?

On the way walking to the town park nearby,

Anna's heart was racing and her emotions did fly.

"Raphael," she whispered quietly to the wind,

hoping to find the tree that creaked from within.

She asked herself, "What did Raphael mean by that?"

Anna found a park bench and down she sat.

Tonight the moon was tucked away,

under dark skies with a hint of blue-gray.

She sat and listened to the sounds of the night:

dogs barking, crickets chirping and cats in a fight.

Then, all of a sudden, all the sound went away.

She seemed to hear footsteps coming her way.

She thought, "This is a bad place to be out all alone,"

and the visions her mind played chilled her to the bone.

Anna stood up to run back to her house, so nearby,

then she heard, "Anna Marie," and tears of joy she did cry.

She yelled back, "Raphael, is that you, my friend?"

the reply was just leaves rustling in the wind.

She yelled his name until she was out of breath,

and felt the pain of a living death.

Now she knows why she's done little things with her life,

because when you lose a friend it cuts like a knife.

She exclaimed, "Mother, dear mother, where can you be?

Why did you take that trip on the sea?

I know it sounded good, winning that trip as a prize,

and the odds of the boat sinking you didn't realize.

But now you're gone, and it's been such a long time,

almost seven years you've been nowhere to find.

In my mind you'll always be alive;

your love and compassion will always survive.

A couple more days you'll be declared officially dead,

at that point I know your will, will be read.

I'd rather have you alive and giving your love so free,

more than the fortune that you have left for me.

Money! Money! What a terrible thing!

It torments the paupers and corrupts the king."

Just as those words escaped her thought,

a woman appeared and a message she brought.

She said to Anna, "Hello. I'm Lyra, Raphael's friend."

The sound of his name echoed in the wind.

Anna looked at her closely, well as close as one could.

She reminded Anna of a statue carved out of wood.

She was in the shadows, yet stood quite near,

but Anna didn't really sense any fear.

She actually looked like the woman from the night before,

the one that hummed the tune filling her soul with horror.

Anna asked her, "Haven't we met? You seem familiar to me,"

She said, "Last night, that was my sister you did see."

Lyra's voice was kind. She seemed so like a friend,

then she said, "Raphael's waiting. Let our journey begin."

Raphael, Raphael, his named burned in her heart.

Lyra took Anna's hand and the journey did start.

They walked and walked, and she said not a thing,

but she whistled a tune that made Anna's heart sing.

Anna asked, "Lyra, what is that tune that you know?"

She replied, "It's an old song from many years ago."

The two of them walked all around in the park

as she whistled her tune, sweet as a lark.

They stopped walking near a dead, old oak tree.

Then Lyra said, "Close your eyes; and count to three."

Anna whispered softly, "One, two," then, "three," she did say,

thinking, "Hide and seek, what a strange game to play."

Before she opened her eyes, someone's hands covered them,

and Raphael said "Guess who?" and she was with him again.

Oh, how quickly she turned to the one she had missed.

He spoke her name passionately, then they kissed.

He turned and said to Lyra, "Don't you have some place to be?"

She answered, "Yes, I must be going. It's a quarter to three."

Lyra was counting one, two, three as she walked away.

Anna thought to herself, "What a strange thing to say."

She had so many questions in her mind that were racing within,

as she stood in Raphael's embrace throwing caution to the wind.

There was one question Anna just had to ask Raphael,

she blurted it out it so fast it seemed like she yelled.

She asked, "Raphael, Raphael, what's happening to me?

I haven't felt so loved since I was about three."

He said, "Anna Marie, look deep in my eyes,

that is the true place your answer lies."

At first she saw his black pupils in the night,

then she saw things like a play in full sight.

There they were: dancing, holding each other near,

in a giant ball room with all the ones she loved dear.

Oh, the sensations of what Anna was feeling,

twirling around under the chandelier on the ceiling.

It took her oh, so far away

from the terrible life in which she stay.

Then, "Anna, Anna," Raphael said passionately,

tearing her from the peace that ran so freely.

"What was that vision I saw deep in your eyes?

It looked like a place where no one ever cries."

Raphael then said, "Tears are for the weak,

they make your life empty, and your heart feel so bleak.

There were times long ago that I did cry,

now I have told my emotions 'Goodbye.'

I have what I have, and I want what I get,

and for this I haven't any regret.

Outside I'm loving and caring to friends,

inside I'm dead, without any sins.

If you can accept this of me,

I know the way to set you free.

Free from this lonely life that you live;

free from a world that won't ever give.

Takers and takers are all that exist,

some of their heads are on the top of my list."

The words he spoke were, oh, so true,

Anna's heart beat in ways she never knew.

Then he said, "Anna, I can take you away from all of this,

and all it takes will be one sweet, deep kiss.

A kiss filled with energy,

bonding us eternally."

He held Anna close and put his lips to her neck.

Closing her eyes, she did not object.

Emotions flooded all over her body,

her blood was boiling and surging so free.

Just as the highest point of her desire,

from Anna's intrinsic sensual fire,

a voice called out and said, "Hey! You two!"

It was an officer dressed in blue.

He yelled, "The park's closed at night,"

and startled Raphael with his flashlight.

This gave Raphael some disgust,

as it extinguished his fiery lust.

He walked up to them and asked, "Can I see some ID?"

Raphael said, "It's a lovely park, now you can play free."

The officer said, "Yes," then began to sing,

then walked to the playground and grabbed a swing.

As he started swinging and laughing like a child,

it seemed that his mind had now gone wild.

Anna looked at Raphael and asked, "What did you do?"

He answered, "That's not any concern to you.

Now lets get back to where we were."

Then her emotions again did stir.

For a second Raphael did take her away,

but then Anna's mind drifted quite astray.
Astray from the love and compassion she felt,
and wondered what cards she was being dealt.
She pushed Raphael away so quickly,
he said, "Come back. I'll set you free."
He stretched out his arms with an angry face,
and said, "Next to me will be your place."
Then Anna knew what she felt was all wrong,
but Raphael's persuasion was, oh, so strong.
He whispered Anna's name into the night.
She broke free and ran with all of her might.
She didn't get far from Raphael's wrath
when she saw Lyra in front of her path.
With her sister from the night before,
she said "Hello. I believe you've met Lenore."
The two of them let out an evil shriek.
Anna's mind was ill, and her heart went weak.
"Oh God, what have I gotten into," Anna said.
The sisters replied, "A world full of dread.
A place you'll beg for death each day,
with a thirst that won't ever go away."
Lenore said, "Poor, poor Anna Marie,
the one with a fortune she'll never see."
"So that's it," Anna said to the both of them,
"You're after my money, but you'll never win."
"Never," Lenore said. "That's such a strange word.

For an eternal being it's kind of absurd."

The fear and gloom deeply began to set in.

The sisters called Raphael's name again and again.

Anna turned and ran till she was out of breath,

fearing what they called a "living death."

She stopped near the swings to find the officer,

and saw him on the ground, and her mind did stir.

He seemed to be lifeless—all pale and white

with two puncture marks on his neck in sight.

"Vampires!" She thought, "oh, this can't be true!"

But the bite on his neck was the thing they all do.

Now her mind was really starting to spin,

"Am I in a battle that I'll never win?

Is this just a plot meant to control my mind,

and drive me insane because of that fortune of mine?

Insanity, hmm, I know that realm well...

It's quite similar to a living hell;

where depression and obsession control your life,

with the only escape are some pills or a knife.

Oh, these three might have met their match,

I don't plan to be easy prey they can catch.

I've never believed in Vampires before,

I guess that just shows, in life, there is more.

More than one can ever believe,

more than one can ever perceive,

more than one ever wants to know,

and more than the mind will ever show.

Okay, now get a hold of yourself, Anna Marie.

You need to think how to get away free.

Oh, my purse! I'm glad I brought it!

Inside is my cross I never forget.

My mother gave it to me when I was quite young,

to protect me from harm and bad things that could come.

She said it would keep me safe one day,"

Anna put the necklace around her neck and started to pray.

Clasping the cross with all of her might,

closing her eyes, oh, so tight.

She prayed to Jesus and God up above,

for some guidance and protection of love.

When Anna opened her eyes, Raphael was standing near.

He taunted, "You think you've won, don't you, my dear?"

At first she was speechless and then she did say,

"In the name of Jesus, I cast you away."

He laughed out loud in a rather hideous tone.

He said, "You can't use Jesus, your heart is pure stone.

Oh, now, Anna Marie, we've got off on a bad start.

Come to me, and let us become one heart."

Oh, once again the passion set in

from Raphael's words, so soft in the wind.

Anna's mind was in terror, but her heart was aglow.

He said, "Come, my love, it's time for the show."

She walked over to him with no will of her own,

her heart was racing, but her mind did groan.

Then as he bent tenderly to give Anna a kiss,

she pressed the cross to his forehead, and it made a hiss.

Back he jumped and shrieked in the night,

the cross burned his forehead and gave him a fright.

All of a sudden Anna felt very strong within.

She whispered, "Thank you, God, for being my friend."

No sooner than he shrieked, Lyra and Lenore were there.

He looked at Lenore and said, "Let me bite you some where."

Lenore bent and surrendered her neck eagerly,

he sank his fangs in her neck and said, "You can't hurt me."

The cross burn had now faded away.

Raphael then said, "Let all of us play."

The three of them surrounded Anna. She felt like it was the end.

But, to their surprise, the new dawn started to begin.

The women shrieked, and Raphael roared.

They turned into bats, and away they soared.

Taking with them the new member of their clan,

flying towards home with the paralyzed policeman.

Anna ran as fast as she could,

but she was drawn to the creaking of wood.

She went to the oak and put her ear to the bark,

closed her eyes and listened in the last glimpse of dark.

The tree seemed to creak from within,

almost like a voice she'd known as a friend.

The more she listened to the dead, old oak tree,

the clearer the creaks and squeaks came to be.

She could almost make out her name

when a voice said, "Hey lady, are you insane?"

"That old tree's dead and hollow within,

the branches are rotten and fall with the wind."

Anna saw that the sun was much brighter now,

and several hours had been lost somehow.

Then she noticed a big red X on the hollow, dead thing

and the closer the man got, the tree seemed to sing.

He had a helmet, some gloves, and a chainsaw in his hand,

some spurs to climb the tree once large and so grand.

"I work for a tree service," the man did say.

"I have to take this one from the top; it's the only way.

Now it's time I started to work on this old gal,

it's been dead seven years." He looked up and said, "Wow!

This one's going to take some time to take down,

it's not only tall but quite big around."

Anna said to him, "Be careful and good luck."

Then two others arrived in a big truck.

She walked away towards her home,

trying to tell her mind not to roam.

In the park she could hear the chainsaw.

The tree seemed to cry out; Anna was filled with awe.

She unlocked her door and went in,

wondering if Raphael would be back again.

She's heard all the stories about Vampires,

from their weaknesses to their unholy desires.

"I'll be safe until the sunset,

until then I'll try not to fret.

Right now I need all of my mind intact,

this fear can destroy me, and that's a fact.

I'll make a list of all the things I need,

to protect me from Raphael and his evil seed.

Do I have the power to conquer this beast,

or will I become a pet or his feast?"

She looked at her mother's painting on the wall

and said, "It Illuminates me for my chosen call.

Now what are the things that I'll need

to conquer this beast and his greed?

Okay let's see: stakes, I need three of them,

sharpened to a point to be driven within.

Crosses, yes crosses, I need all I have here,

even the ones made for my ears.

Oh, I've had it! The game is now to begin,

I have hatred and vengeance flowing within.

I can't wait to see Raphael tonight,

I'll be ready for one hell of a fight.

Where's my black boots and my long, black, leather coat?
For tonight I must battle and not be slain like a goat.
It's not about the money I'm supposed to get.
I've been betrayed; something I'll not forget.
Most of my life I've been betrayed by men,
I'll be ready for my Vampire and both of his friends.
All of my life people have taken advantage of me,
now these three Vampires will have something to see.
I have not the option to let fear in my brain.
That is where many people are slain.
Oh, those two bitches are on the top of my list,
let's see them whistle or hum as they kiss my fist!
I need to bathe and have something to eat,
and create my plan for those I must defeat."
"Oh, damn!" Anna exclaimed, "What day is it today?
No, it can't be that day!
On top of everything that I have going on,
today is the day! What else can go wrong?
Where's that letter the lawyer wrote me
about reading mother's will, and what time it will be?"
She scurried about dumping everything out,
and in total frustration Anna let out a shout.
"Oh, why, why! is all this happening to me?
Vampires and torment, how do I get free?
Okay, Anna, think where you put that letter.
If I find it, I might feel a little better,"

she thought to herself,

it was on the top of a shelf

of that old cabinet her mom had.

Anna found it, she cried and felt very sad.

"Oh, now this is the day they declare mom legally dead.

For seven years I've prayed she'd come home instead."

She opened the letter and read it again looking for the time,

in the footnote the lawyer said, "Around five will be fine."

"Five, five, oh, that can't be done,

when I get home there won't be any sun.

Oh, now what should I do about this thing?"

She called the attorney, and the phone did just ring.

"Damn, damn, to Hell with it all!"

Then she heard someone from the park yelling "She's ready to fall!"

Anna peeked out her window and could see the oak tree,

wobbling back and forth yet still standing free.

She heard one of the workers say, "She's not cut all the way through."

The other one said, "This is my biggest bar. Now what do we do?"

It sounded like someone said, "Shit! We'll have to come back again.

It should be okay tonight, there won't be very much wind."

She saw the three men load up what they had cut.

They jumped in the truck and away they did putt.

Anna thought to herself, "What a comical show,"

and a small bit of laughter gave her a slight glow.

"Well I guess I have no choice but to take a chance.

I'll go to the will reading in a vigilant stance.

Blue jeans and a shirt is all I will wear;

I'll dress for comfort, will anyone care?

Besides, this might be my last day alive,

if I fall prey when Raphael and the sisters arrive.

Screw it, I'll go and hear mother's will read,

I'll hang a cross on my door for the undead.

Okay, I'm dressed, now where's my car keys?

I'm such a mess! God, help me please...

Damn it," she screamed, "this ain't my fucking day!"

She looked at the table, and her keys there did lay.

Anna took the keys and a large crucifix out the door,

along with her purse, and three stakes she made from her floor.

She kissed the crucifix and put it under her rug

and thought, "Stand on this, you unholy thug!"

She ran to her car, got in and locked it up tight,

started the motor quickly and drove out of sight.

Just as she was leaving the giant oak tree gave way,

it crashed in the park after the three men drove away.

Thinking for a second it could have been a tragedy,

all the children were in school, so it fell safe and free.

Anna turned on the radio to calm her mind down,

only sad songs were on the stations she found.

Then the song "Rebel Yell" started to play.

She thought, "How appropriate for this day."

Anna and Billy rocked 'til she was at her destination,

then pain was now the only real sensation.

She turned off the engine, got out, and locked her car up tight.

The lawyer met her on the steps and said, "Are you alright?"

She thought for a second, "What should I say to him?

No matter what choice; my options are grim.

Vampires! I can just hear him look at me and say, 'Wow!'

Then pick up the phone and say, 'I need an ambulance, now.'"

Anna said, "I'm fine. I just have had a bad day,

can we get this done and see what mom had to say?"

They walked to his office, and they both sat down.

He began to read as she looked at the ground.

He said, "This is lengthy but I've studied it well,

why don't you read it at home and see what your mom had to tell.

Everything's yours. You're in total control,

there wasn't any other living soul."

Anna thanked him then ran out to her car as fast as she could,

stuffed the will in her purse with the slats of wood.

Anna started the engine and spun right around,

trying to get home before the sun went down.

She was almost there when a siren gave her a fright,

in her rear view mirror were red and blue lights in her sight.

Anna thought to herself "I'm so close to home now,"

she floored the gas and into her lawn plowed.

Anna woke a few moments later with a bump on her head,

the cop stood at her window, and his face was all red.

"Now, Anna, look what you've done," as he was pointing the blame.

Then she thought to herself, "How does he know my name?"

He said, "This is a mess. Look at yourself now,

Raphael will be angry if I don't restrain you somehow."

The sun was setting and he said, "Get out of the damn car."

Anna did and made a run for it; her house wasn't that far.

She made it to her door with the cop close behind,

yelling, "Stop, Anna, you're a prisoner of mine!"

"Prisoner? Prisoner! Oh, I'll show you prisoner," she said.

They wrestled around, his gun went off, and he was dead.

She realized how he knew her, she'd met him before,

He looked the same in the park as he did near her door.

Anna thought, "Oh, now look what I have done!

I've got blood on my hands, and I'm holding his gun."

Anna dragged the cop inside, and on her floor he did lay,

as she sat with her hands on her face, and did silently pray.

Then she pulled her car out of the yard and parked his in the back,

locked herself in the house awaiting Raphael's attack.

She could just see the newspaper headline,

"Billionaire heiress loses her mind!"

Now the sun had disappeared.

The moments were coming that she'd feared.

She asked herself, "What should I do,

to ban Raphael and the other two?"

She quickly wrote a note for her door,

preparing for the night of horror.

It read, "Raphael I rescind your invite,"

hoping this would keep him out in the night.

Anna opened the door just a very small crack,

stuck the note on the door with tape on the back.

Then locking the door as quickly as she could,

she said, "That will keep him out," knocking on wood.

She took the three stakes and went to her easy chair,

turned on the tube and watched with a blank stare.

Running yesterday's events in her mind,

asking herself, "Why," time after time.

Anna must have fallen asleep because the clock struck ten,

with every single chime she vibrated within.

There was not a sign of Raphael so far,

then she remembered the cop and his car.

Anna thought to herself, "What should I do,

about the this dead man dressed in blue?"

Now was the time to conceal their deadly fight,

under the cover of the blanket of night.

But in order to try and cover up what had taken place,

she'd have to go outside with the possibility of Vampires to face.

Then there came a tap at the door,

suddenly, Anna was filled with horror.

She looked out the peep hole and saw only black,

is this Raphael and his specters' pending attack?

Then a voice called out, "Anna Marie,"

it sounded like her mother but this cannot be.

"Raphael, I know it's you outside. I'm not a fool."

The voice said, "Anna, remember your first day in school?

Ask me some questions that only I would know the answer to.

Then, after you're sure it's me, I'll reveal my new self to you."

New self, hmm, that idea burned in Anna's mind.

What is beyond the door for her to actually find?

Anna thought and thought, again and again,

"Will all of this confusion ever end?"

Then the voice asked, "Tinker Bell, Tinker Bell, remember that name?

And back when I called you Gertrude, it drove you insane?

Oh, Anna, oh, Anna, it's truly me here outside of your door.

Remember your first glasses? You looked in the mirror with great horror.

Yes, I know everything there is to know about you,

open the door so I can reveal my true self to you.

When I changed I was sixty-four years old,

now I have a lovely new form to behold.

I look more like I was at only twenty-three,

just like in the painting over the mantle of me.

Remember that oak tree that fell in the park?

I stayed seven years inside of it in the dark.

My grandmother and I planted that tree.

We set it in the soil when I was three.

It's roots went down and down, and it did grow,

from the power of the Underworld so far below.

When I was on that cruise, just before it went down,

I transformed into a locust and flew to safe ground.

Then I came back here to rest from my trip,

into a knot hole in the oak I did slip.

I buried myself deep in the heart of the tree,

waiting for the day I would be set free.

Slowly I drained energy from the giant oak,

as it creaked from within it's life I did choke."

Anna screamed, "Stop! You're no mother to me!

The things that you say could never be!"

Then the voice said, "Anna, Anna, my lovely dear,

open your heart and listen without fear.

Our family has quite a deep, hidden gift."

When Anna heard that, her curiosity did lift.

"Okay, Mom, if that's who you are, I have a question for you:

What happened to me when I was only two?

If you answer that question correctly, I'll open the door,

but before I do you'll have to tell me lots more."

"Yes, my dear, when you were two,

remember that fire you lived through?

Your doll you called Alice, do you remember her?

What about the dog we called Champ? He was quite a cur.

And the first time you went to the prom,

all dressed up with that hillbilly named Tom?

What about the first time I let you drive?

You almost hit a semi, thank God we survived!

Oh, Anna, I can go on and on about you!

I know every moment of life you've been through."

"Mother," Anna said "I'm confused and so afraid,

can I trust that it's you and not be betrayed?"

"Anna, go grab one of the stakes that you've made,

if I'm not your mother, plunge it into my heart like a spade."

Anna grabbed the door knob with a stake in her hand,

wondering if this could be the right plan.

She jerked the door open and to her surprise,

there stood Raphael with red, glowing eyes

Anna took the stake and plunged it deep in his heart,

he gave her a smile, and a transformation did start.

Slowly Raphael melted away just like sand,

Then, in front of Anna, her mother did stand.

Anna's mother said, "You've conquered your fear for now.

That was just an illusion to show you how.

Raphael's been around for such a long time,

it will take some of my powers to keep him in line."

Then she said, "Yes, Anna, it's really me.

I know that I look like I'm twenty-three.

This is a power that you one day can possess,

but for now let's worry about all of this mess."

She looked at the dead officer laying on the floor,

said a few strange words, and he was no more.

Right where the policeman had just been

was a knight's armor that was empty within.

Anna's mother said "I've converted one of Raphael's legion to mine,

now lets go outside and turn his police car into some vines."

Her mother said a few words once again,

then the car turned to vines blowing free in the wind.

"Mother," Anna said, "what is this that you do?

Is it some kind of witchcraft coming from you?"

She smiled sincerely and let out a giggle,

she laughed so hard she started to wiggle.

Then she said "Anna, dear Anna, I'm not a witch,

my powers come from a whole different branch of that
switch.

Remember those stories we would often read,

about knights in armor fighting man's greed?

Remember the magicians and sorcerers?

I'm a sorceress holding spells and great cures.

Okay, now let's go in and let the vines do their thing.

Before they're done growing they'll surround this house in
a ring."

When they got back to the front of the house,

Mother made the officer's blood become a mouse.

"Wow!" Anna exclaimed. "Is there anything you can't do?"

"Yes, I can't keep harm away permanently from you.

There will be a time when you have to make a choice,

to be yourself or become part of one voice.

In order for me to bear you, my dear Anna Marie,

I had to give up most of my powers, you see.

For so many years I was growing old and wasting away,

it took seven years to get most of my powers back to stay.

That's enough about me, Anna, how have you been?"

Anna answered, "Quite lonely and without a true friend.

I tried dating, but no one could be true,

they were just after the money I was getting from you.

Now that you're back, I feel such a great relief!

The things that you have done removed some of my grief.

But Mother, what now? Everyone thinks that you're dead,"

"Well, I'm no longer Katherine, I'll go by Ingrid instead.

Ingrid, your friend from Germany.

We met in college. Tell the others you see.

Speaking of others, you've been a recluse too long,

let's go have a few drinks and hear a few songs."

"Mother, are you forgetting about Raphael and the other two?"

"Anna, you'll be safe as long as I am with you.

Now don't worry and let's go have some fun,

The bars are still open. Quickly, let's run!"

Anna grabbed the stakes to take them with her.

Ingrid said, "Before the night's over, you'll trust your mother.

Now drop those old stakes, and let's go paint the town,

I've got a thirst I must try to drown.

Alcohol isn't the only thing I need,

my loins are on fire and begging for seed."

They walked out the door, and Anna locked it up tight,

then went to the car, Mom said, "What a sight.

Anna, this old wrecked car just will not do."

She said, "Tsk, tsk, tsk," and the car was brand new.

Wow, this was really starting to be a lot of fun!

Ingrid said, "Start the motor and listen to her hum."

As Anna turned the car around,

and pointed it towards the town,

the head lights hit the vines that had grown,

encompassing everything that they owned.

The sorceress said "Don't worry, just drive right through,

the vines will yield the path to you."

Anna drove ahead and the vines gave way,

then her mother and she were off to play.

It seemed like an instant, and they were in town.

Ingrid said, "Let's see if there's any naughty boys to be found."

Anna looked at her and said, "You sound like you're horny."

Ingrid replied, "You'd be too, if you spent seven years in a tree.

Pull up to that bar that's called the Dead End.

Let's go in and see if we can make a new friend."

Just as they both went through the door,

Anna saw Tom up on the dance floor.

He made eye contact and started towards Anna Marie.

Ingrid said, "You've caught one already, I see."

Anna said to Mom before he got where they were,

"He tried to swindle me. He's not very pure."

Mom said, "Oh, just my favorite kind of man."

One could tell by her eyes she was making a plan.

Tom walked up, and said, "How do you do?"

Anna said, "This is my friend Ingrid. I already know you!"

He could tell by the way she had said that to him,

that they wouldn't ever be together again.

"Ingrid," he said, "what a lovely, sensual name,"

Anna knew right then, he'd play into her mother's game.

Tom said, "Let's grab a table and talk a while,"

Mom said, "Sure," with a devilish smile.

They sat at a table in the back of the club,

Tom's hand was on Ingrid's leg, and he started to rub.

She said, "Whoa! Tom, you don't waste any time!"

Tom moved his hand and asked the waitress for wine.

"Ingrid and Anna, what flavor would you like?"

Mom put her hand in his crotch, and his voice it did hike.

"What's the matter, Tom? Can't two play this game?"

He tried to think of an answer that wouldn't sound lame.

Then he said, "I like a woman that's not a cold fish."

Tom smirked at Anna. The sorceress replied, "Make a wish.

But be careful what you ask for, because wishes can be a curse,

they can wreck your life, or let you end up in a hearse."

Inside, Tom was thinking, "I'd like to screw you."

Then Ingrid replied to him, "Is that what you want to do?"

Tom said to her, "Whatever do you mean?"

Ingrid replied, "Let's go outside, the night's so serene.

Anna, I'll be back when I've had my fill.

Just sit here, relax and try to chill."

She watched the two of them walk out the door,

and looked at the people on the dance floor.

"Ingrid," Tom said when they were outside,

"I haven't seen you around, where do you hide?"

Ingrid said, "Tom, let's drop the small talk,

show me you're a real man or I'm going to walk."

Tom bent down, kissed her and grabbed her right breast.

She said, "That's a nice start, I hope you live through my test."

Ingrid held Tom's hand and opened the back door of Anna's car.

She said, "Get in the seat we're not driving very far."

She pushed Tom down on the seat and said, "Get ready,"

then pulled out his cock and started sucking it steady.

He grabbed her head and began to push it down,

she started humming, an interesting sound.

"Oh, my God!" Tom exclaimed into the night,

his body was trembling in total delight.

Ingrid kept sucking and sucking some more,

humming all the while, Tom was in his galore.

Then Tom said, "I can't stop," and pushed Ingrid's head all the way down.

Ingrid bit his dick, spit it out, and said, "There's a new girl in town.

You'll no longer use women like you did my friend Anna Marie,

and, if you want to climax, it will be only with me."

She sat up, smiled, and licked her teeth wickedly in delight,

as Tom laid there limp and in pain, Ingrid yelled, "What a night!"

Then she said, "You silly, silly, selfish, little boy,

For what you did to Anna, I'll make you my toy.

Now put that thing away and zip up your pants,

lets go back in the club it's time for a dance."

Tom said, "Fuck you, all you are is a whore bitch!"

Then Ingrid's tone of voice made an evil switch.

"Look," she said to Tom with a deep raspy voice,

"I can be nice or be mean; I'll give you the choice."

Once again Tom called her a whore, and then a cunt,

that became a very painful, excruciating stunt.

Every muscle in his body was now in pain,

and the worst centered in his favorite membrane.

He screamed in agony with all of his breath.

Ingrid said, "Play my game, or the next step will be death."

Tom did his best to utter, "Okay."

Then in a flash, the pain was away.

"Well, Tom," Ingrid asked, "Would you like to be my friend?

And if you don't, I can bring the pain back again."

Tom nodded and mumbled, "Yes," in total despise.

Ingrid said, "I'd better not hear you say any lies.

Talk to me and Anna only when you are spoken to,

or I'll give you the worst pain that you ever knew.

Oh, by the way, the pain? That terrible pain that you felt

was the pain of the women you've wronged, and the cards
you have dealt.

Now, let's go back in, I'm in the mood for a dance

and you'd better not move like you have lead in your pants."

Inside they walked, holding each others' hand.

Ingrid said to Anna, "Tom's become a brand new man."

Tom just looked and didn't say anything at all.

The bartender yelled, "It's time for last call!"

"Get us both a drink, Tommy-boy," Ingrid said.

Tom headed to the bar, and his face was blood red.

"Give me two wines please," Tom said to the barmaid.

She looked at Tom, and said, "You look so afraid."

Tom asked, "Who is that bitch with the red hair,

sitting with Anna over there in that chair?"

The barmaid responded, "I haven't seen her in here before."

Ingrid cleared her throat and stood up on the floor.

She yelled, "Tommy! Tommy-boy, my friend!

Get your ass here before I start over again!"

Remembering the pain he had just went through,

he hurried back with the drinks. Ingrid then said, "Thank you,

Tommy. I believe you're not sincere with our deal,

I'm in total control with the way that you feel.

I'm only going to ask you this once my newly found friend:

do you want all that pain to come back again?"

He shook his head "no" with tears in his eyes.

Ingrid looked at her watch and said, "Oh, how time flies.

It looks like we all have to be on our way.

Come home with me, Tommy, so we can still play."

Anna said, "Ingrid, you don't know how Tom can be."

Tom looked bewildered and stared so blindly.

"Oh, Anna, I've got Tom figured out quite well.

I'll take him home, everything will be swell.

Isn't that right, Tommy, my friend?"

Tom just nodded as Ingrid did grin.

"Okay, let's get out of here, I want to go home," Anna said.

Tommy drug his feet to the door; his face was still red.

They got out to the car, Ingrid said, "Now, drive us home."

Tom got behind the wheel, and away they did roam.

Just like they left, they were back in no time.

They went inside. Ingrid said, "Pour us some wine."

Anna said to Mother, "I'm going to bed,

I've got an aching pain inside my head.

These last few days have been too much for me,

I'll leave you alone so you and Tom can be free."

"Good night, Tinker Bell. I'll see you around dawn."

Tom said, "Good night," and started to yawn.

"Oh, no, Tom, you don't get tired, you see,

because it's your turn to satisfy me."

"Ingrid," Tom said, "we've gotten off to a bad start.

You're so beautiful, I want to give you my heart."

"Tom, Tom, with the silver tongue, weaving many lies,

we'll see if you're a man when you're between my thighs.

Now take off your clothes, and let's go to my bed,

you owe me a lot for that marvelous head.

It's been a long time since a man's been in me.

If you please me, I might set you free.

Don't get over zealous, treat me like your queen.

If you act like I'm a whore, I promise you'll scream."

"Okay," Tom said, as he kissed her lips,

rubbing her breasts and holding her hips.

He licked her nipple until it became tight,

massaging her mound and fighting his fright.

He began to kiss Ingrid, it was okay.

She said, "Just *fuck* Me! You don't know how to play."

He slid his shaft deep in Ingrid's crack,

it went in further when she clawed her nails in his back.

Ingrid said, "Now, Tom, it's time for you to perform,

I don't want a sprinkle, I want a thunder storm."

She was undulating with every thrust,

her body was alive and filled with lust.

Tom started moaning and nearing the end,

Ingrid said, "If you're too fast, we'll do it again."

He slowed his rhythm, and kissed her tongue to tongue,

then she clamped down and sucked out his cum.

"Tom, it's over, I'm through with you for tonight.

Now get out of here, I don't want you in sight."

Tom said, "How am I supposed to get back to my car?"

She said, "Just start walking, it won't seem very far.

But you'd better be careful, there's things in the night,

that can do worse than me with their painful bite."

Tom quickly went out the front door,

slammed it, and yelled, "Ingrid, you're a whore!"

Ingrid just laughed and drifted off to sleep,

Tom had broken the promise he said that he'd keep.

As he walked out of the house and towards the huge vines,

they opened and he left with Ingrid's torture on his mind.

Tom was exhausted and half-way to his car

when he saw three people up ahead, not too far.

He yelled out, "Do you have any wheels?"

There were two women filled with giggles and squeals.

He thought, "What the fuck is up with these three?"

It wasn't too long before he did see.

They walked up to him in the moonlight.

he asked, "Is there a costume party tonight?"

Raphael was the first one to speak,

"It looks like the sorceress has made you weak."

Tom said, "Sorceress, oh yeah, you got that shit right!

You wouldn't believe what she did to me tonight!

I'd call her more of a witch or something like that."

Raphael laughed and said, "Did she have a black cat?"

Then he said, "Why don't you come with us, and have a bite to eat

and regain some of your strength to help you down the street?"

Tom said, "I'm kinda hungry; I could use a meal."

The sisters both laughed and let out a squeal.

Then they walked over and took Tom by the hand

and said, "The feast we have in mind will be quite grand."

Raphael said, "Let's be on our way,

before we start a brand new day."

They walked down the street a couple of blocks

to a house made of boulders and of huge rocks.

Tom said, "This really looks like a ran down place."

Raphael said, "Inside is charm you can almost taste."

They opened the door and took Tom within,

then locked it up behind their new friend.

Then Lyra said, "So, what's your name stud?"

He replied, "Tom," but his mouth was like mud.

All of a sudden, he sensed something was wrong,

then the other woman started humming a song.

It ran cold, cold chills right through Tom's heart.

He knew that it was time for him to depart.

Then Raphael said, "One, two, three.

It's time for dinner. The feast is on me."

Tom thought, "That was a strange thing to say."

Then Raphael said, "Girls, it's time to play."

They rushed upon him like a cat on a mouse,

then the door burst open on the stone house.

Ingrid was standing in the doorway.

She said, "Do you really want to play?

Raphael, I knew that you'd take the bait,

and all I had to do was just sit and wait.

You're not as smart as you want to be,

now tell those bitches to let Tom go free."

They let Tom go and he let out Ingrid's name in a yell.

Ingrid said, "Tom go out the door and run like hell."

Tom was gone like a striped-ass ape.

Raphael was pissed that he had escaped.

"Oh, Raphael, are you mad at me?

I think we're even for my trip on the sea.

You didn't think I knew it was you that set me up

with a cruise on the sea and a bow that was corrupt?

You'll have to try a little harder, you see,

to fool a sorceress as powerful as me.

So do we continue this game of wit my friend,

or call a stalemate and turn our backs to the wind?"

"Ingrid, that's a very nice name," said Raphael.

"And the form that you've chosen, I bet the men just say 'Wow.'

Your beautiful, long, flowing, red hair and green eyes,

your shapely breasts and awesome thighs.

Why don't you come over and give me a kiss?

I'll show you the love you've always missed."

Ingrid replied, "Oh, look, you're trying to mesmerize me;

if I was mortal that might work, you see.

But thanks for the compliments; they felt almost real.

You really thought you could have me as a meal.

Your wyrding way won't ever work on me.

Why don't you move on and let Anna and I be?"

"Ingrid, I believe you know what it is that I truly seek,

your billions of dollars would make my life not so bleak.

By the way, all that fortune, did you conjure it up?"

"No, Raphael, sorceresses cannot be corrupt.

Yes, we can manipulate all kinds of things,

and move people around to make paupers into kings.

But as far as money, I have to earn it myself.

Yet living forever, you can amass so much wealth.

Okay, enough about my fortune, lets cut to the chase."

Raphael had a big smile on his face.

His fangs began to show, they gleamed in the night.

He now took his stance for the oncoming fight.

"Well, Katherine, or Ingrid, what should we do?

Anna would taste so sweet since she came from you.

I'd love to bite her throat and turn her,

before her latent talents do occur.

Then there would be four of us in the night,

with one ever powerful that you'd have to fight.

The thought of you and your daughter fighting in the breeze

brings me so much joy, it's almost a tease."

"Well Raphael," Ingrid said, "I guess you've made up your mind.

Now it's time for the sisters to dine.

Lyra and Lenore, you now belong to me,

and Raphael you can't move at all now, don't you see?"

Raphael thought Ingrid was totally insane,

but he couldn't move an inch after she said his name.

"Okay sisters, it's time for a real feast.

You, go to your maker and bite like a beast."

Lyra and Lenore attacked Raphael.

He pleaded for mercy as they sucked on his shell.

Ingrid said, "Take all but his last, little drop,

and when you get there, the both of you stop."

Raphael was drained by Lyra and Lenore,

he stood there weak, then fell on the floor.

Ingrid said to the sisters, "You're both through.

Now down to the Underworld with the two of you.

Down into the darkness between this life and hell,

down where your thirst will grow and continue to swell.

Endlessly you'll search for the blood that you need,

feeding off each other till you no longer bleed."

In a flash the sisters were no longer in sight.

Raphael tried to stand with all of his might.

He managed to get up on all fours and Ingrid said,

"I could use a black cat. I think I'll call you Fred."

She whispered a few words silent and discreet,

then Raphael was a cat, meowing so sweet.

She reached down and picked up the black cat at her feet,

and said, "You thought I was the one that you could

defeat?

Now let's you and I go back to my home

and, if you're real nice, I'll let you outside to roam."

When Ingrid got home Anna was awake.

Anna looked at the cat and began to shake.

"Mother, what is that cat doing here?"

She said, "It's Raphael. Let's keep him near.

And his other two friends are gone now for good,

I gave them a fate worse than being killed with sharp wood.

Now I need to rest, Anna, my dear.

If Raphael misbehaves just pull on his ear.

It took a lot of energy for what I have done.

Tonight we'll go into the town and have us some fun.

Maybe we'll bump into someone else that has wronged you.

I've got this nice young body and have many things to do."

She winked at Anna and went off to her room.

Raphael was hiding in the corner behind a broom.

As he silently thought about his situation,

his temper flared from total frustration.

Raphael waited until Anna left, then came out from behind the broom,

then paced the floor, investigating every inch of the room.

He noticed the knight in armor that wasn't there the night before,

then ran across the room and clawed wildly at the door.

"Oh, I'll get even with that bitch," Raphael thought to himself.

Then he jumped up and knocked items off of the shelf.

Ingrid was awoken from her sleep and went into the room.

She saw what Raphael had done and headed for the broom.

She grabbed it and swung it at Raphael with spite.

He jumped upon her shoulder and clawed her with delight.

His claws went in her neck and she started to bleed,

quickly Raphael licked it, hoping to be freed.

Ingrid let out a laugh, and said, "Freddy, you silly cat.

It will take more than this to remove you from where you're at.

I guess it's time I show you who is in power here."

She threw him out the door and said, "Make sure you stay near."

Raphael hit the ground running, trying to escape his situation.

He made it to the vines that encompassed his location.

As he walked nearer, the vines began to grow.

Then he was entangled from his head down to his toes.

He chewed at the vine madly, trying to get free,

but for every inch that he tore off, a new one did grow free.

Ingrid said, "Didn't I tell you to stay close to the house?

Now you're trapped and as helpless as a mouse.

I could let you be, and the vines will consume you,

but I think I'll save you because our game's not yet through.

Now all you have to do to get free from the vines,

is remove your anger towards me from your mind.

If you can do that, the vines will let you go…

And if you can't, a pain will tend to grow.

I'm going back inside to finish up my rest,

you can stay here while I leave you to your test."

Raphael roared out in a hateful way,

the vine increased the pain just as she did say.

Ingrid went to her bed and went right back to sleep.

She knew Raphael would be the vines' to keep.

In her dreams she thought of her prisoner, Raphael,

and how for seven years he had made her life hell.

She tossed and turned all through the night,

as Raphael was trapped in a non-winning fight.

It wasn't long, and the dawn did begin to break,

Raphael was thinking that this could be a mistake.

He wondered what will be when the sun comes breaking through.

That fear caused him to think, "Ingrid, I will forgive you."

It's not very often that a Vampire does forgive,

but they do have a want and desire to live.

Just as he forgave her, the vines set him free.

Ingrid met him at the door, and said, "You've forgiven me"

She let him in the house and gave him some bloody meat to eat.

With one bite he regained his original form and Ingrid said, "You look so sweet.

I have always thought that you were quite a handsome man,

but I couldn't deal with your evil, selfish plan.

As long as you respect me, you can have your true form.

The minute that you don't, you're in for a real storm."

Raphael nodded at Ingrid while swallowing most of his pride.

Then he said, "I must rest. Do you have a place I could reside?"

Ingrid said, "Yes, I have a place arranged for you.

It's an old steamer trunk that has some soil you knew.

You'll find it in the basement. Go down the stairs and sleep.

Just remember when you awake, your will is mine to keep."

Raphael nodded again in a respectful, somber way,

then went down in the basement and in the trunk he did lay.

Ingrid went to Anna's room, and said, "Wake up, you darling thing.

The sun is up, the flowers smell fresh, and the birds have begun to sing."

She said, Raphael is no longer a cat,

immediately Anna threw off her blanket and up she sat.

"Raphael, Raphael!" Anna said in a frightened tone.

Ingrid said, "Don't worry. The basement's now his home."

"You transformed him again?," Anna said to Ingrid in a voice of fear.

Ingrid said, "He's learned his place. We will keep him near.

I restored his form. Because he has more value to me that way.

And if he ever disobeys, the next game won't be for play.

Now get a shower and put on some clothes; we have some things to do.

Today is a brand new day just meant for me and you.

After you're dressed, we will go have lots of fun.

We'll shop all day, then go out and party after the evening sun.

It's about time you bought yourself some new clothes to wear.

Now with my mass fortune, you can spend without any care."

Anna said, "Mother, but it's your money, not mine."

Ingrid said, "I don't need money. Let's go have a good time."

The two of them jumped into the car and headed towards town.

It was the off-season; there weren't many other shoppers around.

Ingrid said to Anna, "This looks like it will be quite fine.

With so few shoppers we won't have to stand in line."

Anna chuckled as they pulled up to their first store.

Ingrid jumped out and made a bee line for the door.

She went in and said, "Where the hell's the damn clerk?"

The lady in the store thought to herself, "What a fucking jerk!"

That wasn't a good thing for the clerk to do,

for Ingrid looked at her as if she knew.

Ingrid smiled and said in a devilish voice,

"This isn't much of a store; there's not much choice."

Anna said, "I'm going to look around,

maybe there's something nice to be found."

Then Anna saw the clerk; she went to college with her in the past.

She was a really snotty bitch who tormented Anna in class.

Ingrid said, "Good luck with that,"

as she picked up an ugly hat.

She looked at the hat and said, "Is this for a witch?"

Again in her mind the clerk thought, "What a fucking bitch!"

Once again Ingrid smiled at her,

then for a second the clerk's eyes did blur.

Ingrid said, "Ma'am, is there something wrong with you?

You look like you can't see. Is there something I can do?"

The clerk snapped at Ingrid and said, "I don't need help from you!

I'll be just fine in a second or two."

Ingrid smiled and said, "Did I offend you, or something?"

Then the clerk's ears were starting to ring.

Anna said to Ingrid, "Hey, come look at this book.

I believe I've found something that's worth a look."

Anna showed Ingrid the book. and said, "It's filled with poetry.

It's called *Return to Stantasyland*. It might be worth a look-see."

Ingrid said, "I didn't know you liked poetry, my dear child."

She said, "It's the title; it seems kind of wild.

A book called *Stantasyland* by a man named Stan."

Ingrid said, "That's kind of cute. Is he Stan the Man?"

Then Anna said, "I want to see where this guy's head's at.

I've never seen such a clever title like that."

Ingrid said, "Cool! Open it up, and lets see what we find.

I'm always open to hear words from a poet's mind.

After all, Anna, in the beginning it was the poets and philosophers that taught the world to see.

Their logic, love, and inspiration were the basis for this world to be."

Then she said, "Wait, Anna, I have a better plan;

I believe this idea will be quite grand."

Ingrid said to the clerk, "Miss, we would like some help here.

Would it be too much for you to help Anna, my dear?"

The clerks eyes cleared, and the ringing ceased.

She thought to her self I can hear and see now at least.

She replied "I'd be happy to do anything for your friend and you"

As she thought if it gets you out of my store when I'm fucking through.

Ingrid snickered, "Oh, that's so sweet and kind of you!"

The clerk thought, "I'll do anything to get your damn shopping through."

In the clerk's mind, she was kind of confused with what was going on,

but thought again, "I'll do anything to get these two bitches gone."

Then Ingrid asked, "What do you think of this book.?"

The clerk replied truthfully, "I haven't gave it a look."

Ingrid said, "How the hell are you suppose to sell items in here?"

Since you don't know anything about them my dear!

If you have things in here you know nothing about?"

The clerk was to the point she wanted to shout.

Ingrid asked of the clerk, "Do you like poetry?"

The clerk responded, "It's not my cup of tea."

Ingrid said, "Anna, please give the book to the nice clerk.

hopefully she can read it with a nice perk."

Now the clerk was really getting pissed.

Ingrid said, "If you have a heart attack, do you think you'll be missed?"

The clerk yelled at Ingrid, "You crazy bitch!" She couldn't refrain.

Then she had a pain in her chest, and thought, "This is insane!"

Ingrid said, "I'm worse than any bitch you'll ever know…"

The pain in the clerk's chest continued to grow.

Then in terror, the clerk dropped to her knees;

clutching her chest, and she whimpered out, "Please."

Ingrid smiled, and said, "That's much better now.

Will you read us that poem if you know how?"

In agony the clerk uttered, "I know how to read."

Ingrid said, "Stand up, and from the pain you'll be freed."

The clerk stood up, and the pain went away.

Ingrid said, "Pick a poem, or the pain will be back to stay."

With trembling hands the clerk opened the book.

Ingrid said, "Start reading; you don't have all day to look.

Do you need me to give you a little shove?"

The clerk said, "I've found one; it's called Dark Love."

"Dark Love! Oh that's a perfect one for me," Ingrid said.

"Now read it with all of your heart, or you'll end up dead."

The clerk cleared her throat and got ready to read the poem.

It took all of her strength to stand there alone.

She said, "I'll read it to you and try my best."

Ingrid said, "That's great because it's a test."

The clerk began to read:

"I awoke to a gong, wandering on my basement floor.

It vibrated my every cell, I was trapped behind the door.

There were candles burning that I did not light.

Thirteen flames in the smoky room gave me little sight.

There was a foul smell from below my gaping wounds.

Dizzily I wondered if my basement would be my tomb.

I heard a whisper up ahead, but I live alone.

Who is this person I must find, that's cut me to the bone?"

The clerk paused for a second and said, "Am I doing okay?"

Ingrid said, "Fine. I like what he has to say."

The clerk began to read the poem again,

as she still thought of her pain within.

"I stopped and grasped the gashes where my flesh once had been.

I stood half-conscious in pain, wondering if the whisper was the wind.

Again the whisper beckons, and now I must go see.

What kind of a man or beast could do this harm to me?

I stumbled to the wet, west wall and leaned back in curiosity.

There's several black candles burning, did I light them for me?

I never buy black candles. They're seeds of demon spawn.

Oh, the pain and faintness, how much longer can I go on?

I must lie down. I'll lay on that lighted table near the left wall.

I go through the webs, the table beckons, 'Come lie before you fall.'

I lay upon on the table. It felt almost like a bed.

It was softer than the pain and thoughts deep inside my head.

I closed my eyes in agony, my dreams took me away.

I awoke to shorter candles, wondering if it was the same day.

I wished I was sleep-walking, and this nightmare would end.

Yet, this was a wasted wish, I'm trapped in deadly sin.

My eyes were blurred from loss of blood and all the pain within.

On each side a black and white candle burned dimly in the

wind.

The black was to my left, the side of Satan's hand.

Why the Hell I'm here, I do not understand.

As I laid upon the table, and the light pierced the night,

my eyes came into focus and gave me such a fright.

Whites of eyes were glowing and all focused on me.

If this isn't a dream, please, God, come set me free.

There was like an evil force which I couldn't get free from.

It bound me to the table as I wondered what was to come.

I tried to keep my senses and get a hold of my mind.

Yet, things that were in my basement, now I couldn't find.

Where did that old manikin go, over by the south wall?

Where's all my books and boxes and my bowling ball?

It seems as I lie here, reality has went array.

What do these specters want of me on this painful day?

All of a sudden someone was near, I didn't see them come.

I trembled trapped with pain and fear, yet I couldn't run.

He laid upon me, yet I didn't feel any weight.

My body started trembling and pleasure now gestates.

He bonded with my body in the candlelight.

He kissed my wanton lips with pleasures of delight.

This Demon beast from Hell that I could not fight,

seduced me with Dark Love and took my soul that night."

"Wow!" exclaimed Ingrid. "This guy knows how to write,"

as she looked at the clerk so filled with fright.

"Anna," Ingrid said, "we have to buy this thing."

Then looked at the clerk and said, "Can you sing?"

The clerk replied, "I've sang just a little bit."

Ingrid said, "For what I have in mind, you're perfectly fit."

Now the clerk was really getting scared; she wanted to run

because now she didn't know what was to come.

Ingrid said to Anna, "Oh, do look at the time.

We need to be on our way. It's almost time to dine.

Now pay the nice clerk for the book, and we'll be on our way.

The sun's still up, it's not too late, we need to go play."

Anna went to the register and paid for the book.

The clerk could only stare at her with a frightened look.

"Didn't we go to college together," the clerk asked Anna Marie.

"Yes," Anna said, "and all you did was torment me."

Ingrid said to the clerk, "I believe it's closing time."

The clerk replied, "Miss, I don't get off until nine."

Ingrid said, "Call me Ingrid, you're now a friend of mine.

Now close the store, and lets go play,

unless you want this to be your last day."

After all she had been through, she still was wondering why.

The clerk said, "Things are kind of slow; I guess we can fly."

Ingrid said, "That's a good choice, I believe you're starting to learn."

The clerk closed the shop and left, filled with concern.

Ingrid said to the clerk, "You're now not in the store.

Do you have a name, or should I call you a whore?"

The clerk said, "I have a name!" in a spiteful way.

Ingrid smiled at her, and said, "Be careful what you say."

There was a hint of pain coming over the clerk's chest.

Ingrid said to her, "You've only passed the first test.

Now I would like you to drive Anna and me around,

and a whore like you should know a party to be found."

The clerk said, "I have a name; I'm not a whore!"

Ingrid said, "Don't get testy with me, or you'll be no more!

Screw your name, I'll just call you Easy,

you're just another mousey bitch that's always been so sleazy.

You are but an ant in the human race,"

Ingrid said with a smile on her face.

"Now start the car; we have things to do.

I'd like to take the scenic view.

Take the first back road out of town,

I have an old friend that needs to be found."

Easy said, "Okay,"

and they drove away.

They drove thirty miles outside of town,

without a single house or car to be found.

Easy said, "We're not gonna find a party out here."

Ingrid said, "Oh, just keep driving, my dear."

Then up ahead in the road, not very far,

was a man off the shoulder standing by his car.

Ingrid said, "Stop, I believe this boy needs a ride."

Easy pulled up, and Ingrid said, "Get inside."

Then the man let out a wild scream and started to run.

Ingrid got out of the car and yelled, "Tommy, my son."

Oh, that was the last voice he wanted to hear.

He could barely move as he trembled with fear.

Ingrid said, "Tommy, don't you want to go play?

You know you have to do what I say,

or have you forgotten all that pain?

I can give it back, or even make you insane."

Tom stopped and turned around, knowing he had no choice

by the pitch and tone of Ingrid's voice.

He walked back to the car, and said, "I'm glad you came by."

Ingrid said, "Tommy, Tommy, why must you lie?"

He said, "Okay, I'm not really glad to see you,

I was hoping that you and I were through.

I had packed my car and was trying to run as far as I can.

Those things you did to me I don't understand.

Those beasts that you saved me from in the night,

also gave me such a terrible fright.

All that pain that you put me through,

I knew there was only one thing to do.

So yeah, I was running out of fear."

Ingrid said, "Oh, Tommy dear,

how can I punish you for telling me how you feel?

Jump in the car. You don't need your wheels."

In Tommy's mind, he thought, "I got off free."

But then his car burst in flames for him to see.

He screamed, and said, "That car had everything I own."

Ingrid said, "Tommy, you can live in our home.

After all you were trying to steal it from Anna Marie.

Now you can live in it with her and me."

Tom was furious at Ingrid, and started to yell.

Ingrid said, "Tom, your balls hurt like hell!"

Tom doubled up in excruciating pain and fell to the ground.

Ingrid said, "You can ride in the trunk, or with me if you don't make a sound."

Tom did his best to bleat out, "With you, please."

Ingrid said, "Tommy, you're such a tease.

Now get in the car, in the back seat with me,

You've got some making up for me to see."

Anna was watching and loving the show all along.

Easy was thinking, "I hope I can sing a good song."

Ingrid said, "Easy, take us home, dear."

Now Easy was trembling with fear.

Easy turned the car around,

and headed back towards town.

She drove past her store,

as her mind filled with horror.

Ingrid said, "We live on Circular Drive.

Take your time we want to get home alive.

Besides, I love to look at sunsets,

especially when I am with my pets."

Anna thought to herself how much she loved this side of her mother.

She had things she possessed like no other.

She also thought how nice it was to have someone to avenge

all the things for which she, herself, wanted to seek revenge.

Actually, Anna was so pleased, she began humming a tune,

then she realized it was Raphael's music she'd heard in her room.

The sun was almost fully down.

Anna's emotions were stirring around.

She knew it was Raphael's powers again,

as she heard her name whispered in the wind.

But this time she didn't feel as weak as at first,

yet she still had a touch of a thirst.

Anna said to Ingrid, "Raphael's doing something to me again."

Ingrid said, "When we get home, I'll take care of your friend."

A few moments later, Easy drove through the vines

and, as always, they closed in behind.

She said, "Okay here's the party, let's go right in.

I'd like you to meet a very close friend."

When Ingrid opened the door, Raphael and her were face-to-face.

His eyes were on fire, his fangs exposed, because he hadn't learned his place.

Ingrid said, "Hmm, so once again you want to take me on."

Raphael said, "Get out of my way, and I'll just be gone."

Ingrid said, "Fine, but remember the vines.

Is that where you wish to spend some more of your time?"

Raphael said, "I'll change into a bat and just soar away."

Ingrid said, "Fine, if that's what you want, have it your way.

You're free to fly

If you wish to try.

But I wouldn't if I were you,

for your servitude isn't quite through."

Raphael laughed at Ingrid, and said, "You're just a fool!

I'm the powerful one that in the end shall rule."

Ingrid said, "The only power and energy that you have right now is from me.

If it wasn't for the soil I let you lay in, you wouldn't have the will or energy to try to get free."

Raphael said, "What are you going to do? Turn me back into a black cat again?

That's not going to happen. I'd rather be a bat and fly free in the wind."

With that, Raphael folded his arms on his chest, turned into a bat, and flew by Anna's hair.

Raphael circled several times, flew over Anna and the others, squeaked, then rose high into the air.

He headed towards the vines to make his escape, thinking he was going to get away,

but a vine stretched out high in the air, ensnared him, and he was there to stay.

He struggled in the vines once again, trying to get free from their grip,

but the more he struggled, the more and more his energy did slip.

He transformed back into his human form with the last of his energy.

He then was lowered, vine to vine, until he was on the ground for all to see.

Ingrid yelled, "Raphael, Raphael, who has no concern?

You are mine to keep. Will you ever learn?"

The vines tightened as they did before when he was a black cat.

Then Ingrid said, "There's dead limbs there that could pierce the heart of a bat."

Vampires are so prideful, Raphael actually considered telling Ingrid to kill him,

but he knew that to her this was a game that she intended to win.

His only chance was to bide his time, and obey Ingrid's rules,

and play along, while hoping she gave him the tools.

She has a large library with many books to read.

There has to be one that says how to get rid of a sorceress's seed.

Ingrid hollered, "Raphael, we're going in. I have some things to do,

but when I'm done, my friend, I'll be back to check on you."

Raphael burned on the inside, filled with such hate,

but for now he would not struggle. He could only wait.

Ingrid said, "Anna and everyone, let's go inside.

You and Easy can chit-chat while Tom gives me a ride."

Tom just looked at the floor knowing not to say or think anything,

because he knew the extent of what Ingrid's power could bring.

Ingrid grabbed Tom by his hand, and said, "Let's go, my big man.

It's a long time before morning, and I have lots of plans.

Anna, if you wish, you and Easy can go into town,

but if she runs away, let her know she can be found.

Tom is living proof that you can't run from me,

and to give me what I wish is the only way to get free."

Anna said to Ingrid, "I think I'll go to bed.

Raphael's persuasion still messes with my head."

Ingrid said to Anna, "That will be okay.

We have so much time that we can play."

Ingrid said, "Easy, make yourself at home,

but don't get brave enough to go outside and roam.

If you leave the house, there's something in store for you,

and going out my door would be a dumb thing to do."

"Do you have any alcohol, Ingrid? Could I please have a

drink?"

"Wow, Easy, yes, you can. I like the new way you think.

It looks like maybe we can get along."

Easy thought to herself, "That's where you're wrong."

Ingrid gave her a big smile, and said, "I'm off to play with Tom.

Get you a big bottle and drink until it's gone."

Tom said softly, "Can I have a couple of drinks with you?"

Ingrid said, "Sure, if you've earned them, when we are through.

Now get your ass in my room, and we'll see how it goes.

You need to rock my world and curl up my toes."

They went into Ingrid's room far down a hall.

When she turned on the lights, there were mirrors on every wall.

Then she said, "Tom, get your scrawny ass in my bed,

and now it is your turn to give me the head."

Tom took off his clothes and dropped them on the floor.

Ingrid turned around and shut the bedroom door.

Ingrid said to Tom, "I know I've been a real bitch to you,

but like I said, it's payback for what you did do.

Now Tom, I'll ask you a question and you'd better not lie,

because if you do, you'll pray to die."

Tom said, "Okay, I'll try to be as honest as I can."

Ingrid said, "That would be your best plan.

I've lived many years, Tom, lonely years because of what I am.

I know people's thoughts and their every plot and plan.

I've lived centuries and centuries, form after form.

I have a kind heart, but a life like a storm.

Besides Anna Marie, there's only been one other person in my heart,

and when we were separated, it tore me apart.

I never speak his powerful name; for just the mention of it alone,

can cause earthquakes and volcanoes that could destroy every human and their home.

I know if I yelled out his name, he would come to me,

but I know if I did, there would be no world left to see.

He rules the Underworld above Satan's fiery Pit.

I could be his queen, and on his right side I'd sit.

But I choose to be with the living, with their selfish goals,

than be a queen with the lost and misbegotten souls.

For in every living being, there is a form of grace.

Most of the time they have just forgot their place.

Tom, I know your mind and your misbegotten deeds.

I know your selfish heart, all so full of greed.

You've never loved anyone in all your life—it's true—

but I'll give you the chance to start your life anew.

When we had sex the last time, you were just there.

Fucking is just fucking unless you care.

I will give you the chance to love me and grow,

but if you betray me, to the Underworld you'll go.

All the pain I've showed you is not even a glimpse

of the pain you'll know and won't have any defense.

There are two Vampires, Lyra and Lenore.

They belonged to Raphael, but now they're in my horror.

I have them tucked away in the Underworld below,

and they have a thirst that daily will grow.

So I'll give you a chance, if you wish to try,

but you will be gone in a flash if I catch you in a lie.

So if you wish to be my lover and take me by the hand,

remember what's on the plate. Do you understand?"

Tom said, "Ingrid, what if I don't want to try with you?

Wouldn't it be better if I didn't try, than fail, with what you can do?

Are you trying to threaten me into loving you? How absurd!"

Ingrid said, "Oh, my God, Tom, you really are a bastard!

I knew what your response would be.

I opened up my heart to replace what is lost to me.

I told you everything, and I had a slight chance that I actually believed you would choose differently.

You're not a man, Tom. You're a succubus. You drain the life out of those that offer love unconditionally.

I'm quite capable of love, Tom. I'm probably the best lover that will ever be, yet my heart is torn.

When my only true love, the most powerful man I've ever known, made love, the stars were born.

You! I can't believe you actually rejected a chance at that!

You pompous, fucking spoiled, selfish, self-centered brat!

Okay, enough with the romance thing, Tom, since it's not

your style, I see.

Now it's time, Tommy-boy, that you service me."

The brass rails snatched Tom's arms and legs, and he laid spreadeagled on the bed.

Ingrid mounted Tom's face, dropped her mound on it, and said, "It's your time for head."

Tom lay there with his mouth closed in defiance, Ingrid said, "You'd better begin, or I'll rip out your tongue."

Tom stuck out his tongue and started to lick Ingrid's pussy. Ingrid said, "That's not as good as I gave you," then she started to hum.

Instantly Tom's cock was rock hard, and getting harder and harder, the more Ingrid hummed.

Ingrid stopped humming, and said, "You know, Tom, you better try harder because you're making me sort of feel bummed."

"Bummed," Tom thought as he was near agony from his raging hard-on.

Ingrid said, "Tom, if you don't please me, you won't like me when it becomes dawn."

Tom calmed himself and started actually trying, centering his concentration on licking Ingrid's clit.

She said, "That's a little better," as she freed one of Tom's hands, placing it on her tit.

Then he gently squeezed Ingrid's nipple on her beautiful breast.

Ingrid was rocking and undulating on Tom's face, and whispered, "You might pass the test."

By now Ingrid was all in, her new body that was young and fresh, needed sensation.

Putting all her anger and disgust for Tom aside

momentarily, she gave up her frustration.

Ingrid said, "Stop, Tom," just before she came all over his face.

Then fear came over Tom and his mind began to race.

Ingrid gave him an evil grin,

turned towards the foot of bed, and mounted him.

Slowly she lowered her wet and throbbing pussy on top of Tom's cock.

Lowering slowly, in small degrees, teasingly, until it was all the way in, and she began to rock.

Once again she began to hum, and Tom grew more.

Then she stopped, and said, "Remember when you called me a whore?"

She had her back to Tom, and said, "I'll fuck you, but you don't deserve to look at me."

Tom was in pain, mixed with total ecstasy.

Ingrid started to moan, slowly, then faster and faster, then she started saying, "Yes, yes, yes!"

Ingrid then burst on top of Tom. The sensation was so spectacular, Tom exploded his mess.

Ingrid got off Tom, with his semen dripping down her thighs, and looked at his now limp dick.

She said, "I ought to make you lick this mess off my thighs, you prick.

Did I say you could cum? You're the poorest excuse for a man I ever saw. Get dressed.

I'm going to take a shower and wash off. You've failed your test."

Tom got dressed and went into the other room where Easy was half drunk in a chair.

Tom stood there confused, looking at Easy with a blank stare.

Easy mumbled, "Don't try to leave. Ingrid warned me."

Tom said, "I've had all of that crazy bitch that I want to see."

He poured himself a drink to get up his nerve to try to make a run.

He went to the door, grabbed the knob, and Ingrid said, "Tom, my son."

He said, "I just wanted to look outside. It's too much for me in here.

I just wanted to get some fresh air. I'm consumed with fear."

"Fear! Fear! You don't even know what fear is, Tom. I believe you're kind of dumb.

Remember what I said I'd do to you if you lied to me? Your worst fear is soon to come."

Ingrid pushed Tom away, grabbed the door knob, and opened it,

looked Tom in the eyes, and said, "You make me want to spit."

Ingrid stepped out on the porch, and said, "Raphael, dear,

transform yourself and get back in here.

Are we going to fight all night,

or would you like to come in for a bite?

I'm sure that you could use a little snack,

before you're drained and lay flat on your back."

Raphael swallowed his pride and said, "What do I have to do?"

Ingrid said, "Nothing, just come in, and be the real you."

Raphael said, "I'm a little confused,

and I refuse to just be used."

Ingrid said, "Damn it, Raphael, come in and see.

The vines have now set you free."

Raphael stepped out of the vines, brushed off his clothes, and tried to get back some of his dignity.

Thinking, "What is this sorceress's plan now, and what does she want from me,"

he walked to the house and went in the door.

Tom's jaw dropped, and his eyes were filled with horror.

He said, "Ingrid, that's the Vampire you saved me from!"

"Well, Tom, this time things look a little more glum.

So, Raphael, how do you like your steak," Ingrid said.

Tom's face instantly turned to a nice, beet red.

Raphael said, "Oh, this one looks like it's cooked all the way through.

Ingrid, I hate to say it, but this is nice of you."

"Oh, but with me, Raphael, there's always a fee.

This piece of shit you must turn for me."

"Ingrid, he's not the Vampire type of man."

Ingrid said, "Just turn him, and let me go on with my plan."

Raphael said, "Tom, you want to go easy, or the hard way?

I can chase you around like a cat and mouse play.

You want to take it like a man, or squeal like a little girl?"

Those last words made Tom's will begin to curl.

"Adrenalin, wow! My favorite aphrodisiac!"

Raphael said, "The game's over. It's time to snack!"

Raphael said, "Look into my eyes."

Ingrid said, "Too many lies."

Raphael said, "Tom, come over to me."

He held him in his arms, and said, "One, two, three.

The first bite's for laughter, the second is for fun,

the third bite's the one the living death comes from."

Oh, Raphael bit Tom like he had never fed before.

When he finished, Tom fell like a rag doll onto the floor.

Raphael knelt, and said, "I've taken almost every drop you have to give.

You have to drink of me if you want to live."

Raphael bit his wrist and the blood started to drip,

and he said, "Drink of me; it takes only one sip."

Tom was hesitant at first,

but the smell of the blood gave him a thirst.

He put his mouth on Raphael's wrist but started to think,

"What will happen if I take this drink?

Will I become one of the living dead,

cursed to live forever in dread?"

The blood trickled between his lips and teeth.

It touched his tongue that lay beneath.

The first drop had a terrible taste,

then it sweetened, and not a drop he did waste.

It was the sweetest taste he had ever had.

Raphael said, "Stop, before you make me mad."

Raphael jerked his wrist away,

and said, "Ingrid, he's yours. And, Tom: have a nice day."

Tom managed to stand and he said, "Ingrid, you're a bitch!"

Then Ingrid said, "Tom, now you've dug your own ditch.

Do you remember Lyra and Lenore,

the two I talked about before?

They've been away awhile, you see.

I believe they need your company.

Now to the Underworld you must go."

Tom yelled out, "No! No! No!"

The next thing he knew he was in a cave,

but it was more of a living grave.

His fear was like a pheromone to Lyra and Lenore.

They rushed to him, and his flesh they tore.

They thought they'd found a living feast,

until they realized he was a beast.

The walking dead like the two of them,

in the Underworld to be condemned.

For right now the new blood tasted fine,

and Tom thought he'd lose his mind.

He screamed with each and every bite

as the sisters fed in awful delight.

He cried out, "Oh, God, please help me!"

The sisters said, "We're your God now, you see?"

Back at the house Raphael said to Ingrid, "That was kind

of you.

Not only you gave me back my strength, but you gave Lyra and Lenore something to do."

Easy was in a stupor during the whole thing.

Raphael said, "Is this another treat you did bring?"

Ingrid said, "I haven't decided what to do with her yet,

but if she becomes disposable, she'll be another you get.

Now don't let yourself think that I'm your friend.

If you get complacent, we'll start all over again.

The first rule is stay away from Anna Marie,

and we might just get along, you see."

Raphael said, "Ingrid, for now, I'll live by your rules,"

in the back of his mind he knew he needed tools.

Raphael said, "Do you mind if I play the piano? I'd like to calm down."

He went to the piano, and said, "What is this book that I've found.

Stantasyland, that's kind of unique in a way,

but do his words sound so gay?"

"Well, Easy read us one at her store.

It was kind of dark and filled with horror."

"Horror?" Raphael said, "I might like this guy's style.

Horror usually gives me a *big* smile.

Horror is just fine with me.

Let me open it and see what I see.

Ingrid, this one's called 'Satan.' What a strange one to open to.

If you'd like, Ingrid, I'll read it to you."

"Oh, Raphael, you know I love your voice,

and you couldn't have picked a more appropriate choice."

Raphael began, "In my fiery pit below,

where my fire is the only glow,

they'll forget the world they know,

when all the torment begins to show:

gnashing of teeth and burning flesh,

forever tormenting without rest.

Oh, the pain and horror they find,

cannot be felt in a living mind,

for in my kingdom known as Hell,

burning as a molten well,

all my demons laugh and tell

each new prisoner of their cell.

They beg and cry and scream and yell,

tailored for each one from above,

filled with torture absent from love,

in their cell for eternal time,

they'll be tormented by their own mind.

Walking with burning, blistered feet,

within my dominion, down so deep,

they know not to pray to God above,

for he has closed His heart and shunned His love.

Now they're my toys for which to play,

as my torture grows, day by day,

and all the fear that's in my fire,

just heightens my defiant desire.

I fear not the one above this pit,

where as the king I do sit.

Our battle has not yet began,

and I'm free to torture man

anyway I wish to in my realm,

for I'm in charge and at the helm.

I'm the master of trickery and deceit,

the superior one few humans beat.

So read your Bibles and say your prayers,

or you'll end up here, where no one cares.

If you might escape my earthly grip,

there still will be many that will slip,

fueling the energy hotter than the sun

in a place with nowhere to hide, nowhere to run."

Raphael said, "Wow! You're right! This guy's pretty damn good!

Some of this new age poetry can be barely understood."

Ingrid said, "I've crossed paths with Satan, actually,

but the next time we meet, he'll see a battle from me.

He's taken away the one thing I adore.

It's only a small amount of time before we have our war."

Raphael said, "You know how many people I've bitten over the years,

that screamed out, 'You're the Devil!' but I don't understand fears, and the Devil, he's made out to be one bad dude with class.

All he does is wait for a person to fuck their own self up the ass.

I believe they give him too much credit, you see.

The real fear should be from skin walkers like you and me.

But, hell, with the movies and the Vampire romance novels, list after list,

they've glamorized my kind to where it seems we don't even exist."

"I hear you," said Ingrid. "The whole world's a zoo.

I'd rather go back to the old world I knew.

When a king was a king, and a queen was a queen,

and heads would roll, and blood flowed down the streams.

God, I miss the good old days when justice was really blind,

that was when the times were so truly divine."

"Remember the plague, Ingrid?" Raphael asked.

"Oh man, those times were a blast.

I could feed all night long.

Nobody care if someone was gone."

Ingrid said, "Raphael, I think time has made me a bit bad.

It's been centuries, and I've been, oh, so sad."

Raphael said, "You know, you might be right.

I don't remember the last time I had any fun, except maybe tonight."

Ingrid said, "Okay, what are you trying to do?

Those are kind words coming from you."

Raphael said, "Maybe I've been without happiness so long

that now it's flat notes in an endless song."

Ingrid said, "Yeah, Raphael, I don't even know if I smell the flowers any more.

Am I really smelling them, or just remembering from long before?

You know, Raphael, I've been giving people test after test, then condemning them, you see.

But you know now, I wonder if the one true thing is that I'm actually testing me.

It seems I've always wanted more than another person can give.

I guess that's not really the way one should live.

Even with my daughter, Anna Marie. Her life was never hers, you see,

and since I've been back, it seems it's all about me."

Raphael said, "Ingrid... No, Katherine, let me tell you,

there's always a price for the things that we do.

Whether human or immortal, we all play almost the same game,

and if you don't watch, it will drive you insane.

The thirst I have that drives my kind in the night

has consumed me and drove my heart out of sight.

Long before my maker made me,

I was a kind man whose compassion ran free.

I had a wife and three beautiful children and a lovely home.

Now I'm condemned to a life that in the night I must roam

from place to place looking for a human that's a wreck,

so that I can take their life from the veins in their neck.

There was a time long ago when I felt sorry, you see,

but the longer I thirsted, a monster replaced the real me.

Long ago I loved beauty, life, poetry and art.

That was before a piece of stone became my heart.

You know humans often say, 'I am an old soul.'

Don't they realize all essences came from the same bowl?

So that means all the souls you find

were all created at the same time.

The ones that claim to be old souls or twin flames

have just played more applications of life's games.

You know now that you've separated Lyra and Lenore from me,

I believe I'm becoming a new man, you see.

Maybe it's from the times you have constrained me,

it showed me that we can't always be free."

Ingrid said, "Raphael, I haven't been free in such a long time,

it's a wonder that I have any control over my mind.

My emotions have long, long went away,

now it's cause and effect that leads me each day.

In conflict, you know, there's either flight or fight.

I've not soared in so long, I haven't any destination in sight.

Fighting seems to be the only thing that I know."

Raphael said, "Yes, I'm always in for a good fight or a

show."

Ingrid replied, "I could use a good show, you know.

I could use a true man to set my emotions aglow."

Raphael said, "What do you mean?"

Ingrid looked at him, kind of serene.

Raphael said, "Are you looking for a real date?"

Ingrid replied, "Yes, I have an empty plate."

Raphael said, "Let's go out and have a night on the town."

Ingrid replied, "I think I'll keep you close 'til your loyalty can be found.

I'm not going to let you past my ring of vines

until you've proven you are a friend of mine."

Raphael said, "So, Ingrid, what will that take?"

She replied, "When I know you don't need rules I must make."

Raphael sat at the piano and said, "What's your pleasure?

I know many pieces I believe you'll treasure."

He began playing a beautiful tune.

Ingrid said, "Now this lights up the room."

Easy stood up and began to dance.

She moved as though she was under a trance.

Ingrid began humming, and Raphael's emotions did stir.

He thought to himself, "How peculiar."

The more he played, the faster Easy did dance.

The more Ingrid hummed, he got a rise in his pants.

Raphael said in kind of a sensual way,

"Ingrid, would you like to play?"

Ingrid said, "Don't you know that I already am?"

Then she walked over and took his hand.

Ingrid said to Easy, "Go sit at the keys, dear.

Let's see if you can bring joy to my ear."

Easy said, "I don't know how to play."

Ingrid said, "It's better that you start that way."

Easy sat nervously at the keys.

Ingrid said, "Go ahead, please."

"I can't! I can't!" Easy screamed with fright.

Raphael said, "I'll help her, if it's alright."

Raphael walked behind Easy, and said, "My little wench,"

then sat down beside her on the piano bench.

He said, "Look into my eyes, Easy,

and the keys will be your friend, you see."

Easy looked in Raphael's lifeless eyes,

then there were notes that began to fly.

Her fingers hit the keys like a woman possessed.

Ingrid said, "It looks like you're helping her pass my test."

Raphael stood and walked over to Ingrid and took her hand.

They began to dance for the music was grand.

Slowly Ingrid melted into Raphael's arms,

thinking to herself, "What can this harm?"

She let the moment serenely take her away,

as the dance and the music was pure romance at play.

They danced almost the whole night through,

then Ingrid said, "I must say goodnight to you.

Now to the basement you must go,

for the sun is already beginning to show."

Raphael smiled and kissed Ingrid's hand softly,

and said, "You've brought new life to me.

Now I'll go and get my rest,

and tomorrow night we'll continue your test."

Raphael went down the basement stairs,

as Easy stood up and collapsed in a chair.

Ingrid said, "Wow! It's a new day:

the seventh one, when they all pray."

She went and tapped lightly on Anna's door,

and said, "I feel like a sinner; I need to pray some more."

Anna said to Ingrid, "Mother, what the hell do you mean?"

She said, "Please get dressed and wear something that looks pure and clean.

I'll get dressed too.

I'm torn between blood red or midnight blue."

Anna said, "Mother, it's not even nine."

Ingrid said, "Great, we'll be at church on time."

Anna said, "We're not going to see Father McKay, are we?"

Ingrid said, "There's no better church around for me."

Anna said, "Oh, do we have to go there?"

Ingrid smiled, then her eyes got a glare.

Ingrid asked, "Anna, do you have any clothes that will fit Easy?

I want her to go, but she's dressed so sleazy."

Anna said, "I believe I can find her something to wear."

Ingrid went in and said to Easy, "Get out of that chair."

Easy popped up like she was sitting on a spring,

wondering what type of torture Ingrid was about to bring.

Ingrid said, "Go to Anna's room and get dressed.

We're going to church; this isn't a test.

Well at least not a test given from me,

but you still have the one from the Almighty."

Easy asked in a real low voice, "Do you believe in God, Ingrid," as almost afraid to ask.

Ingrid said, "Yes, I do, and for everyone He has an individual task.

There's not one person nor grain of sand

that doesn't fit into his master plan.

None of us really knows if we're doing God's will

when we smell one flower or another we kill."

Easy couldn't help it, she just had to say,

"Ingrid, do you believe God wants you to do things your way?"

Ingrid said, "Long ago that question would have made me angry,

and you would have felt the whole wrath within me.

But now I try to be a little more kind,

and let people torture themselves from their own mind.

Unless they're just pawns that get in my way,

then I give them a new board on which to play.

I have not yet taken one single life,

but I have filled many beings with pain and strife.

Enough talking, we must be on our way.

I want to hear some words from Father McKay."

Easy went to Anna, and said, "Do you have some clothes for me?"

Anna opened her closet, and said, "Now, let me see...

Oh, here's a beautiful green dress.

And there's a brush; your hair is a mess.

Over in that corner sits all my shoes,

I'm sure there's a pair that you can use."

Anna went into the other room with Ingrid and said,

"Man, my back aches. I need to get a new bed."

Ingrid said, "You look, oh, so nice, my love,

and the clothes make you look as pure as a dove."

"Come on, Easy," Ingrid gave a yell.

She stumbled into the room, and said, "These shoes hurt like hell."

Ingrid said, "I'll take the pain away,

if you'll be a nice little lady today."

Easy said, "I'll be as nice as I can be."

Then, from the pain, her feet were now free.

Ingrid said, "See how nice things can be,

if you're good and listen to me."

Easy said, "Yes," and it was all she could say.

Ingrid said, "Fine, now we must be on our way."

Anna said, "Wait just a minute, Mother. I have something for you.

Since you've came back, you have done just what you wanted to do."

Ingrid said, "Anna, maybe I've gotten carried away,

after we go to church we'll try things your way.

Maybe we can take a trip and have some fun.

We can visit the places from which your dreams have come."

"Mother," Anna exclaimed. "I know why you want to go to see Father McKay.

You want to punish him for what he did to me back in the day.

But why, Mother? Why are you just now doing these things to get even for me?"

Ingrid said, "Because there needs to be a reckoning before your latent talents run free.

Anna, right now you're like a moth sleeping in it's cocoon,

and your metamorphosis will start to bloom soon.

Then you'll feel like you've taken a brand new breath,

but with the slightest whisper, you can send a man to his death."

Anna replied, "I've got way too much going through my head.

It seemed much simpler when I thought you were dead.

Now my life seems like a huge black hole,

and I'm being sucked in with my heart, mind, and soul."

Ingrid said, "I know, but we must be on our way.

I have a date with Father McKay.

Easy, you're driving. Let's head towards town."

Easy said, "Yes ma'am," while trying to hide her frown.

They went to the car, and the three of them got in.

Easy started the engine, and away they did spin.

They pulled up outside the church's front door and parked the car,

then walked up the marble stairs that didn't go very far.

Just before Ingrid went in the church, she bent and kneeled,

She crossed herself as if her deal was sealed.

She then arose, and said, "Let's go in.

I can't wait to see my preacher friend."

They went through the doors, and everyone turned to look.

Anna had a frown on her face, as Easy stood there and shook.

The three of them sat down in the third row.

Ingrid snickered, "This will be quite the show."

Onto the pulpit walked Father McKay.

He cleared his throat and began to pray.

The Lord's Prayer was where he did begin,

then the whole congregation chimed right in.

Father McKay then said, "Today's lesson will be on sin."

This gave Ingrid a really big grin.

The Father had a loud, thunderous voice, filled with inflection, but he was a small, frail man who couldn't handle rejection.

He began talking about the deadly sins of the flesh.

Ingrid thought to herself, "Those, my friend, will be fun to refresh."

The service went on with the singing, communion, and the last prayer.

Then Ingrid's green eyes started to get a red glare.

Anna said, "I'm glad that's over now. Let's go to the car, Easy."

Ingrid said, "I'll be right there after the priest takes a confession from me."

Anna and Easy went outside to wait

as Ingrid sat and prepared her bait.

She watched as one after another came out of the booth,

and couldn't wait until her turn, to reveal the truth.

She waited until she was the last person to confess,

then went into the booth to prepare the priest for his test.

She said, "Forgive me, Father, for I have sinned..."

He answered, "How long has it been, my friend?"

Ingrid said, "Long, long ago when I was a child,

ever since then I have been kind of wild."

Father McKay said, "Oh, please, do go on..."

Then Ingrid started weaving a familiar song.

"Oh, Father, I have hurt children in many ways over the years."

The priest's eyes began to fill with huge tears.

"I've violated their trust and took advantage of them,

and left them with pain, and their pureness condemned.

Living relationship after relationship with their agony within,

never, never ever being able to trust anyone again."

The priest cleared his throat to hold back his tears

from all the pain he'd caused over the years.

Ingrid said, "Father, will God forgive me for what I have done?"

The words sounded just like his own mouth they had came from.

The more she talked, the more she sounded like him,

revealing all the guilt he had hidden within.

Ingrid said, "How does one violate a child's trust

and do perversions for their own lust?

There's got to be an answer. Now tell me! You must!

Or it's ashes to ashes and dust to dust."

"I can't! I can't," yelled out the priest.

Then Ingrid said, "You are a fucking beast!

You're worse than the demons that spawn down below."

Then Father McKay's anger started to grow.

He said, "Who are you to judge a man of God?"

Ingrid just smiled and started to nod.

Father McKay kept going on and on.

His words sounded like a well-rehearsed song.

Ingrid said, "It seems you've practiced well for this day.

I can see it and hear it in the words that you say.

So obviously you must have known you were doing wrong

as you tormented those children all along.

Now grab on tight to your rosary beads

as I return your lustful seeds.

All the pain that you have given

is returned for you to forever live in."

The priest let out a shriek of pain,

then growled, "What is your name?"

He ran out of his booth and jerked open the other booth door,

then fell to his knees and screamed and trembled in horror.

For the person in the booth that caused his greatest fright

was his own image, gleaming a smile of delight.

He trembled and shook and began to pray.

Ingrid said, "It doesn't matter what you say.

For each and every deed we pay a price,

often balancing the scales isn't very nice.

Payback or karma by any other name

is the poetic justice that rules this game.

All of your life you've told people about sin

while having your own sprouting within.

Take all the pain that you have given

back into your mind to forever live in.

The pain of the living and the pain of the dead

is now all you can feel in your head."

Ingrid got out of the booth and walked towards the door

as the father laid contorted and in pain crying, "No more!

No more!"

When Ingrid got to the car, Easy and Anna were listening to the radio.

Ingrid said to Anna, "You missed one hell of a show.

Father McKay has now payed the price

for living a life that wasn't very nice."

Anna looked at her mother and said, "Who's Father McKay?"

Ingrid said, "That's exactly what I knew you would say.

Now Easy start the car and find us a club,

I've got a sensation a man needs to rub."

"Mother," Anna yelled, "What the fuck about me?

Did you already forget what you said would be?"

Ingrid smiled, and said, "No, I haven't my dear.

We'll drop you by the airport; it's rather near."

Anna said, "Drop me by the airport, but I have to gather my things and pack."

Ingrid said, "With your money, the same clothing never need touch your back."

Anna said, "I don't want to just jump on a plane, and go somewhere.

I need to think over where I want to go before I get there."

Ingrid said, "Okay, that's fine. We'll just go back to our home,

then you can decide where you want to roam.

Easy," Ingrid said, "I believe I'm through with you for now.

If I need you again, I'll find you somehow.

Now get out of the car and be on your way,

unless there is something that you have to say."

Easy thought for a moment how far her home was away,

but didn't have the nerve for any words she should say.

She got out of the car, and said, "Anna, goodbye."

Ingrid hopped behind the wheel, and said, "It's time to fly.

Anna, would you like to have something to eat?"

"Yes," Anna said, "How about something sweet?"

"Oh, sweet is always good for me, Anna, my dear.

Do you want to find something that is near?

Do you have a favorite place in mind,

that since I was gone you did find?

We have a lot of catching up to do

for all of the times you thought I was through,

and you had to face the world all alone,

making decisions all on your own.

I believe it's a good thing it happened that way.

It gave you independence and your own say.

Just like at the church, when you made that scene,

That is a daughter I've never seen.

I'm so glad you've came out of your shell,

and have the strength to bitch or yell.

For, Anna, this world that we live in,

sometimes it's hard to find a friend,

and you end up walking in it all alone,

taking scraps of friendship thrown like a bone.

Sometimes it's easier to be your own best friend

than have acquaintance after acquaintance and never win.

Even a mother's own birth-child

abandons them and runs so wild,

not worrying about their family name,

not caring if they bring it shame.

The honor in the world seems to have gone astray.

It's been replaced with greed of one's own way.

'Honor thy father and mother' was so written,

but in life today it's continually smitten.

Nursing home after nursing home are filled instead

with the parents of those who see them as the living dead.

To outlive one's usefulness is a terrible pain.

Yet in our society, it's the name of the game.

Anyway, now that I'm all done with my ravings,

what type of sugars do you have in your cravings?"

Anna said, "No, Mother, it is fine.

I know there's things that torment your mind

and I fully understand how you feel inside,

for in those same thoughts I do confide.

Anyway, how about ice cream, and maybe some chocolate cake?"

Ingrid said, "Oh, maybe I could go with a shake."

Anna said, "There's a little shop right down this street,

and the man that runs it is, oh, so sweet."

"A sweet man," Ingrid said, "there's nothing better I'd like in my bed, with dreams of only pleasing me in his head."

Anna said, "Fuck! Mom, is that all you have on your mind?"

Ingrid replied, "Why would I waste a body so fine?"

Anna said, "Mother, do you know how long it's been since I had a man?"

Ingrid said, "You never have. That's why you don't understand.

All you've had is boys with their toys,

saying they'll love you and bring you joys.

It takes a lot to make a real man who's true from within,

and who has the compassion that makes you soar like the wind.

We haven't talked about sex, have we, Anna Marie?"

Anna replied, "No, and this isn't the time for me.

Now let's have some ice cream before you spoil my mood."

Ingrid said, "Fine! I don't want to watch you brood."

Anna thought to herself, "Oh, you can be a real bitch!"

Ingrid smiled at Anna and gave her nose a twitch.

"Damn it!" Anna said, "Quit reading my mind!"

Ingrid just nodded and smiled so sublime.

She stopped the car in front of the ice cream shop.

She read the sign, and her jaw suddenly dropped.

Tristan's Treats was the name of the place.

Ingrid looked like she was lost in space.

Anna said, "Mother, is there something wrong? Please talk to me."

All Ingrid could say was, "This just cannot be!"

"What do you mean, Mother?" Anna asked silently.

Ingrid said, "Let's go in. I must look and see."

Anna went in first and sat at a table by the window,

wondering what it was that she didn't know.

Ingrid came in and sat with Anna Marie.

A waitress walked up, and said, "What will it be?"

Anna said, "I'll have the same thing I always have, Judy."

Ingrid said, "Is there a menu or a list I can see?"

Then she heard a man whistling a tune she knew,

and her eyes went from green to passionate blue.

She hadn't heard that tune in years.

Her heart raced, and her eyes filled with tears.

Anna asked. "Mother, are you okay?"

Ingrid didn't know what to say.

Then from the counter came a man with a menu,

still whistling that beautiful song she knew.

She looked at him, and said, "Hello."

With her emotions aflight and heart aglow,

she tried to speak, but words wouldn't come

and down her face the tears did run.

The man stopped whistling and looked at her.

All she could see was him as a big blur.

Then the tears did subside,

and her eyes opened wide.

It was a man that she once knew

who had loved her, oh, so true.

But things happened as they always do,

and life had to separate the two.

His life was never actually his own to live.

He had to please his parents so their love had to give.

First, it was off to college, then into a war

that left his mind in horror galore.

Then he crawled into a bottle and faded away,

and fate brought the two of them back to this very day.

Yet, once again things were out of sync,

as Ingrid looked at his old face and began to blink.

Every blink seemed like a decade going by,

and she tried her best not to cry.

It took everything she had to say,

"I believe I will have a shake today.

Just vanilla, with a hint of mint."

The old man's eyes gave a small squint.

Then he had a twinkle in his eye,

as he thought of days gone by.

Back when he had a girlfriend named Katherine,

and they sipped shakes in summers way back when.

She always had to have a hint of mint.

Then his mind wondered where the years had went.

He looked at Ingrid, and said, "You remind me of a friend."

Ingrid said, "Oh, really," with a heartfelt grin.

"Yes, someone I knew long ago;

someone who set my life aglow.

I've never been the same since we parted,

and with a living hell our separation started.

I'm sorry," Tristan said. "At times I get carried away."

Ingrid said, "Oh, at times, we all do. It's okay."

Tristan said, "One mint shake, and the usual for you, Anna Marie."

Anna said, "Yes, please, but this time make mine fat free."

Then Tristan said, "I'll be back in a flash."

And Ingrid said to Anna, "Do you have any cash?"

Anna said, "Mother, it doesn't matter here.

Tristan lets me charge. He's quite a dear."

Once again the whistling began and was moving Ingrid's heart.

She started singing silently and with these words she did start:

"Long ago a maiden was betrothed to be

to a handsome man who sailed upon the sea,

Oh-yee, Oh-yee, rum-de-rum-de-rum.

Who knows what destiny has to come?

The lassie was so fair, she set every heart aglow,

but she was betrothed as everyone did know.

Oh-yee, Oh-yee, rum-de-rum-de-rum.

Who knows what destiny has to come?

Then there was a war that needed all the ships,

and her sailor man was sent on deadly trips.

Oh-yee, Oh-yee, rum-de-rum-de-rum.

Who knows what destiny has to come?

The lovely maiden waited four long and lonely years.

Her face was torn with pain and her eyes were filled with tears.

Then late one evening came a rap at her chamber door

and the message it contained said her lover was no more.

Oh-yee, Oh-yee, rum-de-rum-de-rum.

Who knows what destiny has to come?

The maiden wept and lived out her life alone,

as her sailor had a watery grave for his home.

Oh-yee, Oh-yee, rum-de-rum-de-rum.

Who knows what destiny has to come?"

Anna said, "Mother, that is a really sad tune."

Ingrid said, "Don't call me Mother in this room."

Ingrid's eyes flared and her face turned red.

Anna asked, "Was it something I said?"

"Yeah!" Ingrid snipped. "You wouldn't know beauty if it bit you in the ass.

Songs existed like that when the world still had class."

"Oh, give me a break," Anna said in a snide tone.

"I can't wait until I get back home."

Tristan came to the table, and asked, "Is everything alright?"

Anna said, "My friend, Ingrid, is just a little uptight."

"Well here's your order. I hope it makes you feel better, dear."

Ingrid said, "Thanks," in a voice filled with cheer.

"What time do you close, Tristan? Anna says you're a sweet man.

Would you like to go with us afterward, if you have no plans?"

Tristan said. "I close at 8 PM.

I need to go home and tuck myself in.

I'm not as young as the lovely two of you,

and the next day seems to come before I know this one is through."

Ingrid said, "You don't look that old. You're quite a handsome man."

"Oh, but life's taken its toll on me," as he touched Ingrid's hand.

"Maybe we can make it another night," Tristan said in a kind voice.

Ingrid said, "Sure, we'll do it on a day of your choice."

Tristan said, "Okay, I'll let you know the next time you come in the shop.

I hope you two youngsters don't keep me out until I drop.

Now I have to get back to work; enjoy your shake."

He walked away, and Ingrid's heart felt it would break.

Anna said, "I told you he was a sweet man."

Ingrid said, "Sweeter than you'll ever understand.

Now let's go home. We have things to do.

We have a Vampire that needs tended to."

They walked out of the shop, and Tristan yelled, "Goodbye!"

Ingrid looked as if she could cry.

Ingrid said, "Anna, do you mind driving us home?

That old song made me feel so alone."

"Sure, I'll drive," Anna said, and away they went.

Ingrid said, "I just need time to vent.

Do you have any cigarettes in here?"

Anna said, "No, but there's a convenience store near."

They got to the convenience store, and Ingrid jumped out.

An old homeless wino gave her a shout,

"Spare change, ma'am. Can you spare a dime for a lost soul like me?"

Ingrid put her hand in her jeans, and said, "Let me see."

She pulled out a dime and gave it to him.

Then she gave him a sinister grin,

for in his head he thought, "You tight-wad bitch!"

She said, "It's your lucky day! You're in for a switch."

The wino said, "A switch! I could use one of them.

My life has been hell for so long, my friend."

Ingrid went in the store and bought some smokes and wine,

came out, and said to the wino, "It's party time!"

She asked, "Do you need a ride anywhere," handing him a bottle of wine.

He said, "I sleep in an alley, but this bottle will be fine."

She said, "How would you like a nice place to rest,"

baiting the man for one of her tests.

"You can have a bath and something to eat."

He said, "Oh, ma'am, oh, ma'am, you're really too sweet."

He thought to himself, "What does this bitch think,"

as he opened the bottle and slugged down a drink.

Ingrid smiled, and said, "Get in the back seat.

We'll take you home and give you a treat."

He got in the car, and Anna said, "He smells like shit!"

Ingrid said, "Drive the car," so the gas Anna hit.

Anna said. "Is there any other foul people you want to pick up today?"

Ingrid said, "No, this gentleman's fine. Let's be on our way."

The wino said, "Gentleman! I haven't been called that in years.

You think we could go back and get a few beers?"

Ingrid said, "Sip on your wine; I'll get you some after while."

The wino said, "Thanks," and gave a big smile.

They arrived at the house and got out to go in.

Anna said, "How about your wino friend?"

Ingrid said, "I'll get him," and opened the car door.

The wino said, "It's all gone. Do you have any more?"

She took his hand, and helped him to the door.

He started yelling, "Give me more! Give me more!"

Ingrid opened the front door, and helped him in.

Anna said, "I need to stay out in the wind."

Ingrid said to the wino, "What is your name?"

He said, "Charles Adams," without any shame.

"Well, Charles, I think you need to take a shower and get

clean."

He started yelling, and screaming, and making a scene.

"Shh!" Ingrid said, "You'll wake everyone here."

He said, "Fuck you, bitch! Now give me that beer!"

"Raphael," Ingrid called "I have you a new friend."

He entered the room, and said, "Let the party begin."

He looked at the wino, and said, "Is this all you've got!

Some drunken fool the world has forgot?

I deserve better than this foul, disgusting excuse for a man."

Ingrid said, "You'd better be grateful and take what you can!

You're still not showing any respect to me.

You'd better learn how if you want to hunt free.

Like I said before, you can come and go and have what you will take,

when there aren't any rules that I have to make."

Raphael said, "Rules? Fuck your rules! I don't have to listen to you."

Ingrid said, "Oh, my! Is it dawn? The sun seems to be piercing through."

Raphael looked at the window, and dawn was breaking.

Ingrid said, "This one was yours for the taking.

Now you have to rest, hungry and weak,

until your attitude becomes more meek."

Raphael left for the basement, hissing and cussing.

Ingrid yelled, "Get over your fussing!"

Anna came in, and said, "Where did the day go?

I blinked my eyes and dawn started to show."

Ingrid snickered, "Whatever do you mean?"

The drunk once again started making a scene.

Ingrid pushed him into a chair, and whispered, "Sleep."

He fell into dreams without making a peep.

Anna said, "Mother, I'm going to go rest

and, when I get up, I'll pick the trip that's the best.

I need to get away from all of this for a while."

Ingrid said, "Yes, you do," and gave her a smile.

Anna went to her room and put on a lace gown

and fell asleep as soon as she laid her head down.

Ingrid looked at the drunk, and said, "He'll be fine there,"

went to her room and started brushing her hair.

She slipped out of her clothes and laid on her bed

but couldn't get Tristan out of her head.

"Even for an older man, he still looked good," she thought.

"Even after all the trials and tribulations he's fought.

He still had that warm glow,

the very one I used to know."

When he touched her hand she felt the warmness of his caresses.

It reminded her of his gifts: flowers and all of the dresses.

The two of them were almost as close as she had been

with her one, true lover that the Underworld had taken within.

For a mortal, Tristan seemed like the perfect man,

and she was proud to walk holding Tristan's hand.

Side by side they watched sunsets and stars in the night,

holding each other very closely in delight.

Her lips pouted for his tender kiss.

Her hips moved for the times of bliss.

She was in agony from thoughts of all his wonderful sensations,

laying in her bed lonely and full of frustrations.

She shrieked, and then cursed God and time,

for taking away her man so fine.

Her emotions were stirred. Her passion was filled with desire.

She thought to herself, "I need to quench this fire."

She got up and put on a silk robe,

and went about the house to probe.

She went to Anna's room and peeked in.

She was asleep, so she let her plan begin.

Ingrid said, "Nightfall—return to a moment before,"

then she went down the basement door.

She rapped on Raphael's trunk, and said, "I'll give you another chance."

She opened the lid, and said, "I need a dance."

Raphael said, "Is this another game you're playing with me?"

She said, "No, come on. Let's go upstairs. You quickly will see."

They went upstairs, and Ingrid said to the wino, "Awake.

There's a shower you need to take.

Go down the hall and water yourself down,

after your shower put on my gown.

Come back here when you are through.

I have a task for you to do."

Ingrid looked Raphael in the eyes sincerely.

This is something Raphael never thought he'd see…

Raphael said, "What is it you want of me?"

She said, "Just hold me tenderly.

Can we set our differences aside a while?"

Raphael gave her back a smile.

He took her and held her close to him.

She let out a silent loving whim.

He bent to kiss her wanton lips,

as he placed his hands upon her hips.

She said, "You can kiss me all the night,

but if you try to bite, there will be a fight.

Yet I will surrender myself to you,

if your passion is really true."

Back into the room, Charles came.

Ingrid then called him by name,

"Charles, you smell nice and clean,

and you said things to me that were mean.

I bought you what you asked for at the store,

but you thought I should have gave you more.

This is a friend of mine. Say 'Hello.'"

Raphael's eyes began to glow.

He said, "Charles, I need a little help, my friend.

Some of your blood I need within.

Would you mind if I took a bite?"

Charles said, "That would be alright."

Raphael let go of Ingrid, and walked to Charles,

sunk his teeth in his neck with lavishing snarls.

Ingrid said, "Don't take it all.

He'll be back again to call."

Raphael stopped, and Charles fell to the floor.

He said, "You won't be a drunk anymore.

The next time you come back for me to feed,

your blood better be sweet, virgin seed.

Now Ingrid, where were we?"

She smiled, and said, "Now let me see…"

She walked over to Raphael, French kissed him, and said, "Stop."

Then she said, "You didn't swallow that last drop."

She had never tasted human blood before

and found it to be a taste she could adore.

They kissed deeply, and she said,

"How would you like to share my bed?"

Raphael said, "Lead the way."

Ingrid said softly, "Okay."

They walked into Ingrid's room of mirrors.

She said, "Do you have any fears?"

Raphael said, "What do you mean by that?

You've already made me into a black cat."

She laughed, and then they laid on the bed.

Tristan's memory was still in her head.

She disrobed, and said, "Do you like what you see?"

Raphael said, "Yes, it pleases me.

You have picked a beautiful look.

The first time I saw you, my breath was took."

"Raphael, I've always thought you were an adorable man,

Now kiss me, and give me all that you can.

Mmmmm! That's nice. Mmmmm! So tender,

and so full of passion; so full of splendor."

Raphael stood up and took off his clothes.

Ingrid looked and saw something had arose.

She said, "So you're not pretending you want me

as now I can plainly see.

Now lay in my bed next to me,

and take me to realms of ecstasy."

Raphael laid on top of Ingrid kissing her madly.

She took his hard cock in her hand and started stroking it steadily

He began kissing her neck. The more he kissed her flesh,

the closer the two of them were starting to mesh.

Soon like wild animals clawing and biting eagerly.

Raphael bit his wrist and said, "Taste of me."

Ingrid opened her mouth and drank of him,
and felt a burning fire forming within.
She screamed, "Now! Now! Put it in! Put it in!
And it better stay stiff and not even bend!"
Raphael slid deep inside,
and like a wave they began to ride.
She clasped her hands upon his rear,
pulling him deeper and, oh, so near.
They kissed and his fangs touched her lips.
She undulated happily under his hips.
Gyrating and pulling him further in,
over and over and over again.
Then Ingrid starting yelling, "Yes! Yes! Yes!
This new body is the best!
Fuck me! Fuck me," she yelled at him.
Then he gave her an evil grin,
and sunk his teeth deep in her neck.
Her body then became a wreck.
She exploded in sheer ecstasy
and moaned, "You're sucking the life out of me!"
He dug his fangs deeper in,
and sucked with all his might within.
Completely possessed not to stop,
until he had drained her of every drop.
She went limp beneath him,
he had taken all her blood within.

He got up and dressed and called her a bitch.

She sat up laughing and said, "There's been a switch."

He said, "No, this can't be true.

I sucked all the life out of you."

She said, "Yes it is, my little friend.

I told you it's a battle you cannot win.

I asked you if you had any fear,

now you have to look in my mirrors.

The bite that you tried to bestow on me

is now on your neck for you to see.

Worse than that, my Vampire friend,

your human days will now begin."

Raphael looked and in every mirror he was surrounded by his reflection.

Ingrid said, "This is a curse I've gave to you for giving my love rejection."

Raphael fell to his knees in horror—he was now definitely Ingrid's slave—

and now he would age and die and have to await the grave.

This now mortal that had been powerful for hundreds of years,

let his thirst for power end him up full of tears.

Weeping, he said, "What of me now? Oh, help me, GOD!"

Ingrid said, "I'm your God and, when I say to do things, you'd better nod.

Now get that wino dressed, put him in my car and take him back to an alley somewhere.

Then get back here as soon as you can, we need to start discussing our new affair."

"Okay," Raphael said. "Okay," she asked. "It had better be 'Yes, ma'am' from now on,

or in the blink of an eye to the Underworld you'll be gone.

I'm sure Tom, Lyra and Lenore would just love to see the new you,

especially with all that fresh blood that your veins have flowing through.

Now go and do what I say,

unless you have another game to play."

"No, ma'am. I'll go," Raphael said with tightly clenched teeth.

Ingrid said, "You better work on that smile and what's hiding beneath."

Raphael left with the wino and headed towards town.

Ingrid said to herself, "I'll take a bath, then I'll lay down."

She went into the bathroom and ran a nice, hot bath,

then thought of what had transpired and let out a laugh.

She lay in the hot water, warm and serene;

closed her eyes and started to dream.

She drifted back in time hundreds of years,

back when they called it *ale* instead of *beer.*

She was in a small pub in England,

sitting with Iris, her dearest friend.

Then a shot rang out and black powder smoke filled the air,

and a man nearby laid slumped over in his chair.

Everyone started screaming and running out the door
and the man that had the gun said, "No more, no more."
Then he fell to his knees and began to cry,
and looked up to the heavens and said, "Why? Oh, why?"
He dropped the pistol and it fell to the floor by his side.
His eyes were transfixed and open so wide.
He sat shaking and weeping like a young kid,
then ran to a corner and there he hid.
He said over and over, "He's the one
that fed that monster my daughter and son!"
Iris said to Ingrid whose name then was Ann,
"What does he mean? I don't understand."
She replied, "There are things in this world, my dear,
that can take your life or leave your mind trapped in fear."
"What do you speak of," Iris said.
Ann replied, "The living dead."
"Living dead," Iris replied
with both of her eyes now opened wide.
"What does it mean to be called 'living dead?'"
"They call them Vampires," Ann softly said.
"They will bite your neck and drain the life out of you,
and make you like them if they want to.
Then you'll live a life forever cursed,
with the taste of human blood as an unquenchable thirst.
Then you'll sleep by day and live by night,
seeking out some poor soul to bite."

Iris said, "Oh, what a fairy tale!"

Ann replied, "No, it's not," trying not to yell.

"Come with me and I'll show you

that my story is, oh, so true!"

She grabbed Iris by the hand

and walked over to the dead man.

She said, "Here, take a look at this poor being."

Pulling his collar back, she said, "Do you see what I'm seeing?"

She said, "Now do you understand?"

Looking at the bite marks, Iris said,

"So he's what you call the living dead?"

Ann said, "No, this man was a minion—a servant to his master—

but I don't understand why his life ended in disaster.

Normally their host keeps their minions out of harm's way

so they can look after them while they sleep during the day."

"Oh, this is almost all too much to believe," Iris said.

"Blood sucking monsters and the evil undead?"

"Iris, I've been around such a long time.

If you knew what I know it would destroy your mind.

I have seen so many terrible things,

from the slaughter of nations to the murders of kings."

"Whatever do you mean," Iris asked in a confused tone.

Ann replied, "There's things about me you have never known.

If I tell you my secrets can you keep them to yourself?

If anyone finds out it would be bad for our health."

Ann said, "I hope you understand,"

as she took Iris by the hand.

Then she said, "Close your eyes and clear your mind

and I'll show you new things that you will find

will help you to understand

that there's more to this life and land."

Iris closed her eyes and started to see

all of Ann's hidden mysteries.

They were just blinks in time,

some as horror and some divine:

castles, knights, dragons, and streams,

angels, fairies, and demons with wings,

candles, potions, and fires in the night,

roses, crosses, and butterflies in flight,

bites, boils, and all that festers,

kings, queens, and joyful jesters.

Through Ann's mind Iris saw

all these things that filled her with awe.

Then Ann softly said, "Come back to me.

You've seen all that you need to see."

Iris opened her eyes and said, "The light's so bright."

Ann replied, "Because you have new sight.

You now see things as they truly are,

things that weren't visible to you so far.

Now I have given you a gift my friend

that will be with you until the end.

Each and every day it will grow

into the powers that I know."

"Powers? What powers," asked Iris.

Ann said, "Powers like this...

Sir? Oh, sir," Ann said to the man in the corner weeping.

"Sir, come over here and talk with your friend who is sleeping."

The man came over and sat down at the table with the dead man.

Ann said, "Now, please do take this poor man's hand."

He did as he was told but didn't understand.

"It's time we started a brand new plan,"

she said. "It's time for the clocks to start to rewind,

and there won't be any murder to find."

In an instant everything was as it was before,

there wasn't a dead man or a gun on the floor.

Iris and Ann were back at their own table again.

Ann got up, walked over, and said, "Don't do it, my friend."

The man with the gun just went over and sat down,

and ordered an ale so his pains he could drown.

Iris was now in total confusion from what she had seen:

the man that was covered in blood was alive, fresh, and clean!

She said, "How the hell did you do that, Ann?"

Ann said, "The longer you're with me, you'll understand."

Ann went and sat with the minion and said, "Hello."

She looked over at Iris and said, "It's time for a show...

Hey mate, do you have a name?"

He answered, "Albert," but wished he'd refrained.

"What do you do, Albert," asked Ann.

He said, "I work for a man called Sebastian."

When he spoke he had a quiver to his voice,

as if his words were not of his choice.

Ann then said, "You care to give us ladies a good time?"

Albert said, "That would be divine.

Gather your coats and we'll go where I stay."

Ann asked Iris, "Do you want to go play?"

Iris said, "Yes, it would be a delight,"

wondering what else would transpire in the night.

She now was wondering what else Ann could do.

Ann said to her, "Let's be on our way and I will show you."

Iris said, "How did you read what I had on my mind?"

She said, "I have even stronger gifts you will find."

Albert said, "Gifts? What do you speak of?"

Ann replied, "Oh, it's nothing, my love."

They went out to a street of cobblestone

and started their walk to Sebastian's home.

There was a full moon out and the air was damp and cold.

Iris thought to herself, "This venture is kind of bold."

She was starting to believe everything Ann had said

about Vampires and the living undead.

The visions she had seen from Ann's mind

gave birth to new thoughts she could never find.

All the years she had known Anna she seemed normal as could be,

but now Iris knows there's much more to see.

They had walked several blocks and not a word was said,

then Albert spoke and said, "It's not much further ahead."

They kept walking and then they began to hear

the faint sound of a violin and music so dear.

The closer they got, the notes were more sweet.

They walked more like dancing as they moved their feet.

It removed any form of fear or fright,

as the two of them ventured into the night.

Ann said to Iris, "Before we get where were going, my dear,

I need to show you how to not have any fear.

Usually it takes years and years for this to take effect,

but I might need your help so I don't end up Sebastian's subject.

Albert, stop right where you are at."

He came to a stop and down he sat.

She said, "Now, Iris, I will speed up time

so that your powers will be almost equal to mine.

Close your eyes and let the powers in,

you're part of the earth, the fire, and the wind.

Anything now that you wish to do

is all within the powers given to you.

I've never given anyone this gift before,

it's much, much more than luck or lore.

It comes from the elements and the soul of creation,

now open your eyes and receive confirmation."

Iris opened her eyes and said, "I feel so old."

Ann said, "It's the age of the powers you now hold.

All you have to do is say what you wish to do,

and there won't be anything that's not attainable for you."

Iris yelled at Ann, "So what have you done? Made me a witch?"

"No. I've made you a sorceress, you bitch.

I've given you a very powerful gift because you're my friend,

and you yell at me before any of your powers even begin."

"I'm sorry," said Iris. "Things are happening so fast to me tonight.

I'm torn between anger, fear, power, and delight."

Ann said, "Oh, so you feel it coursing in your veins, I see.

Now you can live your life totally free.

You can live forever if you wish to.

Or you can number the days until the end of you.

There's a lot more I need to say,

but for right now, let's go play.

Albert get back on your feet and let's pick up the pace.

I can't wait to see Sebastian's face!"

Albert stood and they went on their way,

with the sun long set and hiding the light of day.

The violin music was getting even louder as they got nearer,

and the soothing music was the sweetest thing Iris did ever hear.

She began to hum along with tender melody.

Ann said to her, "This man I have to see."

Iris said, "Yes, his music sets me free;

free from the pain I have endured through all the years,

free from all the nights when I was drowned in endless tears,

free from this life I live that seems to get worse each day,

free from all the hurtful things that most people say,

free from all the loneliness that has filled my world with strife,

free from all the things that made me want to take my life."

Ann yelled, "Stop, Iris! Just stop! Don't you see what's happening to you?

If you let him in your head the both of us could be through!"

"But Ann," Iris said, "I haven't felt this well in ages!"

Ann replied, "Iris you don't understand this Vampire is full of rages.

I need you to be with me in everything we do,

or Sebastian will consume both me and you!"

Albert said, "We're here," as he came to a stop at the huge steps of granite.

Ann looked at the house and said, "Sebastian has taste, I have to admit."

Iris said, "Look at all the stained windows and how they

glow in the moonlight."

Ann said, "Lets go into this lair, Iris, but be ready for a fight."

Albert grabbed the handle and the hinges let out a piercing squeak,

at that very instant Iris's happiness turned very bleak.

She screamed, "I won't go in," then ran and hid behind Ann.

Ann said, "It will be okay," as she took Iris's hand.

Ann said, "I've given you almost all my gifts, Iris, my, oh, sweet dear,

but the one gift I can't give is how to conquer your fear:

fear that one thing that hides us from achieving our goals,

fear that one thing that destroys our lives and consumes our souls.

Fear and doubt, fear and doubt...

Oh, how they surge about!

One blinds you,

the other binds you.

Teetering back and forth, back and forth.

Neither one has a half penny's worth!

Yet they grow like giant festers within your mind,

blinding your true direction to find.

Now come, Iris, and let's go;

you said you were up for a show."

Iris said, "No," and turned and ran away.

Ann yelled, "Okay. I guess I'll just play."

Just as Iris was out of Ann's sight,

a voice said, "What a wonderful night."

Out of the darkness Sebastian appeared,

he was a handsome man with a well-groomed beard,

long blond hair and eyes—his eyes, they were serene.

Unlike most other Vampires eyes, they looked pure and clean.

They had a soft blue hue with sparkles of gold.

Ann thought to herself, "What a lovely man to behold."

"Are you just going to stand in the doorway," Sebastian said.

"Or are you going to run away like your friend, instead?"

His voice was soft and tender to the ear.

Ann replied, "I won't run. I have no fear."

"Albert," Sebastian said, "go ready the study for our guest."

Ann thought to herself, "Now begins the test."

Sebastian said, "Would you like wine, my dear guest?"

Ann said, "Yes, I would, but I prefer the best."

Sebastian said, "Albert, you heard her request;

now prepare my study, then you can go rest."

Ann said, "Yes, it's been a long night for him,"

as it took her all to hide her evil grin.

Sebastian closed the door and took Ann's hand.

She said, "Your hand's kind of cold for a man.

Most men I've met had warm hands, but a cold heart."

He said, "Maybe we're off to a different start.

Walk this way. I'll show you around my domain."

As they walked down a huge hallway all lit with flames,

there were huge paintings on each of the side of them.

Ann asked, "Who are these people?" He said, "They're my kin.

Three hundred years of ancestors hang on these walls.

It was the highest of honors to be remembered in these great halls."

As they were walking, Ann stopped and said, "Isn't that Lord Bane?"

Sebastian said, "Yes, you know of his name?"

"Only stories I've been told

when I wasn't very old."

"I'm intrigued," Sebastian said. "Please do tell me of the stories.

You won't offend me, I promise; no worries."

Ann began, "Lord Bane was said to have been one of the fiercest men to walk the land.

They said his sword was yielded by the devil's hand.

He fought both on the land and sea

and always achieved victory.

He was quite a calculating man

when he chose a battle plan.

He would look at each and every option before

he would send his army into a war.

And each every one of his men were trained

by this man some called insane.

They said he would drink the blood and eat the meat

of the poor souls that his army would defeat.

He would ravage women and plant his seed

into the women of the fallen breed."

Sebastian said, "Interesting... You seem to know quite a bit about him,

but there's some errors in your stories. Where should I begin..?

Oh, never mind. We have better things to do

than me to correct the stories that were told to you.

My study is just down the hall ahead.

Let's go have a toast and break some bread."

Bread and wine, that sounded very good to Ann.

As she walked down the hall with Sebastian hand-in-hand,

she wondered why he had stopped the conversation about Lord Bane

and what hidden stories that still did remain.

She tried to peer into his mind but then she felt weak

and wondered if her options might turn out bleak.

"Here's the study," excitedly Sebastian said.

She looked at the decor, it was all crimson red.

There was a table with fruit, bread, and wine.

Sebastian said, "Go ahead, I'll play while you dine."

Grabbing his violin, Sebastian stroked the strings with the bow.

He said with a smile, "This might be a tune that you know."

A first it wasn't familiar, then it began to grow.

It wasn't very long that it set Ann's heart aglow.

She started dancing as if she was possessed.

He played ever faster. Ann said, "I think I need to rest."

But as long as he played Ann could not stop her dancing.

He struck one more note and said, "I think you need romancing."

Just as he stopped, Ann collapsed into his arms.

She thought to herself, "This could lead to harm."

She knew she was so weak that it could lead to her death.

She said, "Please, let's sit down. I'm so out of breath!"

Sebastian walked her over to a chair,

helped her sit down, and stroked her hair.

"I love your hair," Sebastian said.

"I've always been fond of red."

Ann, still out of breath and weak, wondered what was next to come.

She was so drained, she knew she couldn't run.

Sebastian bent down to her and said, "Look in my eyes, dear.

You don't have anything that you must fear.

You wanted to meet me, so here I am.

I guess things didn't turn out like you did plan.

But there's more to me than you see,

I have a curse, but I live my life free.

I have never drank the blood of any man.

Animals keep my thirst in hand.

Yes, I have to drink more and more

to quench my thirst and fight the horror.

I've searched over and over on this earth

for a way to kill this curse and give me rebirth."

"Who are you trying to fool," Ann said.

"I know that you are one of the undead,

and all of you are pretty much the same.

You just have different ways you play the game.

Some of you are kind and some are cruel,

but there's always the golden rule.

Whether a Vampire's in your heart or your head,

the best type of Vampires are the ones that are dead."

Sebastian said, "You're an evil bitch, aren't you?"

Ann said, "Evil to the core, through and through.

But I didn't start out this way,

life made the game I play."

Sebastian said, "Yes, I was once a tender man, myself,

serving humanity with no wish for wealth.

But that was many years ago

and into that story I'd rather not go."

He said, "Yes, it's a story I'd rather forget.

Just the thought of my maker makes me sweat."

Ann said, "So do you have any other stories you'd like to share?"

He said, "What about Ursula," and Ann's face turned as red as her hair.

"Ursula? That bitch! What do you know about her,"

as she asked the question her emotions did stir.

Sebastian said, "She was condemned thousands of years ago

to the Underworld where nothing but pain does grow!"

Sebastian started to say something to Ann,

there was a knock on the door and Raphael said, "Ma'am."

Ingrid woke from the daydream shaking and cold,

her bath felt as icy as the stories of old.

Shivering, she yelled, "What the fuck do you want?"

Raphael thought to himself, "She's really a cunt!"

Oh, that was very serious mistake

that Raphael just did make.

"I'm a *what,*" Ingrid yelled out back at him.

Then Raphael had pains that set in.

It started at the top of his head,

and went through him so bad he wished he was dead.

He curled up on the floor in a fetal position,

trying to shield the ever painful condition.

He murmured, "Please, Ingrid, please stop... please stop..."

She got out of the icy water and dried off every drop.

She put on her robe and opened the door,

and looked at Raphael curled up on the floor.

He had tears streaming down his face.

Ingrid said, "Will you ever learn your place?"

He said, "Yes, yes, please make the pain quit."

She took his hand and said, "Let's go have a sit."

As soon as she touched his hand,

the pain was gone. It felt so grand!

She walked him into her bedroom and said, "Sit down, my pet.

It seems that it's so easy for you to forget.

Is it so hard to remember that I am in charge of you

and you have to do everything I say for you to do?

If you keep up this game you're going to lose

and 'Raphael Went to the Underworld' will be the new news."

Just as she said Underworld the name Ursula popped in her mind,

and *vengeance* and *payback* were the words she did find.

"I wonder," she thought. Then she said, "Raphael, I have a question for you,

and if you don't answer truthful you know what I'll do.

All of you Vampires are like one, giant nest.

There's the name of a siren I truly detest.

If I ask you her name can I trust you

to tell me about her with things that are true?"

Raphael, now still remembering the pain

said, "Yes, you can. What is her name?"

Ingrid blurted out, "Ursula," in total spite.

Raphael shook and closed both of his eyes tight.

He clenched his teeth and tried to decide

whether if this was a story that he should hide.

Ingrid said, "Answer me now; I command you!

Or you know what is the next thing I will do."

Raphael said, "And if I don't, you'll torture me."

Ingrid said, "Either way, you're dead, don't you see?

Close your eyes, Raphael, and go see your friends

and I'll show you how real torture begins."

No sooner than she spoke, he was in the Underworld with Lyra and Lenore.

Tom was clutching a huge rock and was ravished with horror.

The sisters looked at Raphael and they both said, "Hello."

They smelled his fear and their thirst began to grow.

Raphael said, "Wait! I want to help you get out of here,"

but even Tom realized Raphael was hiding his fear.

Lyra said, "One," then Lenore said, "Two," then Tom said, "Three,"

and Raphael thought to himself, "This is the end of me!"

He yelled, "Ingrid I'll tell you about Ursula," at the top of his voice,

then he was back with her and she said, "So you've made your choice."

Still trembling with fear Raphael said, "Yes, I'll tell you all I know."

Ingrid said, "You'd better, or it will be back to the show."

Raphael began, "Legend has it that Ursula was a hideous siren,

that her beautiful voice mesmerized so many men,

and the more she mesmerized the more power she would

attain.

The ones she couldn't conquer, she drove them insane.

Thousands of men fell prey to her power, so they say.

She could sing her spells twenty-four hours a day.

She didn't need to sleep or even to eat,

the souls she consumed tasted sweeter than mincemeat.

Nations all over the world had heard or her deeds,

they sent knights and warriors, armed on their steeds.

There wasn't ever one single fight;

the armies fell prey to songs of delight.

Sorcerers and warlocks all tried their hand,

nothing could evict Ursula from their land.

But, just as total power can be a curse to one,

Ursula won so many battles her loneliness had begun.

She longed for love from a true man.

She went into isolation and created a plan."

Ingrid said, "Blah, blah, blah, Raphael. I've heard all of this.

Tell me something unique," she said, almost like a hiss.

He hesitated a moment and then said, "What, exactly, do you wish to know?"

Ingrid said, "How did she get out of the Underworld down below?"

To his surprise, Raphael didn't know that Ingrid knew of her escape.

He said, "It took her hundreds of years and she wasn't in very good shape.

When she came back here she was almost nearly dead,

and the world was full of wars and everywhere was bloodshed.

This was a time of feasting for Vampires; no one missed anyone.

They were too worried about if they had a future to come.

Ingrid said, "Yes, humans are such a quibbling mass of jelly.

Their only concerns are sex and their belly.

Women popping out breed after breed,

not having any concern where they get their seed.

Children not knowing where they fit into which race,

having nowhere to belong, wandering place to place.

At least our lineage is from pure and true blood flowing within,

not showing any guilt or anything that the humans call *sin*.

Oh, my mistake, Raphael, I said *our* linage. I seem to have made an error,

you're now a human again and now you must care.

Care about aging, care about love,

care if there's a devil or a God up above."

"Oh, you bitch," Raphael exclaimed.

Ingrid said, "Do you want some more pain?"

He said, "No, you have me at your beckoning call

and I have to do every task, how large or how small.

But, I swear to you, it won't always be like this."

Ingrid made an angry face and let out a hiss.

"Now, get back to the story about Ursula, I command you."

He said, "Don't you have better things for me to do?"

She said, "Maybe later, Raphael, my little pet;

now tell me what I want or it will be to your regret."

Raphael said, "Why is it so important that you know?"

Ingrid said, "Never mind that, now let your words flow."

Raphael said, "I wish I could run..."

Ingrid said, "Maybe some pain will loosen your tongue."

Raphael shrieked and said, "Please, no! I will tell you!"

Ingrid said, "This is your last chance; the answers had better be true."

Raphael said, "Ursula had a voice that was, oh, so serene,

but it was her face that took lives and crushed their dreams.

She was a truly horrid-looking thing.

Her face killed the people, not what she did sing.

It lured them to her like a rat to some cheese.

It lured men, many of men, with, oh, such a tease.

But when they were close enough to see her face,

she raised her veil and their life was erased.

Their energy then returned to the source of all things,

that timeless and ageless place that just turns in rings.

Speaking of that, I now know that I have to die,

it won't be so bad to be part of the sky.

But I wonder if God will forgive all my deeds,

and all of those I cursed with misbegotten seeds..."

Ingrid said, "Oh, Raphael, is that guilt that I hear?

Isn't it funny how it comes with unknown fear?

Now get back to your story and quit whining to me,

you have the answers that I wish to see.

Do I have to give you a little nudge?

Don't worry about God right now; I'm your judge."

Raphael cleared his throat and began to speak,

never in his life had his words been so meek.

He said, "After all of her years and conquests,

there still was a pain, oh, so deep in her chest."

"Not that boring love thing again," Ingrid said,

"I just want to know if that bitch is really dead."

Raphael said, "She is, as far as I know."

Then Ingrid's eyes started to glow.

She said, "Oh, please, please, do go on,

I want to know how that wench is now gone."

Raphael said, "Why do you have so much hatred for her?"

Ingrid said, "Never mind," and his eyes started to blur.

Raphael rubbed his eyes and said, "What are you doing to me?"

Ingrid said, "Finish the damn story or this will be the last time you see!"

Raphael cleared his throat and then started to speak,

hoping his answer would be the one she did seek.

"Well it was love that lead Ursula to her death,"

he paused for a second and took a deep breath.

"She decided that she would seek out the love of her life,

but she knew that her face could kill faster than a knife.

So she sat and thought and thought and cried;

she had so much loneliness tucked deep inside.

Her tears streamed and streamed down her face,

until there were crevices her sorrow did trace.

One day she went to a pool to have a cool drink.

She laid on the ground and started to think.

She thought, 'How will I ever get rid of this face

and find me a man that shows me some grace?'

Then she thought, 'There has to be a transformation spell,

that will make me more beautiful than words can ever tell.

That's it,' she yelled out, so filled with glee.

Now there was hope for her to be free!

She traveled land to land, looking for the right sorcerer

who could transform her face and take the pain away from her.

Just when her journey seemed like a dead end,

she heard her name echoing silently in the wind.

It seemed to be so far away that it came from,

but she walked towards it and began to hum.

The closer she got, the voice did increase;

it was serene and gave her internal peace.

She walked and walked, mile after mile,

then, for the first time in her life, her lips cracked a smile.

This was a peculiar feeling to her,

the smile made her happy and she let out a purr.

She felt her lips, they were soft to her touch,

and thought to herself, 'This is too much.'

Her lips had always been so coarse and so rough

that, in comparison to her face, leather wasn't even tough.

Now she had soft and smooth, shapely lips,

and to her touch she thrusted her hips.

She had always longed for a gentle kiss.

This, among other things, she truly did miss.

The voice was still calling out her name.

She thought to herself, 'Is this just a game?'

Then the voice stopped and she heard a whistling tune.

Her ears started to perk and her heart made more room.

The more she listened, the better she could hear.

She reached up and grabbed her left ear.

To her surprise it also had changed miraculously,

she wished she had a mirror so that she could see.

Then the tune stopped and she smelt a sweet smell,

then touched her nose and started to yell.

'My God! My God! What's happening to me?

I now have a nose that doesn't feel like three!'

The transformations continued as it neared the night,

then there was a man ahead in her sight.

She yelled, 'Are you the one that's doing this to me?'

He answered back, 'Yes, come! Let me set you free!'

She then started to run like a horse in a race,

running her hands along her new face.

It was soft to her touch, much softer than silk.

She looked at her skin on her hands, as white as milk.

She ran up to the man, said, 'Oh, thank you so much!'

He reached out his hand and her face he did touch.

This was the most beautiful feeling she ever had.

He said, 'I hope your change hasn't made you mad.'

She said, 'Mad? Mad! Are you insane?

All of my life I've lived in so much pain.'

She said, 'What is your name my, oh, so kind friend?'

He replied, 'I've had many names since time did begin.'

Then he said, 'Ursula,' in a soft tone

and her emotions started to roam.

He grabbed her and held her close in his arms,

and said, 'May I have a kiss,' and she thought, 'Oh, what's the harm?'

Then she said, 'After all that you have given to me tonight,

you can have anything that will bring you delight.'

He said, 'That's a very inviting invitation.'

He kissed her wildly, with no hesitation.

Her body started to ignite from within

from all the compassion from her newly found friend.

She gasped and said, 'I've never, ever, felt this way.'

He whispered softly, 'Shh. Let us just play.'

He kissed her with his tongue in her mouth deep.

She had bodily juices that started to seep.

He slowly removed her gown

and dropped it to the ground."

Ingrid said, "Are you going to ramble and ramble on?"

Raphael said, "I thought you wanted to hear how she ended up gone?"

Ingrid said, "Skip all the romance and get to the end."

Raphael said, "It was with romance that her demise did begin.

You see, the man that transformed her had a grudge to fulfill,

but he couldn't kill her until after he had broken her will.

He seduced her and loved her over and over again,

her moans of ecstasy echoed in the wind.

She thought to herself, 'I've found that one true love I've sought,'

and, all the night long, this was her only thought.

Dawn was breaking as she lay on the ground spent,

and she thought to herself how fast the night went.

They got dressed and he gave her a kiss and said, 'Good morn.'

He said, 'We have to leave, there is an oncoming storm.'

He had a horse tied to a bush quite near.

They mounted it together; she was so filled with cheer.

They rode together towards a town not far away.

She spoke to him, but not a word he did say.

She thought that this was peculiar of him,

but she liked the feel of his body next to her skin.

She said, 'What is the name of this town?'

He said not a word, nor turned around.

He rode to the stable and they both did dismount.

She started to wonder to herself what this was about.

He looked at the stable owner and said, 'Take care of my steed.'

He gave a big smile and said, 'Yes, sir; indeed.'

He said, 'Ursula, would you like to go that pub over there?'

She thought, 'Pub,' and her eyes had a happy glare.

They walked in and she had everyone's eye,

and thought to herself, with a blush, 'Oh my, oh my.'

She said, 'I don't know what to call you. What is your name?'

Her friend said, 'Just call me *Revenge,* if it's all the same.'

'Revenge,' she thought, 'Oh my, how strange.'

Then he said, 'I found this one out on the range.'

She said, 'Revenge, can I ask you to do for a favor for me?

Can you find a mirror so my face I can see.'

He said, 'Yes, I'll find you one,' and called to the barkeep.

'Can I have a mirror that is so clear and so deep?'

The barkeep came over with an old mirror.

Ursula said, 'I can't.' Revenge said, 'What is it you fear?'

Revenge said that in a condescending tone.

She thought he was implying that his heart was her home.

She took the mirror and quickly gave it a glance

and the beauty she saw put her in a trance.

She now wanted men, all the men that she could get;

the search for one love she soon did forget.

She did man after man, over and over again,

until her once-evil heart exploded within.

As she lay dead on the floor,

Revenge said, 'She is no more.'

He said, 'Now I have avenged my father's death

that I swore to fulfill until my last breath.

That evil bitch at last is no more.

She died a useless, unfulfilled whore.'

All the men toasted his noble deed,

for removing one of mankind's worst ever grown seed."

Ingrid said, "So, how did Revenge perform his spell?"

Raphael said, "That, I will never tell.

I've answered what you've asked of your enemy,

now let's let the rest of the story just be."

Ingrid said, "Fine. I've heard enough for now,

but, if I want the answer, I'll find it somehow.

You still haven't told me how she came back to Earth,

so that whole damn story had little worth."

"I'll never tell you how she came back here.

You'd then have too much power, my dear!"

Then she gave him an evil grin,

he knew this was a quest that she would win.

"Well for now we'll just let this question be,

I'm sure there will be a way for your words to come free."

Then Ingrid said, "Raphael, go check on Anna Marie.

See if she wants to join you and me."

Raphael said, "So, why did you hate Ursula so?"

Ingrid said, "That you don't need to know.

Now do what I said.

Go get Anna Marie out of bed."

Raphael left her bedroom and went to Anna Marie's door,

he counted as he knocked, "One, two, three, four."

Anna Marie said, "Who is there?"

He said, "Raphael," and her fear did flare.

"Where's my mother," Anna Marie shrieked.

He said, "In her room," with words so meek.

Anna thought to herself, "That's a different tone..."

She thought he sounded all alone.

She said, "Raphael, what is it you need?"

Almost in tears, he said, "I want to be freed."

Anna said, "Raphael, is this a trick?

You're normally quite a pompous dick."

He said, "No, something's happened to me,

now open the door and I'll let you see."

Then Anna went and grabbed her cross in her hand,

just in case he had a sinister plan.

She went to her door and opened it wide,

looking at him on the other side.

She said, "You look so different, almost like you're in pain."

He said, "Ingrid's transformed me; it drives me insane!"

"Transformed you," she said in a questioning way.

He said, "Yes. Now I'll be human 'til the end of my days."

Anna noticed his face had color and his eyes were serene,

this wasn't the Vampire who made her just want to scream.

She noticed a tenderness from him that she did once feel,

but the only words she could find are, "So, what's the deal?"

"What's the deal," he asked. "Well, I had a fight,

now stands a human before your sight.

I tried to make Ingrid into a servant for me,

she reversed my plan, and now I can't ever be free.

I guess this is what they call karma, Anna Marie.

It seems all my deeds have been returned to me.

Now I'm a slave to your mother; there's no way to be free

unless my maker comes here to rescue me.

I know she's aware of what's happened to me right now.

We're all connected to each other, but none of us really know how.

There's a psychic bond between a maker and his minion.

I believe it's from the heart if you want my opinion."

"Heart," Anna said, "what heart do you speak of?

When you were a Vampire, your heart felt no love."

"Anna," he said, "this is what I kind of believe:

we're all our makers' children since there's no way to conceive.

Yes, we can have sex and passions of the flesh,

but though our bite can we add loved ones to the mesh."

Anna asked, "When you lose a loved one, you do feel some pain?"

He said, "Yes, it is so bad it would drive a human insane.

We feel the exact pain that led the other to it's fate,

the exact same second on that given date.

But the pain we feel is so intensified,

we almost ignite from the pain felt inside."

Anna said, "So, you think it's some kind of fucked up maternal bond

that tortures you so badly when one of your legion is gone?"

Raphael said, "I guess you could put it that way,"

and then his mind started to stray...

Drifting back so long ago in time,

he found a forgotten memory in his mind,

one that time had seemed to erase,

but now it is one that he must face.

There Natasha was in his mind, as plain as day,

trying to take his fever away.

She had a cold bucket of water from the well,

and was dousing his fever that was hot as hell.

In and out of consciousness he slid, time after time,

as she whispered, "Oh, my darling, you will be fine."

She held him close with his head on her lap

and looked at his trembling lips, so dry, and so chapped.

He was shaking all over and trembling within

as she wondered what had done this to him.

For three long days she never left his side,

and had no idea what was growing inside.

Then on the evening of the fourth, torturous day,

his fever broke and the symptoms went away.

He stood up and said, "This seems like a strange place."

She said, "You'll find only friends here," with a smile on her face.

"Here," he said, "where, might I ask, is here?"

She said, "It's your new home, so soft, and so dear."

"Home? Home," he loudly exclaimed.

He said, "Where's my family," with a grimace of pain.

She said, "There's no trace of your family to remain.

You're lucky that I was able to save you from the plague,"

with words that had little emotion and seemed very vague.

"Now that you're better, let's go to the dining table and have a seat.

You've been without food too long, so it's time to eat."

He walked into the dining room with her in the huge house and sat.

He said, "My family's gone," and she said, "Let's don't talk about that.

Right now you need food to regain your strength.

To save your life I've had to go through great length.

That last four days has taken it's toll on me.

He said, "Why didn't you let me die and be free?

Now I have to live without the ones I did love.

Is this a curse from God up above?

Why did you save me? Why did you care?"

She just smiled and gave him a blank stare.

She said, "I know you're in pain and I understand,

now you must eat. Doesn't the food look so grand?"

He replied, "Yes, the food looks grand and smells sweet."

She said, "Yes, now forget the past and begin to eat."

He began eating like he'd never eaten before,

then there was a loud knock on the door.

She said, "Excuse me, I will be right back."

He said, "Okay," and continued his attack.

With every bite that he did eat,

the food grew, oh, so sweet.

He overheard her at the front door,

a man said, "May I come in," and she said, "Not anymore."

Then there was yelling and screaming between the two,

Raphael kept eating wondering what he should do.

She called out, "Raphael, could you come here, my dear?"

He came to door and the stranger said to her, "He is
nothing to fear.

He looks like a rat that's lived in the gutters too long."

She said, "Give me a few days and he'll be quite strong."

She clenched her hand and hit him with her fist,

the stranger grabbed her arm and bit her on the wrist.

She pushed him away and closed and locked the door,

and said, "Soon we'll be ready if he comes back for more.

Now, dear, let's go so you can finish your meal."

He started to speak and she said, "It's not a big deal.

Just go back to the table with me and eat,

I have in mind a dessert you'll find very sweet."

He thought to himself how much pain he did feel,

but he was mesmerized into eating his meal.

The woman seemed to have some kind of power over him,

and with every bite she would just smile and grin.

He felt kind of strange, but was so compelled to eat,

as he wondered what was the mysterious meat.

It had an aroma that his nose had never smelt,

with a consistency his tongue had never felt.

Every bite of this unknown morsel he ate,

made him put more and more on his plate.

She said, "Have you tried your drink yet,

I know that you'll love it, what do you bet?"

He grabbed the goblet with inquisitive thirst,

but wondered if he drank it if he would be cursed.

Once again he thought this woman had a strange power
over him.

He looked her in the eyes as he thought this and she gave
him a grin.

Now his feelings and emotions started to roam,

wondering what will come next in this peculiar new home.

She said, "Are you nervous? You don't have to be.

You're a big, strong man; I'm just little, old me.

Would it be okay if I left you alone?

I haven't bathed in four days. I feel filth to the bone."

Raphael said, "Yes, ma'am, that would be fine with me."

She said, "You're not only good looking but you have manners, I see."

Then slowly she left the room, leaving Raphael to his feast.

He chuckled to himself, "Well, she's complimentary at least."

He continued to eat and drink, more after more.

It wasn't very long before she came through the door.

She asked, "How do I look?" His reply was, "Just great,"

as he was adding more food to his plate.

He said, "Why is it the more and more I eat,

my stomach still feels like an empty street?"

She said, "It must have been the plague, it drained you so much."

Then she walked over and gave his shoulder a touch.

The instant she touched him the hunger went away,

now he had a new hunger that was starting to play.

He looked at her in the black lace gown, it was almost see through.

Then she said, "Is there something you have in mind for us to do?"

With those tender words his mind went astray,

wondering what kind of game she wanted to play.

She took his hand and said, "Come with me,

I have a nice surprise for you to see."

She led him to the bathroom and a hot steaming tub.

She said, "Get undressed and I'll give you a scrub.

You smell like an old goat that's been left in the rain.

Please let me bathe you and remove some of your pain."

He undressed and lay down in the tub.

She grabbed a sponge and gently did scrub.

She started at his neck and went all the way to his feet,

she added oil that made the bath water smell sweet.

She touched his face and said, "This will not do,

I have to remove all these whiskers from you."

She grabbed a sterling cup with a shaving brush,

and whipped up a lather and gently said, "Shush."

She took a razor that looked like it was made of pure gold,

and said, "When you're clean shaven you won't look so old."

Gently she took the razor and, stroke after stroke,

she said, "Just lay back there and try to soak."

As he lay there his mind drifted away,

and thoughts of his family started to play.

Just as he started to think about all of them,

he felt a sharp pain and she said, "Did I cut you my friend?"

He touched his face after what she had said,

there on his hand was a slight touch of red.

She said, "Oh my, I'm sorry, but it's just a nick."

She gently bent over and gave it a lick.

"Mm," she murmured and the bleeding did quit.

She said, "Get out of the tub and lets go have a sit."

He stood and she wiped him dry with a soft cloth.

He noticed a few holes in it made by a moth.

She took a black robe and gave it to him

and said, "Now see? Your life isn't so grim."

She said, "Let's go to my bedroom and the both of us rest."

They went and lay down then she put her head on his chest.

She said, "You have a strong heart, I hear it pounding inside."

He began to have urges that he could not hide.

Then he thought he'd never been with anyone but his wife.

When he did this, she dug her nails in his back like a knife.

She said, "I thought I told you to forget your past.

Do it, Raphael, or I'll give you pain that will last."

Now he was seeing that she wasn't a savior like he had once thought,

and he knew there were soon going to be battles that will have be fought.

She jumped on top of him like a woman possessed,

holding his hands over his head, into the mattress she pressed.

He struggled to get free but she was too strong for him.

She let out a laugh as she had hold of his limbs.

She said, "After four days of me caring for you,

you have no appreciation for the things I did do.

I was hoping you'd pay me back with something for me...

Don't I look pretty enough for it to be?

Don't you find me pleasing to your eyes?

Don't you want to be inside of my thighs?

Men! Men! You're all the same:

after you get what you need, it's the end of the game.

I've given ninety-six hours of my life to you,

now you're going to love me until I am through.

Unless you want me to do something that you will regret."

Then, showing her fangs, she said, "I can make you my pet."

Just as she said "pet," he awoke from the daydream,

and then he let out a disheartened, childish scream.

Anna said, "Raphael, what is wrong with you?"

He said, "Oh, how wish my life was through."

He started crying and saying over and over again,

"Will this torture ever come to an end?"

Anna said, "You're a fine one to ask for torture to end.

What did you want to do to me, you hooligan?

Now that the shoe's on the other foot, how does it feel?

I guess you don't like my mother's new deal.

You know, there for a while, I thought she was unkind.

Now that I see you like this, I'm changing my mind.

I'm tired of tyrants and evil creatures like you

picking on the weak with everything they can do.

If you're seeking pity, you'll find none from me;

you're the most pathetic thing that I ever did see."

With those last words Raphael's temper flared,

he grabbed Anna by the throat and she looked really scared.

She yelled, "Stop it," with all of her might deep within,

then Raphael flew back as he was pushed by a great wind.

He rammed into a wall and slowly slid down.

Anna said, "Look, one of my latent talents I've found!"

This event filled Anna with excitement and with joy,

she knew that Raphael could be her toy.

Now she had no more fear from him.

This brought to her face a devilish grin.

She said, "I wonder what else I can do?

You counted to three. I'll just count to two,

then we'll see what I can make you do."

Anna was feeling that rush of power,

one that one feels when they test that hour

when a person's latent talents evolve,

and the powers of others they can dissolve.

She said, "One is for me and two is for you,

now you will dance until I say you are through."

Raphael picked himself up off of the floor

and started dancing like he had never before.

Ingrid came and said, "What is this I see?"

Anna said, "Raphael's under total control from me."

Ingrid said, "My, my, well look at you child,

I see the power, it makes your eyes go wild.

Just remember, my daughter, try to keep it in control

because, if you don't, it will consume your soul.

Raphael," Ingrid said, "go have a seat."

He thought to himself, "I now have two to defeat."

Ingrid said, "You'd better watch what you think,

or you know where you'll be in less than a blink.

Now, Anna, it's a new day for you. Let's go celebrate!

I have waited so long for this date.

Where is it that you would like for us to go?"

"How 'bout for some ice cream," and Ingrid started to glow.

Tristan popped in Ingrid's head and she said, "It's a date!

Let's go celebrate your next step in your fate."

She looked at Raphael and said, "Try and make yourself at home,

I have no idea how long the two of us will roam."

Raphael said, "Yes, I will try and do that."

She said, "Not 'Yes, ma'am?' I kind of miss my black cat."

Instantly he said, "Yes ma'am," and she said, "You're so sweet.

See? It's not that hard to really accept your defeat."

Then she said. "Well, Anna and I must go fly.

Don't wait up for her and I."

He said, "Yes, ma'am," as they went out the door,

and muttered under his breath, "She is a real whore."

They went to the car and sped away,

Anna was driving like it was her first day.

The whole world seemed so different to her now.

She thought of her newly found powers and let out a "Wow."

Ingrid said, "Now, that's my girl.

Let's go have an ice cream then make this town whirl."

Back at the house Raphael sat thinking

of his new life and his world that was shrinking.

He stood up and thought, "Maybe I'll just go outside

and enjoy the sunshine from which I used to hide."

He opened the door and the sun was so bright,

his eyes had became used to only the night.

He went back in and found some sunglasses to wear,

then outside he went into the sunny, fresh air.

He walked to a gazebo and sat down at a table,

enjoying the sun. It had been centuries since he was able.

This was an unreasonably warm, late December day.

He laid his head back and drifted away,

back to Natasha where he had daydreamed before,

back to the woman who filled his mind with such horror.

She said, "Do you want to be my pet?"

He didn't know how to answer the words he met.

He said, "What do you mean by 'pet,'" as he tried to get free.

She restrained him even tighter and said, "You're not leaving me.

Not until you pay back all I have done for you,

not until our loving bond is through.

So if you want to see my fangs go away,

I suggest you please me in every way.

I could control you and have you do anything to me,

but I want your love and compassion to be free.

Now, I'll let you go, I suggest you don't fight,

or I will give you one hell of a bite."

Raphael said, "Okay, please let me free,

maybe there's just things that need to be...

Are you what I think you are? " Raphael asked her.

She said, "Yes, I'm a Vampire," almost like a purr.

He said, "So why did you save me from my grave?"

She said, "Because, I needed a lover, if not a slave.

The choice is simply yours to make."

He said, "God, help me, for goodness sake!"

"Goodness," she said, "from God up above

that has killed so many in the name of love?

Don't make me laugh. I'm much too old for that."

She stood up and on the edge of the bed she sat.

"Now, tell me, dear child, just what's in your mind,

and don't give me shit about what they call so *divine.*"

"Okay, I think you're a blood-thirsty beast."

She sneered, "Well, so you're honest at least.

Let me tell you, my friend, how we all play the game:

humans kill wild creatures just like the tame.

They have to kill something in order to live.

If it's not for meat, the plants have to give.

So you see either it be meat, plants, or grain,

everything kills to survive or it will not remain.

Even if you eat a grain of corn,

you stop a life that could have been born.

So the next time you wish to call me a beast,

try to live on water as your only feast.

Now have I made my point to you?"

He replied, "No! You shouldn't take the human lives that you do!"

She said, "Sometimes I take their life, and sometimes I don't."

He said, "How do you decide who you will and you won't?"

She said, "Mainly I kill those who fuck with my plan

and, when I drain their life, the sensation is grand.

There's some I just feed on and those that I turn,

but only the ones that will help my concern."

"Concern," he said, "what could that be?

Trying to enslave people like me?

Making them have to bend to your will,

under the threat of their life that you'll kill?

Kill me you wench! Just set me free!

I want to be with my family!"

She said, "Your family is much closer than you know."

With those words her eyes turned red and started to glow.

"Are you ready to meet your pathetic God?"

He looked at her sternly and began to nod.

"Oh," she said, "you really have bravery,

before I kill you I'll condemn you to slavery."

He yelled, "I will never be your slave!

I'll find a way to go to my grave."

She said, "So you're really convinced you can?

Let me help you my, oh, so strong man."

She walked to her dresser and took out a knife.

She said, "Here. Go ahead, now, take your life."

He took the knife with a trembling hand

and wondered what his captor had planned.

She said, "Go ahead. Plunge it in your heart,

but I promise you will not depart."

In total defiance, he plunged the knife deep in his chest.

She said, "Now, for bravery, you've passed my test."

She bit her wrist and took a mouth full of blood in,

and said, "I'll save you from dying in what they call sin."

She had blood dripping down her face,

and said, "This is an injury I will erase."

She kissed him as he was fading away,

and spit her blood in his mouth and said, "Why don't you stay?"

He swallowed a few drops and his mind went astray.

Then, as he was slowly drifting away,

she said, "Sleep now, you need your rest,"

and thought to herself, "This one is best."

She left him there, lying limp in her bed,

and had lots of thoughts inside of her head.

She walked into her living room and laid on the couch,

and thought how this one was far from a slouch.

Then she called out, "Thomas, will you come here my dear?"

He came in the room and sat by her, quite near.

She said, "I'm famished; it's been a long night.

Do you mind if I have just a little bite?"

He leaned over and surrendered his neck, tender and meek.

She caressed his face and gave him a peck on the cheek.

Then she let out a scream and dug her fangs in so deep,

sucking out almost every drop of blood his body did keep.

Weak and so drained, he fell down on the floor,

and muttered, "You've never bit me like that before."

She said, "Oh, forgive me; I got carried away."

He just laid there with nothing to say.

He could see in her eyes, she was a woman possessed,

as she whispered to herself, "He is the best."

Then she said, "I don't need you any more."

It took all his strength to get off of the floor.

Dizzy and drained, he slowly walked away,

and she said to herself, "I can't wait to play."

She sat staring at the embers in the fire,

glowing hot and heightening her desire.

She went back to her bedroom and said, "Raphael, dear,

I thought I'd come back and give you some cheer."
Raphael stirred and slowly sat up in the bed.
"What the hell happened?" were the first words he said.
"Well you killed yourself with my knife, my dear friend,
but I won't let you die until I say it's the end.
The blood that I gave you sustained your life.
It's much more powerful than a simple knife.
Now we're connected. My blood flows in your veins,
and I'm now the one that has control of the reigns.
You'll find many new sensations to say the least."
He sniped, "Why didn't you let me die, you evil beast?"
Natasha said, "Oh, my, my, you're still testy, my dear.
Soon my voice will bring pleasure to your ear.
You won't be able to control the fire deep down inside.
You won't be able to control the emotions you can't hide.
So, Raphael, it looks like I'm your final date.
You can be my lover or try to choose a new fate.
But no matter how hard you try to escape me by death,
I will keep restoring what you think is your last breath.
So you can learn to play nice and treat me like your mate,
or you can live over and over with no hope of your fate.
Do I make myself clear, or do you need another test?
before you realize that I will never let you rest?
Now that you drank my blood from me,
I can turn you into a Vampire easily.
But, I like you human. You're much more sexy to me.

Now, accept your place and let be what be."

He said, "I'll never love you, you bitch! I've only loved one woman before

and, as far as I see, you're just a blood-sucking whore."

"Oh," she said, "those words would have sent anyone else to their grave,

but I'm very patient. I know, after time, you'll learn to behave.

Well, dawn is nearing. I must go have my rest.

Would you like to cuddle with me in my nest?

Well," she laughed, "I guess it was a good try,

But for now I have to bid you goodbye."

She left the bedroom and walked down the hall

and said, "Thomas is my servant. If you need something, just call."

He yelled, "Rot in Hell," as she was walking away,

she answered back, "What a nice thing to say.

I'll be back at dark if you wish to continue this fight,

but dawn has now broke. It's time I say goodnight."

Raphael started to say something and she said, "Can't it just wait?

Don't you think you've already put too much on your plate?

If you must say something I'll listen to you,

yet I can't tell you what actions I'll do."

Raphael thought to himself, "Maybe I should just be silent.

I don't want to see what she can do if she becomes violent."

She looked at him and said, "Now that was a good choice,"

in somewhat a romantic, yet sinister, voice.

"Now, my dear friend, this is my final goodbye.

I need my rest. You won't escape, so don't even try."

In a flash, she was out of his sight,

almost as fast as a shooting star in the night.

He then started worrying about what he should do,

thinking he was as captive as a pet in the zoo.

He left the bedroom and started walking around,

the house seemed so empty, there wasn't even a sound.

He went to the front door and opened it wide,

hoping he could leave the situation inside.

Just as he stepped out onto to the stoop in the sunlight,

Four huge dogs came running, they looked like they'd bite.

They were growling and drooling as if he was a fresh meal.

He yelled out to them go away. He even tried, "Heel!"

Nothing he said broke their stride,

and quickly he went right back inside.

Shutting the door, remorse began to set in.

He thought, "This isn't how I thought I would end."

He went to the kitchen and looked for something to eat.

He found cheese and wine and some salty dried meat.

He took all of it and went to the living room,

and tried to drink away his sensations of doom.

He drank the whole bottle and sank back in a chair,

and thought, "How much more of her can I bear?"

He laid back in the chair and fell asleep,

and soon the last of the sun sank slowly and deep.

He awoke to her saying, "Are you ready for my bed?"

He looked at her and said, "No," while holding his head.

"My head's never hurt like this before...

What was in that wine? Tell me, you whore!"

She said, "Hmm, I see you haven't lost any of your spite,

I thought you might have calmed down when I saw you tonight.

But I see that, with you, it's going to take lots of time,

before you bow down and make yourself mine."

"'Mine?," he said. "Are you totally insane?

I'll never be yours! Isn't that plain?

The only woman I've ever loved is dead,

There won't be another! Get that through your head!"

She said, "Never! Oh my, that's such a long time.

When dealing with humans it's so quick to find.

But for an immortal creature as powerful as me,

I just have to have patience. One day, you will see.

So now we have ourselves a stand-off."

He looked at her and let out a cough.

Clearing his throat he said, "Yes. Yes, we do.

There won't be any of myself given to you."

She said, "Fine! So have it your way.

I'm bored with you, it's time I must play."

She walked out and left him sitting there.

He curled up in a ball in his cold chair.

He sat there for hours dreading his fate,

wishing for death to be his final date.

He thought to himself, "She's cruel, and evil inside."

Then he buried his face in his hands and, oh, how he cried.

She came in the room and said, "I'm going out for a bite.

Would you like to join me, and enjoy the night?"

He thought for a second and then answered, "Yes, that offer I'll take,"

knowing if he was outside of the house, he could make a break.

She called out, "Thomas, ready my carriage for me,"

as Raphael had now a glimpse of hope that he might be free.

Thomas answered, "Yes, ma'am, right away!"

In just a few minutes they were on their way.

Raphael looked for landmarks to tell him his location,

as they rode along he probed her for information.

"So," he said, "how far is it to the nearest town?"

She answered back, "There's many to be found."

He asked, "What's the name of the town we're going to?"

She answered, "I see the night air has made a conversationalist out of you."

Natasha asked, "So, Raphael, how old are you, my friend?"

He answered, "What does age have to do with a life you can't end?"

"Yes," she said, "you have a very good point there.

If you drank my blood daily you'd never see a gray hair."

He asked, "So, this gift of life that I get from your veins,

how much will it take before I'm in your reigns?"

She answered, "Well that's different for everyone;

some just take a drop, others a gallon.

But I can only give it in small doses from me.

If you drink too much, I'll no longer be."

He said, "Then why did you say a gallon?" with a confused face.

She said, "It stays in your body, to the smallest trace."

He said, "You told me if you bit me, a Vampire I'd become."

She didn't answer, sat back, and began to just hum.

Then she said, "Isn't it beautiful out tonight?

If it wasn't for you I could have went for a flight."

Raphael said, "So you can really turn into a bat?"

She said, "Oh, my friend, I can do much more than that."

He said, "Well do you mind telling me of your powers?"

Natasha said, "This is not the time, the place, or the hour."

Once again he decided to try and get in her mind

to see if there were any answers to find.

He said, "You know, by the way, you have a beautiful name..."

She smiled and said, "Are you trying to play a game?"

"Game," he thought, "this is like no game I've known.

Fear and anguish are the only things she has shown."

She said, "Let's concentrate on having some fun,

it won't be long before the morning sun.

The town we're going to is just up ahead,

there's lots of people there that need to be bled."

Raphael thought to himself, "Oh, what does she mean by that?"

because after she said it, she purred like a cat.

Raphael asked, "Why do you do this to these people here?"

She replied, "It's their fate for what they did to my maker my dear.

Years, many years, ago I was normal like you,

Just a simple mortal, doing things that they do.

In this town was a man and he was quite the prize.

He was definitely well kept and wise.

But he was to wed a woman he didn't love one bit,

He knew she and he would never be a perfect fit.

So one day a stranger approached him and said, 'Hello.'

He looked at her and their hearts started to glow.

They call it chemistry, I believe that's the word,

because, when he spoke, no sweeter sound had she heard.

His voice was full of compassion and sounded so kind,

and to look at his body, it was so divine.

His clothing was tailored and he had not a hair out of place,

and she had never seen before such a beautiful face.

She stood there and smiled as they talked for a while,

He said, 'I am Kian,' and gave her a big smile.

Deep inside of her there was a flame that started to glow.

He felt the same thing, it's something a woman just knows.

They talked and they talked standing in the middle of town.

It was like there weren't any other people around.

Then, just as the moment came, it was taken away,

because in a loud shriek a woman did say,

'Who's this whore that you're talking to?

If I tell my father, you know you'll be through.'

'Whore,' Sally said, 'Oh, those are fighting words, you bitch!'

Then they both grabbed each other and rolled down to the ditch.

Rolling and gouging, clawing each other, time after time,

all the while she was screaming, 'He's mine! He's mine!'

There was a large crowd that gathered and watched the two of them fight.

Her fiance stood there watching them with a look of delight.

They were both covered with mud and with blood from head to toe,

then there was a voice that yelled to the crowd, 'You all have to go!'

When the crowd dispersed there was a constable there,

looking at Sally with wide eyes filled with glare.

He said, 'I don't know who you are but I'll not have this fight.

Now come with me, you're getting locked up for the night.'

He took her hand and they started towards the jail.

Sally said, 'It's *her* fault!' Then yelled, 'Go to hell!'

Kian's fiancee took his hand and said, 'Lets go!'

He said, 'Okay,' and Sally's anger did grow.

She broke free from the constable and went after Kian's fiancee again.

The constable hit her with his nightstick and said, 'This fight I will win.

'Then by her hair he drug her away to be jailed,

all the way there she cried and she wailed.

He opened the door and took her to a cell,

then he sat in a chair saying, 'Well, well, well...'

Then he said, 'Now, aren't you the prettiest thing I ever did see?

I'll have my way with you many times before you can be free.'

She looked at him and said, 'Oh, no, you won't! I'd rather die

than have an ugly man, like you, between my thighs.'

He replied, 'Oh, honey, don't be so cruel to me,

after a while you'll do anything to be free.'

'Don't I get a trial,' she yelled out at him,

then he just gave her a Devilish grin.

He said, 'You know that lady you were fighting a short while ago?

Her father is the judge here, I guess you didn't know.

So if you have any plans of being free,

maybe you should be a little nicer to me.'

She thought to herself, 'I'm really in a mess.

I'll have to anything he wants, I guess.'

Sally said, 'Oh, I'm sorry, constable, I guess you are right,

I shouldn't have ever gotten into that fight,'

hoping to ease the tension she made with him,

but all it did was widen his grin.

He said, 'My name is Talbert, but you can call me Tally.

What is your name?' She said, 'Just call me Sally.'

'Tally and Sally, how cute does that sound,' he said.

She tried her best to keep her face from turning red.

He said, 'Well, Sally, looks like you need a bath and some clothes.

There's some here left over from my last guest, named Rose.

He opened her cell door and took her by the hand,

then he burst out, 'Cleaning you up will be quite grand.'

He led her to a room back in the jail.

It was dimly lit and smelled like Hell.

He said, 'Now, undress, don't be so shy.

There's no one to see you, it's just you and I.'

Hesitantly, Sally undressed and was shaking inside.

She knew that fat bastard was wanting a ride.

As each and every piece of clothing hit the floor,

all he would say is, 'More, baby, more.'

When she was naked he said, 'Now do a good scrubbing.

I want you nice and clean when I'm giving you loving.'

She went into the bathtub and gave the rusty knob a turn.

The water was so hot, she hoped it didn't burn.

He said, 'Oh, now we're getting somewhere,'

as he stood there with a demented glare.

He slipped his hand down his pants and started to groan,

saying over and over, 'Oh, Missy, you're home.'

'God,' she thought, 'What have I got myself into.'

He said, 'You're clean enough, we have things to do.'

He walked over and grabbed her hand tightly,

tugging her out of the bathtub, saying 'You're lovely and sightly.'

He threw Sally down on a feather mattress bed,

and yelled, 'Now Bitch give me some head?'

She cursed at him and said, 'You bastard! I'd rather die!'

Then he punched her in the right eye.

He hit her over and over again,

all the while keeping that demented grin.

The harder he hit her, the more she resisted his plan.

He said, 'You can take this beating just like a man.

You've got plenty of spite inside of you.

When I break your spirit, I know you'll do.'

Once again she said, 'I'd rather die.'

He hit her again and said, 'Why don't you cry?'

'Crying,' she said, 'is that what you want from me?

I know that crying won't let me be free.'

He was just about to hit her again,

then she cried out, 'Okay, you win.'

In her mouth she tasted her salty blood,

flowing there from a want-to-be stud.

'Okay,' she said, 'so what do you have in mind?'

He giggled and said, 'Some bump and grind.

If you please me I'll go easier on you,

and make your stay here comfortable too.'

Sally looked at the pathetic piece of horse shit,

and said, 'Okay, lets get on with it.'

He started squeezing her breasts until they hurt,

and said, 'Why don't you put it in my mouth until you spurt.'

He said, 'Oh, now, now, this sounds like a trick,

when I put it in you'll bite off my dick.'

That was exactly what she had planned,

and to do it to him would be so grand.

But thinking of it actually made her hot

and one day it will be her most devious plot.

He grabbed her hands and held them over her head,

and inserted his cock as she wished she was dead.

Oh, the pain from the beating was nothing to her,

compared to the abuse to her dignity from this fucking cur.

He was pumping and growling like a mongrel dog,

as she lay on her back as stiff as a log.

He yelled, 'Missy, I can do better than this with my hand,

and you're starting to dry out and feel gritty as sand.'

Then he let one of Sally's hands go free,

as he continued to shred her dignity.

He spat in his hand to make her a little wetter,

then wiped it on his cock and said, 'Oh, my, that's better!'

He grabbed her hand and started again,

as she laid there and prayed for him to end.

He just kept going and going as she laid there;

he was drooling saliva into her hair.

He tried to kiss Sally and she spit in his face.

He said, 'Oh, I see you haven't learned your place.'

Spit and blood was running down his cheeks,

he said, 'You'll learn to be nice over the weeks.'

She started praying, 'to be someplace other than here,'

letting her mind go astray with her eyes pooled with tears.

Separating herself from her flesh,

hoping the two would never mesh.

Sally's prayers took her far away,

as her body started going astray.

He said, 'Now that's better your starting to play.'

His voice sounded a thousand miles away.

Her body was now undulating with uncontrolled thrusts,

sucking him dry from all of his lusts.

Almost instantly he was spent.

She thanked God for that place to vent.

He stood and stuck his cock back in his pants,

and said, 'In a few weeks, we'll fuck like a dance.'

'A few weeks,' She thought, 'will seem like a thousand

years,'

as her face was sadly streaming with tears.

He said, 'Now, Sally, let's go back to your cell.

The judge comes in the morning for the story you tell.'

He led her back to the cell and locked her in,

then sat in his chair with that Evil grin.

It wasn't long and he was asleep,

sucking in every snore, oh, so deep.

She could feel his slime oozing out,

the very thought of it made her want to shout.

She thought, 'How long will the judge keep me in this cell,

to be tormented by my captor in a living Hell?'

Her eyes were swelling bad from the beating she took

from a constable who was far worse than a crook.

She knelt by her bed and began to pray,

and thought, 'Does God really hear the words that I say?'

Then she started thinking of all the things she said in church.

There were no answers, no matter how hard she searched.

'Oh, yeah, the God works in a mysterious way

so, if that's the truth, why do I bother to pray?'

Sally laid on the bed, flat on her back,

wondering how long until the next attack.

It seemed only moments and the new day was here,

the constable awoke and said, 'Good morning, my dear.'

'My dear,' Sally said, 'fuck you, you pig.'

He said, 'Looks like a deeper hole you want to dig.

I was going to give you breakfast for being so kind,

but I see you haven't yet learned how to mind.'

She replied, 'Mind? Mind? I'll never be your pet.'

He said, 'Oh, those are words you'll live to regret.'

Then there came a knock on the door,

and a woman's voice yelled, 'Where is that whore?

Open up,' she yelled out.

Another voice said, 'Please, don't shout.

You'll wake everyone in town,

we don't need any more people around.'

'Yes father,' she said, 'I'll control myself for you,

but if it was just me and her, that Bitch would be through!'

'Now, my daughter, is that any way to talk about our guest?

I'm sure the kind constable will give her test after test.

Good morning, Talbert. So, how was her first night?'

'Well, Your Honor, she and I had a fight.'

'Fighting again, and with a man of the law?

This is the worst citizen I think I've ever saw.'

'Yes, Your Honor, she's quite unstable.'

He said, 'Then we'll keep her here as long as we're able.

In a few weeks or months, we'll take her to trial,

I bet before then she learns how to smile.'

Sally stood there glaring at all of them, wanting to burst

out,

but she knew she'd spend more time for every word she did shout.

The judge looked at her and said, 'Do you have anything to say?'

Sally responded, 'No, I don't.' He said, 'It's better that way.

Okay, my dear, let's leave these two alone,

it's time you and I started heading back home.'

'But, father, can't I say anything to that Bitch?'

Sally thought to herself, 'She's quite a witch.

How could a lovely man want to be with her?

She's just nothing but a spoiled rotten cur.'

'Now come on, Mildred, your mother is waiting for you.

There's lots of preparation for the wedding and things to do.'

'The wedding,' those words burned deep down in Sally's soul,

it felt like her heart was turning to coal.

She felt a bitter taste in her mouth, as bitter as bile,

and what was left of her goodness was turning so vile.

She cursed God under her breath and wished to be in Hell

She knew it would be less painful than being in that cell.

Most of Sally's life things were so simple and grand,

She'd lived almost a fairytale life until she came to this strange land.

She was raised by wealthy parents in a wonderful home,

and her father had so much money, anywhere she could roam.

But, from a layover in this town on a coach ride to Spain,

fate took away her freedom and started tormenting her brain.

She was thinking thoughts that one could never dream,

and each and every second she wanted to scream.

Her mind came back to her horrific reality

when the judge said, 'Don't let this one go free.'

Just as he and his daughter went out the door,

the constable said, 'Are you ready for more?'

He opened the cell and started towards her,

threw Sally on the bed, and the rest was a blur.

The next thing she knew he was sitting in his chair

and she could feel his semen mixed in her pussy hair.

She thought, 'I must have blacked out when he had his way with me.

How much more pain and molestation will I have to see?'

The minutes turned to hours, hours turned to days, days turned to weeks,

with every new fucking he would say, 'Are you ready, sweet cheeks?'

Each and every time she would disappear,

leaving an empty shell for him to hold near.

But her shell took on it's own identity,

and began giving the constable love that felt free.

After a few weeks when all her injuries did heal.

He said, 'You've been so kind, let's go out for a meal.'

He let Sally bathe and gave her a dress,

and said, 'You are lovely, I must confess.'

She mustered up a 'Thank you,' it took everything she had,

but the thought of a hot meal made her feel glad.

Stale bread and water was her every meal.

She was in for anything that he wanted to deal.

He looked at her and said, 'If you try to run away,

there will be even worse games you'll have to play.'

She responded, 'No, sir, I'll do what you ask me to do.'

He said, 'Okay, but I have just warned you.'

He reached in his desk and took out some perfume,

and said I want everyone to smell you when you enter the room.

Sally put some in her hand and rubbed it on her neck and face,

the smell of it would have made a whore filled with disgrace.

He said, 'Do you like it? What do you think?'

She wanted to say how much it did stink,

but only said, 'Oh, Tally. Oh, Tally, dear.

It smells so fine, it fills me with cheer.'

He said, 'I'm glad you like it, now let's go get that meal.'

She said, 'Yes, thank you, that sounds like a great deal.'

They went outside and it was already dark,

the air smelled so fresh and the stars looked like sparks.

Sally didn't know how long it had been since she saw outside of her cell.

It felt like she'd been released from the constable's spell.

He walked her to a near pub, it was right down the street.

They went in and sat down, and he said, 'You'd better be sweet.'

She replied, "Oh, yes, Tally. Tally, my dear,

only kind words will come to your ears.'

Tally said, 'I knew it would only be time and you'd take a liking to me.

See how much better our relationship can be?'

She said, 'Yes, dear, you're much kinder than I thought at first.

What are you going to order to quench your thirst?'

He said, 'I'll have an ale. What will it be for you?'

She said, 'Do you mind if I drink the same thing you do?'

He replied, 'So, what's in it for me if I let you drink some ale?'

She said, 'Oh, just wait until you get me back to my cell.'

He gave her a big grin with his ugly, Damn face,

She wondered if he could catch her in a foot race.

Well, maybe for a short while he might be able run.

She looked at him and said, 'Let's have some fun.'

He stood and said, 'I'll get the drinks, my dear.'

Sally said, 'Oh, please sit, I'll go bring them here.'

She went to the bar and said, 'Can we have two ales, please,'

then gave the barkeep a smile and a look that could tease.

He smiled at her and gave her the mugs of ale.

She returned to the table, twisting her tail.

They drank a few ales and the constable said, 'I have to go piss.

Are you going to still be sitting at our table when I return, my miss?'

She said, 'Yes, Tally, where ever would I go?

You've been so gracious, I'd like you to know.'

He smiled and said, 'Okay, I'll be right back, then.

Go order us some more ale, and don't talk to the men.'

No sooner than he was out of her sight,

she jumped on the table and screamed with all of her might,

'Help me! I'm being held against my will in the jail!'

The bar owner said, 'Wow, that's quite a tale.'

Then every one in the pub started to laugh out loud.

She screamed, 'Someone help me,' hopelessly to the crowd.

Then the constable came back from the bathroom,

walking slowly and smiling into the bar room.

He said, 'Oh, I see you've met the people in town,

I believe they're all glad to have you around.'

Then he said, 'Boys, drinks are on me,

and isn't she the prettiest thing you ever did see?

Oh, and this body of hers is so sleek and fine,

and she'll give you a ride with it that's so divine.

Don't be so bashful boys, and just give her a glance,

come over here and ask her to dance.'

They all started yelling, 'I'm first! I'm first!'

He said, 'Take your time, boys, while I quench my thirst.'

She looked him and said, 'I'm not going to dance.'

He said, 'Would you rather I let all of them into your pants?

Now, go be a lady and enjoy your night on the town,

and put a smile on your face and get rid of that frown.'

'What am I going to do? What am I going to do,'

seemed to be the only words that Sally knew.

He said, 'Now go and dance with every man,

since you wouldn't live by my plan.'

Sally walked over a took a big, strong man by the hand,

and said, 'I'll give you something that's oh so grand.'

She started dancing with him seductively,

then started kissing him passionately.

She told him, 'I like a big strong man,'

and started to create her own freedom plan.

As they danced she started to undress,

wondering how Tally will like her own test.

As the music played and they spun around,

she let all her clothes hit the ground.

She jumped on a table and said, 'The constable will not do;

I want to fuck each and every one of you.

Come on and show me what real men are like,

and tell that fat bastard to take a hike.'

Talbert stood up and started towards Sally,

then the big man said, 'She's mine! Leave her be!'

He and Talbert got into a fight,

and Sally started fucking the others just for delight.

After weeks and weeks it felt so grand,

to see Talbert watch her with another man.

Soon the whole bar was into a brawling fight,

knives were slicing wildly in the night.

She had so much blood on her skin,

she licked it off and drank it in.

She thought oh how empowering this blood is to me,

and from that ugly bastard for now I am free.

She managed to to run out the door into the moonlight.

Almost crimson red, she stood in the night.

Sally screamed out, 'Oh, someone please help me!'

A man came and said, 'Come with me if you wish to be free.'

They jumped into his carriage and into the night they went,

he grabbed her hand and he felt heaven-sent.

All of a sudden she found herself apologizing to God.

He said, 'Are you okay,' then she gave him a smile and nod.

They rode into the night until the break of dawn.

He had given her his cloak; it was all she had on.

Just as the sun started to shine it's full light,

She realized it was the lovely man from the day of the fight.

She looked at him in total terror,

because now she was not so fair.

He said, 'Are you okay?'

Sally didn't know what to say.

He had not even a clue

of the terrible things she'd been through.

'What should I say? What should I say?

I don't want to run him away.'

She answered, 'I don't know, I don't know if I'm okay.

I don't even know who I am today.'

'What do you mean,' asked the man.

She said, 'I don't think you'll understand.'

He said, 'Let's stable the horses and get you inside,

it's been a cold night and a lengthy ride.

You need to take a warm bath and rest for a while.'

She looked at him sincerely then gave him a big smile.

When she smiled she felt the crusted blood crack on her face,

then she said, 'Oh, look at me! I'm such a disgrace!'

He said, 'No, you're not, just try to calm down,

you'll be safe as long as I am around.'

'Oh, thank you! How will I ever repay you?'

'Miss, there's nothing I want you to do.

Just go with my maid and she'll take care of you,

I have a lot of things I must attend to.

I won't see you until after sunset,

then we'll try to help you forget.'

Sally said, 'Kian, I'll never forget what happened to me.'

He said, 'Oh, I have ways to set one's mind free.'

'Come, dear,' said the maid, taking her by the hand.

'I'll draw you a bath and cook something grand.'

She took her into the house while whistling a tune,

and said, 'Here, miss, this is your room.

I'll prepare your bath, just yell when you're through.

I believe there's clothes in the closet that will fit you.'

Sally sat on the edge of a four-poster bed,

adorned in fine linens that were almost blood red.

Sally watched the maid come in and out of her room,

emptying bucket after bucket, still whistling that tune.

She said, 'Okay, miss, the tub is hot and full,

if you need me, just give that string a pull.'

Sally said, 'Thank you,' and away the maid went.

From the hot, steaming tub came the most beautiful scent.

She dropped the cloak and stood in front of a huge mirror,

and what she saw made her shudder with fear.

She was almost skin and bone,

from bread and water in her captor's home.

She was still covered with dried blood from the pub,

She ran quickly and jumped in the copper tub.

She lay back and fell asleep for a while,

when she awoke she wanted to smile.

The warm water took some of her pain away.

She wondered how long she'd be able to stay.

The lovely man that she'd met in town so long ago

had now given her a safe place to go.

Then she thought, 'He's supposed to marry the judge's daughter soon.

The constable said it will be in the month of June.

June,' she thought, 'how long is that from today?

How long did they have me locked away?

Oh, my God, what will happen to me if he marries that Bitch?

I wish there was a way that I could get him to switch.

He is the man of my dreams, I know for sure,

How could he marry that fucking cur?

Oh, what am I doing? It's not my place to say,

I'm just so glad he got me away.'

She got out of the tub and went to the closet and opened the door,

it was filled with the most beautiful dresses she'd ever seen before.

A purple one with gold trim caught her eye,

She put it on and on the bed she did lie.

Then drifting away, she started dreaming of her lovely man,

then she awoke and he was holding her hand.

Kian said, 'Hello, Miss, I hope you got plenty of rest.'

Sally said, 'Oh, yes, I did. This bed is definitely the best.'

He said, 'What a nice selection you've picked to wear,

purple and gold have that royalty glare.'

'Royalty,' she said, 'I'm so far from that, kind sir.'

He said, 'The way you look in it makes my heart stir.'

She couldn't help it, she burst out, 'But, aren't you engaged?'

Then to look in his eyes was a sensation of rage.

'Engaged,' he said. 'Oh, you mean Mildred, the evil leech?

I have a plan for her and the judge. It's my turn to teach.

I could be swift and do it quickly, but I prefer to play with my prey.'

Sally thought, 'He prefers to play with his prey?

What a strange thing for him to say.'

'Yes,' he said, 'the judge, Mildred, and the constable too,

they're all three on my list of things to do.

Now, my dear, let's get you out of this bed,

I told you I'd help you remove the pain from your head.'

They walked into a huge dining room with the table set.

He said, 'Maybe some good food will start to help you forget.'

She glanced at the table and it looked like a meal fit for a king.

He said, 'Have a seat,' and he started to sing.

She'd never heard the song before but the words seemed like her own,

they put a smile upon her face and she let out a sweet moan.

He stopped for a second and said, 'Please, eat and drink while I sing,

and if there's something different you want, my maid will gladly bring.'

She replied, 'Oh, no, kind sir, this is more than I deserve to eat.'

He said, 'My fair lady, you don't see yourself as sweet?

Has the judge's cruelty defiled your own self-worth, my dear?

Well don't have regret about it, your life begins anew here.

I've called you *miss* ever since the very first day.

Do you have a more lovely name that you wish me to say?'

She said, 'Sally, actually it's Sally Nicole'

He said, 'Oh, that name warms my soul.

Sally sounds sensual in a mysterious way,

and to my ears it sounds like a musical array.

'Thank you, Kian. I'm glad my name means so much to you.

Also thank you for all the things you did do.

Kian, I've never heard that name; what does it stand for?'

He said, 'Oh, it's just a name, now eat. Would you like the wild boar?'

'Wild boar, that's something I've never ate.'

He said, 'There's plenty, please fill up your plate.'

Sally started putting food on her dish with both hands.

He looked at her and said, 'Your hunger is grand.'

She said, 'I'm sorry, it's been so long since I've seen real food.

Oh, you must see my manners as reckless and crude.'

'No, it's fine, I understand,' he said.

Sally tried to not let him see her face turning red.

She asked, 'What do you do with the food left over from the meal?'

He said, 'I have other guests that eat a deal.'

'Other guests,' she said, 'but I've seen no one around.'

Kian said, 'They come in late and eat what can be found.'

Then he started to sing again

as she was trying not to stuff the food in.

But it all tasted, oh, so tasty and good!

She said, 'I don't want to eat more than I should.'

He said, 'Would like to have some wine

to drink with your meal as you dine?'

She exclaimed, 'Yes, that would be wonderful,

but I better not fill my glass too full.'

He said, 'Drink all you want my dear,

there is nothing here for you to fear.

If you drink and lose your head,

I'll tuck you gently in your bed.'

She filled her glass up to the brim,

then held it high and toasted him,

'To my rescuer, thank you so much

for your courtesy and loving touch.'

He said, 'Yes, thank you, my dear,

you bring my home some long-missed cheer.

You can stay here as long as you wish to,

and my home will be a home also to you.'

She said, 'I don't know what to say...'

He said, 'Just be happy every day.

If you're not, let me know,

and I'll try to set your heart aglow.'

'But what about Mildred; what will you do?'

He said, 'Oh, don't let that worry you.

It will all work out in time,

that wench will soon learn to whine.

Now go rest, Sally, I have to go back to town,

and see what rumors are stirring around.'

She asked, 'But won't they recognize you and your carriage?'

He said, 'No, I'll take the one her father gave me for our marriage.

It was part of her dowry to me,

yet they'll never pay enough to ever be free.'

He sounded so evil when he said that,

then he looked at her and tipped his hat

and said, 'Goodnight, now I must run,

I'll be back before the morning sun.'

Sally said, 'Be safe and have a nice trip.'

He responded, 'You stay here and keep a stiff upper lip.'

He walked her to her bedroom and opened the door,

and said, 'You'll find the nightgowns in the dresser drawer.

Goodbye for now. I'll see you soon.'

Sally closed the door as he left the room.

Kian rode into the night back to the town,

all of the people were gathered 'round.

The constable said, 'We have to find that evil bitch,

we'll search each house, barn, and every ditch.'

Kian yelled out, 'I'll join the search for that whore

that attacked the beautiful woman I adore.'

'Here, here,' they all started to yell.

Kian said, 'Let's find her and send her to Hell!'

The judge and Mildred were standing there,

she ran to Kian and said, 'I want her hair.

Cut every inch off of that whore,

and I'll make us a small rug for our bedroom floor.

That will be a sign from me,

that no woman looks at thee.'

'Oh, my love,' Kian said,

'I'll make sure the bitch is dead.

But I will not take your hand

until she is erased from this land.

I'll hunt her day and night

to avenge that brutal fight.

Then when she's gone, thee I will wed,

this is my vow I now have said.'

'Oh, Kian, that is so noble of you,

I will wait until your vow is through.'

Kian said to the mob, 'Let's begin our quest,

and see which hunter is the best.'

The first day yielded no results,

the judge just spouted loud insults.

'All of you big, strong cocky men

can't find one simple misplaced hen?'

He yelled at his constable, 'What good are you?

Another escape like this, and then you're through.'

Every night, as ordered, they searched for Sally,

but she was tucked away safe far from Tally.

They didn't even have a clue or know

that her protector was running the show.

A few weeks into Sally's safe domain,

came such an earth shattering pain.

It was something worse than her most feared sin,

when she noticed something growing deep within.

She looked at Kian with her eyes so wild,

and said, 'Oh, my God! I'm with a child!'

Then all the pain Tally had caused came back,

because she was now pregnant from his attacks.

She said, 'Now I have to bear his seed,

there is no way I can be freed.'

Kian said, 'My maid can take this burden from you...'

She replied, 'If I kill this child, my soul is through.

One cannot take the life of a child,

without making Satan's flames burn wild.'

He said, 'Okay, Sally, I'll stand by you,

if this is your decision on what you wish to do.'

She said, 'I'd almost rather burn in eternal hell,

than have a child from when I was raped in that jail cell.

But I can't! I have to do what's right!

I know it's going to take all my might.

After the birth I'll give the child away,

I will not keep it one single day.'

He said, 'If that is your wish, I'll see it is done,

and you won't know if it was a daughter or son.'

'Thank you, Kian, what in the world would I do without you?'

'Oh, don't thank me, it's a pleasure to provide the things that I do.

Now go rest I have to go back to town.

My maid has an elixir you need to drink down.

An elixir? What ever is that for, Kian?

It will help you with the child you hold within.

It's full of nutrients that will help it grow,

and there won't be any stretch marks on your body to show.

It will be like you've never once had a child before,

if in the future you find a man you truly adore.'

'Oh, thank you, Kian, that will be a blessing,

then there won't be any past things that I'll be confessing.

You are such a wonderful man,

at times I wish I could take your hand.'

He looked at Sally with a serene look,

and said, 'Maybe I should write your name in my book.'

'Your book,' She said. 'What do you mean?'

'My book of people I'd treat like a queen.

Now, go rest, I must be on my way,

I have a game for the townspeople to play.'

He drove his carriage in the night and arrived back in town.

Just like the night before all the citizens were around.

He stepped down from his carriage

and was instantly met by the one for his marriage.

'Mildred, my love, I've arrived, my dear,

ride with me, please, and fill my night with cheer.

Yes, I'll ride with you, but this hunt is getting old.

There's not been one clue of that bitch to behold.'

'Oh, my love, I feel this is the night.

You being with me will sharpen my sight.

We'll go where the others may have not.

Maybe this wench has a really safe spot.

There's tall, soft grass under the rambling rose

and, if she's made a path, she won't scratch her toes.

The bushes are near enough to town for her to eat from the trash

and, if she feels threatened, she could return in a flash.'

'Kian, why haven't they used the hounds to hunt her with?'

He said, 'She has so many men's scents they won't know what to sniff.

Okay, Mildred, let's go test my theory.'

She said, 'I feel a little bit leery.'

He said, 'You have no faith in me.

Humor me, let's just go see.'

They rode off quickly into the night,

and he said, 'The roses are nearing sight.

The moon is full keep out a watchful eye,

Hopefully we'll see where that bitch does lie.'

He brought the carriage to a stop near the rambling rose,

She said, 'Where's she at,' as her doubtfulness arose.

Then he said, 'Mildred, Mildred my dear,

oh, please look over here.

Look in my eyes and you will see,

the thing that most torments thee.'

She gazed deeply in his eyes and her anger grew,

then he said, 'There she is, just like I knew!'

She dove off the carriage like a woman possessed,

running into the rose thorns and tearing her dress,

Then he yelled, 'Look! You're, oh, so near!'

She ran through the roses like a frightened deer.

The thorns were tearing so deep in her skin,

the more she was cut her anger dug in.

She had ran almost the whole length of the patch,

enduring without pain each and every scratch.

Then Kian yelled, 'Mildred! She's running this way!'

She ran back through the thorns to right where he stay.

She had almost not a stitch of clothing left,

she was profusely bleeding and out of breath.

Her face looked like it was almost torn off in bits,

he pulled her into the carriage and said, 'Have a sit.'

Still her anger was flaring so bad she felt no pain,

she was obsessed with this whore that drives her insane.

They got back to the center of town,

and Kian yelled, 'Oh, God, is there a doctor around?'

'Help me! Help me!, someone, please!,' Mildred did yell,

'I'm cut to pieces and I'm bleeding like hell!'

Instantly she was in earth-shattering, brutal pain,

screaming, 'I saw her, I saw her,' like she was insane.

Kian said, 'I don't know what got into her, we went for a ride,

and there she was, happily at my side.

The next thing I knew, off into the roses she ran,

screaming, "You bitch, you'll never have my man!"

I called to her again and again,

but there she just kept running deeper within.'

The doctor arrived and said, 'Take her to my office, quick,

this is much more than a simple few pricks.'

With that statement Kian chuckled within,

doing everything he could to not grin.

He thought to himself, 'A few little pricks, how true,

if it wasn't for a few little pricks I wouldn't have done this to you.'

The doctor worked all through the night,

Stitching Mildred's gashes up tight.

The judge said, 'Doctor, will she be okay?'

He said, 'Look at her, what can I say?'

The judge looked at his daughter who was once so beautiful to see.

Now cat gut and bandages were her new-adorned beauty.

The doctor said, 'She'll heal, but she'll never look the same.'

Kian said, 'I'll love her still and give her my name.'

The Judge said, 'That's so kind of you after this tragedy,

most men would wait to see what they would see.'

Kian said, 'Oh, I've always loved Mildred for what she had inside.

No matter how she looks, in my home she'll reside.'

'Thank you, my son, I know you're an honorable man.'

He looked Kian in the eyes and then he shook his hand.

Kian said, 'I'll stay with her most of the night,

but I have to be gone before first light.

I have affairs to attend long away.

Oh, how I do wish I could stay.'

The judge said, 'The constable will be here before first light.

Now this has been too much for me, I bid you both good night.'

His daughter was trembling and shaking while lying on the bed.

The judge looked at the doctor and said, 'She'd better not end up dead.'

He bent and kissed his daughter on her new formed lips tenderly.

He had to close his eyes, she was too much for him to see.

'Good night,' he said and he scurried quickly out the door,

as he walked away he yelled, 'Someone better find that whore!'

The doctor and the constable said, 'Well we had better go now.

We'll leave you with your fiancee. Try and comfort her somehow.'

Kian said, 'We'll be okay, I'll see you before daylight.'

The constable said, 'Okay. Try and have a good night.'

They walked out the door and Kian locked it tight.

He said, 'Oh, Mildred, it's just you and me for the night.'

She tried to talk and he said, 'Oh, my love, just rest.

I want your adrenaline to go down before I give your blood a test.

I want to see if your blood tastes as bitter as your heart.

It would never sweeten even if you said "'til death do us part."'

He put his hand on her open eyes and closed them quickly.

He said, 'Now, sleep, as you now become part of me.'

He thought, 'I can bite her anywhere I wish, as often as like to,

with all of those scrapes and punctures no one will know what I do.

She's lost a lot of blood I have to keep my control,

I want many years with her so I can torment her soul.

Okay, I think I'll start with the thigh for my very first bite, but no matter how often I feed on her she'll never feel any delight.

She is going to suffer like all of those she brought pain,

I'll drive her close to madness with every day that I reign.

With that bite I'm curious to see if she is really a virgin,'

his fangs began to show as his thirst was surging.

'Mm, she is a virgin and I can understand why:

no man in his right mind would lay twixt her thighs.

Well, that's enough for tonight,' out loud he said.

'Her blood's tastes bitter, like she's already dead.

I'll marry her and take her home then make her Sally's pet,

and the pain that she caused her will now be hers to regret.

I'd better make sure that she doesn't die on me,

I'll give her a drop of my blood and bind her to me.'

He bit the tip of his finger and stuck it between her lips.

As the one drop fell, she thrust up her hips.

'Oh,' he said, 'that will be

definitely nothing you'll see from me.

You'll live your life and never feel a man,

and wait on me and Sally. Welcome to my plan.'

Weeks went by then the bandages and stitches were removed,

She regained her strength, Kian set a date, and she approved.

He said to her, 'My love, maybe we should have the wedding after sunset,

I want it to be a ceremony that you'll never forget.

I'll lift the veil only high enough to kiss you,

I know not all of your healing is completely through.'

She said, 'But what about your vow to avenge me?'

He said, 'Let's go on with our life and let that bitch be.

Please, again let us go on with our life,

I'll take you away when I make you my wife.'

'Away,' she said. 'Away? But where will we go?'

Kian said, 'To a secret place only we will know.'

She said, 'But what about my father? Can we visit him?'

He said, 'Oh, yes, dear,' hiding his grin.

'Also, we'll visit the constable too,

I know how much he means to you.'

She said, 'Thank you, Kian, you're, oh, so kind;

you're the most wonderful man a woman could find.'

'You are giving me way too much credit, my lovely dear.

You don't really know a man until you live with him is what I hear.'

She said, 'Oh, I'm sure everything thing will be great,

I can't wait now for our wedding date.'

He said, 'Oh, yes you'll be such a lovely bride,

and all of your blemishes you won't have to hide.

I'll give you sanctuary from everything I can,

and your disfigurement won't be seen by another man.'

'Kian,' she said, 'you're so wonderful to me,

I'm so glad that you're love comes careless and free.'

'Oh, my love,' he said, 'you're everything I could ever want and need,

and to have you by my side will be true pleasure indeed.

For now I must go back to my home and work on my affairs,

and ready the things we'll need for us to live there.

Share me a kiss and I'll be on my way,

I try to come back in one or two days.'

He bent and kissed her disfigured lips,

the moment they touched, she thrusted her hips.

She said, 'Oh, Kian, I wish I could go with you right now,

you've always known how to make me feel special, somehow.

Every night since those thorns tore inside me,

I've had desires for you from which I cannot get free.

Somehow I feel even more part of you sensually,

and there's part of your essence that's calling to me.

It drives me so crazy, it's like an untameable desire,

I crave you more and more each second of the hour.

I know that we've been waiting for our wedding night

for me to give up my virginity to the one that's so right.

But, Kian, I'm boiling, and on fire, and bursting within,

if you desire my flesh, my love, I'll easily give in.

Father's away on business and our house sits alone.

Please Kian take me, take me now, let's go to my home.'

'My dear,' he asked, 'are you sure this is what you need?'

'Yes,' she replied, 'I want to make love with you, indeed.'

'But my maiden,' he said. 'What of the gift you've saved for so long?'

She said, 'Oh, my love, I can't wait any longer lets go dance to our song.'

'Okay,' he said, 'let's take my carriage to your love den,

and we'll let our union of love on this night begin.'

Taking her hand he helped her onto her seat,

He leaned, putting his nose to her neck, saying, 'You smell so sweet.'

Gently he nibbled on the side of her throat,

then he raised up the collar on her winter coat.

He gave the reigns a whip and said, 'Let's be on our way.'

She said, 'Oh, Kian, my love, how I've waited for this day.'

The moon was full and the stars were bright

as they trotted along on their way to delight.

Kian would look at her in the moonlight,

some of her scars seemed to glow in the night.

He thought to himself, 'This will be such a fun sight,'

and the idea of tasting her again gave his body delight.

They rode and they chatted all the way to her home,

her constant babbling about nothing let his mind often roam.

But he never lost focus on his master plan with his bride to be,

for her to live forever in torment from which she could never be free.

They stopped at her home and got out of the carriage.

He said, 'You're sure you want this before our marriage?'

She said, 'There's not anything I've ever wanted more!

Kian, my love, you're the man I adore.'

They walked up to the door at her home.

Kian asked, 'Are you sure that we are alone?'

'Yes,' she said, 'my father's away.'

He asked, 'What of the servants? Where do they stay?'

She said, 'Oh, the servants have never stayed in our home.

When their duties are finished, to the streets they all roam.

My father is not a very kind man, you see.'

He thought to himself, 'The apple doesn't fall far from the tree.'

Smiling at her all the time as he thought how evil she was too,

Once again, he asked "are you sure this is what you want to do?"

he said, 'So, my love, aren't you going to invite me in?'

She said, 'Yes, please my love, let's go in and begin.'

Then he grabbed her up in his arms in a loving hold,

and carried her happily in across the threshold.

'Oh, how romantic that was of you,' she exclaimed.

He said, 'There's a few of us gentlemen that still do remain.

Now let's go to your room so I can make love to you,

and we can forget some of the pains that life's put you through.'

Gently they kissed and she took him by the hand,

then she said, 'Let's go upstairs to my room and continue

our plan.'

Up the stairs they went to Mildred's bedroom.

She opened the door and said, 'Let's start our honeymoon,'

then removed the veil she wore over her face.

She was so hot she felt no disgrace.

'Kian,' she spoke softly, 'come lie next to me,

and take me to realms of ecstasy.

The only thing I know of love between a woman and a man

is from the romance novels I've held in my hand

but, from everything I've read, the sensation's so sweet.

Oh, please, come to me so our bodies can meet.'

Kian took off his shoes, and lay on the bed,

and gently stroked the blond hair on her head.

Then he kissed her so deep and so wet,

she to him said, 'This I'll never forget.'

Slowly they kissed as their passions arose.

Soon they were bared from their head to their toes.

Kian mounted over her, looking into her eyes,

then started kissing her neck as she thrust up her thighs.

She could feel his cock hard and touching her mound.

Two hearts and their breathing was the only sound.

She broke the silence and yelled, 'Please, put it in,'

and just at that moment he sank his fangs deep within.

He bit at her throat like an animal possessed,

sucking her vile virgin blood; they generally taste best.

He sucked and he drank until she was almost dry,

then he yelled out loud, 'I won't let you die!'

He bit at his wrist and it started to bleed.

He dripped it on her throat and said, 'Now join with my seed.'

Instantly the large bite started to close and heal in,

then all that remained was a little blood on his chin.

The bed was covered with blood that had dripped from his mouth.

He picked up his new prize and said, 'It's time to head south.'

He carried her down the stairs and walked out the front door,

put her in his carriage and rode off through the moor.

He left the door open so when her father got back,

it wouldn't take him long to find the evidence of the attack.

Off into the night they rode away,

to hide his recently caught prey.

When they got to his castle, he let out a shout.

Then his servant immediately came out.

He said, 'Take this wench.' The servant lifted her with a loud groan,

then said, 'I see you've brought another one home...

Master, what is it you wish for me to do with this woman, sir?'

He said, 'Lock her in my library I'll deal with her when I stir.

It's been a long ride and a tiring night,

now go take that whore out of my sight.'

Daybreak came and then the evening sun did set,

Kian arose from his crypt and yelled, 'So, how is my pet?'

The servant came to him and said, 'She hasn't made a single sound.'

Kian said, 'She'll get real loud when she sees her old friend's around.'

He then walked to the library door and opened it wide,

and there on the sofa his prisoner did reside.

He walked up to her and gently stroked her face,

touching the scars that time will never erase.

She started to move, then opened her eyes and looked at him.

He stood there looking back with such a Devilish grin.

When her senses regained you could see the fear on her face,

she realized that she was in a very strange place.

Weak and disoriented she stood and said, 'Where am I at?'

He said, 'Oh, my little pet, let me worry about that.'

'Pet,' she said. 'I don't like the tone of your voice.'

He said, 'You had better get used to it. You have no other choice.'

She thought for a moment that she must still be dreaming,

then Kian showed his fangs and she started screaming.

'Now, that's better,' Kian said. 'Now you sound so at home.

Get used to it, for no other place will you roam.'

She looked at him in fear and tried to run away,

but no matter what way she went, in front of her he stay.'

He said, 'You need to eat and drink and replenish yourself,

I want you to always be in the best health.

I have some very interesting tasks for you,

and I want you fresh for when I want a drink or two.'

She said, 'A drink or two, what the hell do you mean.'

He quickly grabbed her arm and bit it as she let out a scream.

'What kind of beast are you,' she screamed out to him.

He said, 'Oh, I'm no beast, I'm much more wiser than them.

Beasts only kill for food and have sex for procreation.

I, myself, enjoy the finer things and only kill for sensation.

It's taken me a long time my "love" to get you into my grips,

and if it wasn't for "love" mankind wouldn't make so many slips.'

Holding her bleeding arm she asked him, 'So, why? Why do you want me?

Why did you want to capture me and take me here where I can't get free?'

Kian said, 'Well, the answer lies

on what you can realize.

First my "love" do you know what I am?

Do you know what drives me to my evil plan?

Well let me tell you my "love,"

I do not come from above,

nor do I come from far below,

where fire and sulfur are all they know.

I come from a long lineage of man,

that tried to force the Devil's hand.

For, my "love," there's things in the Bible people don't see,

that caused the living to become undead like me.'

'Undead,' she said,

'what is "undead?"'

'We have had many names in time,

but Vampire is the most used you'll ever find.'

'Vampire,' she yelled, 'they don't exist!'

Then Kian bit again into her wrist.

She screamed in pain from his fierce bite,

he licked his lips and had a look of delight.

'Now do you believe what I'm telling you?

Watch what else I can do.'

He bit his wrist and said, 'Here's my seed,

something that will stop the way you bleed.'

He dripped it on her wound once again,

and the injury began to close back in.

Then Mildred racked her brain about all she's heard

of Vampire tales that seemed so absurd.

But now right in front of her was this creature of the night,

she almost went into shock from her increasing fright.

Once again she tried to run away,

but every way she turned in front of her he stay.

'Mildred,' he said, 'you're now my slave and my pet.'

She said, 'When my father finds you, those words you'll

regret!

He's talked about dealing with your kind before.

To me his stories where quite a bore.

I thought that it was just a fantasy game he played,

so I really never listened to any of the stories he made.

But in what few things I did hear his friends and him say,

I'm sure he'll be able to rescue me and take me away.'

Kian said, 'Oh, you're amusing! Now you're the one with the dreams,

for the only rescue you'll find will be relief from your screams.'

He started towards her and she said, 'Get the hell away!'

He said, 'That's not a very nice thing for you to say.

Just a few hours before this you begged me for my *love*

as we nestled together, as pure as the dove.

I can control each and every move that you make,

but I'd rather make every option as something I take.

We Vampires can mesmerize you and make pain feel like pleasure,

but tormenting you, Mildred, will be the thing that I treasure.

No matter what I choose to do with you,

there will never be pleasure in the things we do.'

'Why, Kian? Why are you doing this to me?'

He said, 'After some time you'll begin to see.

Eventually I'll tell you the root of my obsession,

and I guarantee you won't like my confession.

Now clean yourself up. It's time we go eat,

I have an old friend I'd like you to meet.'

She straightened her dress and pulled back her hair,

and said, 'How do I look,' giving him such a glare.

He said, 'You look fine, but your scars are such a disgrace.

Is there anything you can do with that horrible face?'

Just as he said that, she busted out in tears.

She hadn't cried that hard in so many years.

She ran and grabbed her veil to cover her face.

He said, 'You will not wear that here in my place.

Those scars are your reward for the evil within.

You will never be covering them up again.

Now sit down and wait, I'll send my servant when we're ready.'

She sat in a chair and began to rock steady.

He left and locked the door behind him,

walking away with that devilish grin.

He went to Sally's chamber and said, 'How are you my dear?'

She said, 'I'm fine but I feel the child's birth grows so near.'

'Yes,' he answered, 'it's definitely almost that time.

Let me help you to the table it's time that we dine.

I have a special gift for you tonight,

I believe it will bring you extreme delight.'

He took her by the hand and led her to the dining table and pulled out the seat.

He said to his servant, 'Go get Mildred. Tell her it's now

time we all eat.'

'Mildred? Who's Mildred,' she said to Kian.

He said, 'Oh, my dear, she's your old friend.

But you might not recognize her when she sits at her plate,

it seems her beauty and vanity have been bitten by fate.'

Mildred walked in the room and her eyes went to cold black.

She ran towards Sally with a plunging attack.

Just before she could grab her, Kian had her by the hair.

He said "sit now, you wench," as he pulled out her chair.

She screamed, 'I'll not sit and eat with this whore!'

Kian said, 'One more word and I'll show you real horror.'

Pushing down on her shoulders as he walked away,

he said, 'This is your place and where you will stay.

Now mind your manners and be a good guest,

you don't want to put my anger to the test.'

She sat there staring at Sally, so cold.

Kian said, 'It's impolite to stare, or haven't you been told?

Now eat, the both of you, enjoy the food.'

Mildred said, 'No, I'm not in the mood.'

Kian got up and walked over to her seat

and said, 'This will be the last time you refuse to eat.

If I have to hand feed you like they do a child,

it won't be tender, it will be vicious and wild.

Now I'll tell you again: it's time that you eat,

and your mood for Sally had better turn sweet.'

She yelled, 'I'll *never* be sweet to that goddamn *whore!*'

He shoved a handful of food in her mouth and said, "Do you want more?"

She tried to spit it out but he shoved much more in,

he started to laugh as food ran down her chin.

Sally didn't really know what to think,

out of nervousness she took a big drink.

Mildred turned in her chair and spat the food in Kian's face,

he yelled, 'That calls for pain that you'll never erase!'

Totally disregarding that Sally was near,

he opened his mouth and bit off Mildred's ear.

He chewed on it like a biscuit and swallowed it down.

Sally sat frightened and not making a sound.

Mildred was screaming in terrible pain from what Kian did do.

Kian said, 'You'd better listen twice as hard, you now have one ear not two.'

Sally started to feel ill and so weak,

and the color was flushed from each of her cheeks.

All of a sudden she saw Kian in a new light,

and what she saw gave her such a fright.

The man she had believed to be so loving and kind

now appeared to be out of his mind.

She said, 'Kian, may I be excused? I don't feel so well.'

Mildred yelled, 'Oh, he's bitten off my ear, bitch! Go to hell!'

Kian said, 'Yes, you may, and I'm sorry for what you have

seen;

I didn't intend this to become such a horrible scene.

Now you've seen the dark side of me, the one I try to hide.

It's a curse, centuries old, I am forced to abide.'

Mildred burst out, 'He's a Vampire and evil, through and through!

You'd better look out for what he has planned for you.'

'Vampire,' Sally said, 'oh, no, he can't be one.

The very first day we met in the sun.'

Mildred said, 'Yes, he is, you best listen to me!

He has the both of us trapped so we'll never be free!'

Kian cleared his throat and said, 'Sally Nicole, now go, be on your way.

Mildred and I have to discuss all the things she did say.'

He handed Mildred a napkin and said, 'Cover where you once had an ear,

I wouldn't want you to bleed to death on us, my dear.'

She removed her hand from the wound and pressed the napkin on it.

Kian said, 'I'll walk Sally to her room, you just stay where you sit.

Then, when I am back, we'll finish discussing your behavior my *dear.*'

The way that he said that filled her body with fear.

Sally got up and he took her hand and led her away,

as Mildred felt like a dog that was told to sit there and stay.

As she sat there, she began to think that her father would be home soon, and he'd come with a civilian army to change the name of this tune.

She thought, 'All I have to do is play Kian's game,

because if I don't he'll give me more pain.'

She calmed herself as she sat and she waited for when Kian returned,

and wished she'd listened to her father about the Vampires he'd burned.

Kian returned and said, 'Now, where were we, my *dear?*

Oh, yes, we're talking about my words you don't hear.

So far your disobedience has caused you lots of pain,

and if you don't start to listen that other ear won't remain.'

She said, 'Kian, I'm sorry, I'll listen and do all that you say.

Can you please make this pain go away?'

He said, 'Well if you show me your intentions are true,

I'll remove all the pain that I've caused to you.

But if this is just a game you're playing with me,

there will be more and more pain for you to see.

I'll push your pain limit until you almost lose your mind,

then I'll bring you back, time after time.

Then after so long you'll welcome the pain.'

She started to say, 'That is insane,'

but for now she just bit her tongue and listened to him.

She couldn't stand for any more pain to set in.

She smiled at him with her disfigured lips,

and began to drink her wine in very small sips.

'Kian,' she said, 'so, where do we go from here?'

He said, 'The answer to that question is up to you, my dear.

If you accept the role I have for you to do,

life will be so much easier on you.'

She said, 'I'll do anything you ask without saying a word.

No matter what you wish, even if I think it's absurd.

I've accepted my fate that you've chosen for me,

I know I'm your prisoner that shall never get free.'

Kian said, 'Oh, those words seem so filled with promise for me.

Are you just biding your time 'til you think you'll be free?

Time will tell if your words are pure and true,

but for now I have something for you to do.

Clear off this table and give the dishes a scrub,

after you've done this I'll put you in a tub.'

'But, Kian,' she said, 'what about my ear?

I can't do much with just one hand, my dear.

I know that you can heal me, you've done it before.

Please, it's all I ask of you. It's painfully sore.'

He said, 'Okay, I will, if you'll remember your place

but, if you don't, the next time you'll lose half of your face.'

'Oh, I'll listen! Please set me free!

This pain that I'm feeling is too much for me!'

Once again Kian bit his wrist and said, 'Remove the napkin, my dear.

This gift that I give you will replace your lost ear.'

He dripped a few drops of his blood onto her wound.

The pain went away and it started healing so soon.

She looked at him and said, 'Thank you, my dear.'

He said, 'My dear? That is a word from you I never want to hear.

There is no bond between us and there has never been.

Everything I've said and done was bait for the trap that you're in.

From this moment on you'll address me as "sir." Do you understand?

And your feelings for Sally should be obedient and grand.'

Oh, that idea struck a nerve deep in her brain,

she started to say something then remembered the pain.

She just closed her eyes and took a deep breath,

trying to accept what seemed like a living death.

He said, 'Now go do what you've been told and yell when you're done,

I have more chores for you that won't be any fun.

You're going to have a lot of responsibilities to me,

the quality of your existence depends on what I see.'

He walked away leaving her to her the chores.

As she was doing what he said, her mind filled with horrors.

The fear of the unknown started to torment her mind,

terrible thoughts were the only ones she could find.

Kian went to Sally's room and said, 'How are you, my dear?'

All she could say was, 'You bit off her ear.'

He said, 'What is that you say?

Are you sure you're feeling alright today?'

He took her hand and tried to settle her down,

as she lay in bed in her white satin gown.

He said, 'You look lovely. Do you feel better now?'

She said, 'Yes, I look lovely. I feel better somehow.'

He had used his wyrding way to sooth her mind

and the bite to Mildred's ear she no longer could find.

'It seems that my fears have been taken away.

What where those last words, Kian, that you did say?'

He said, 'Never mind, it wasn't anything my dear.'

Then he bent and whispered, 'Now rest softly,' into her ear.

She drifted asleep and he went to his den

and waited for his pet to join him within.

The clock chimed seven and he heard Mildred give him a call.

He answered back, 'Come join me. I'm just down the hall.'

She walked down the hall and came to his den,

and stood at the door and said, 'Shall I come in?'

He said, 'Yes, if you've done all I told you to do.'

She said, 'I have. Every task is now all through.'

He said, 'Come join me and sit next to my side,'

as he sat on a sofa made of some animal's hide.

She entered the room and sat next to him,

feeling such anger and hatred within.

He looked at her and said, 'You have much anger and fear.'

She said, 'How can you know the words you cannot hear?'

He said, 'Oh, Mildred, that's easy, my dear,

the supreme beast can smell anger and fear.

In nature, the animals that run with the pack,

can smell the weak ones and the vulnerable to attack.

So, that little talk about your loyalty to me

was just a facade to try and appease me.

Did you really think I believed a word that you said?'

She answered, 'Before I surrender to you, I'd rather be dead.'

He said, 'Dead? Don't make me laugh.

For you, my dear, lies a long, painful path.

I'll seduce you and torment you, time after time,

and that virginity you chose to lose you'll never find.

The blood that I share with you to heal what I've done

will never let your wish to die be something to come.

But, unlike me, you'll get old in an immortal shell,

with no powers of your own in a living hell.'

She said, 'Oh, you're wrong. Everything can die.

No creature lasts forever 'twixt the earth and the sky.'

'Well,' he said, 'we'll just have to see.

Your only escape would be to get free from me.

Now let's go to that bath. I like clean and fresh meat.

I prefer my meals to be served so fresh and sweet.'

'Meals,' she said. 'You won't be drinking from me.'

He looked in her eyes and said, 'We'll just have to see.

How soon you've forgotten the pain from your ear.

While you soak in the tub, remember that, dear.'

They walked down the hall to a hot steaming tub the servant prepared,

He said, 'Get in the water.' She stood there and glared.

'Get in the water. I won't say it again.

Or I'll pick a new spot for the pain to begin.

You have some tender spots that are a favorite of mine,

and they'll make a nice snack before I start to dine.'

Tender spots, now those words filled her with fear.

'Yes, sir,' were the next words out of her mouth he did hear.

She disrobed in front of him revealing all the scars she had.

She glimpsed down at them and felt very sad.

Then she thought for a second and said, 'Why haven't my scars went away?'

He looked at her and said, 'What was that that you did just say?'

'My scars, when you heal me why don't they disappear?'

He said, 'Oh, now I understand what it is you're asking, my dear.

The reason they won't go away,

is previous injuries to your body will always stay.

But I could remove each and every one,

but the process to remove them won't be any fun.

I'd have to open up each and every place you did bleed,

and coat your entire body with my healing seed.'

'So you could restore all my beauty to me?'

'Yes, but that wish it's something you'll probably not see.'

The thought of getting back her beauty was grand,

she got in the tub and rethought the situation at hand.

She said, 'If I change and do everything that you ask,

will you consider restoring me as a possible task?'

'Change,' he said, 'that's not an easy thing to do.

Vixens are vixens, all through and through.

All of your life you've planted hateful seeds,

repenting will never relieve you of your evil deeds.'

She started to weep and drop tears in the tub.

He said, 'Enough of that. Get back to the scrub.'

He thought for a second and said, 'There might be a way

that I will restore your beauty some day.

But you'll have to do everything without questioning me,

and I might return all the beauty you wish to see.'

'You will,' she exclaimed in total delight.

He said, 'Maybe, but first you'll have to learn not to fight.

Possibly I'm judging you too harshly, my dear.'

Now those were words she started liking to hear.

He said, 'But never mistake giving you a chance for compassion,

for that is a weakness that I tend to ration.

Finish your bath and put on this robe. I'll be in my bed.

Think about all the things that we have said.'

He left and went to his room and there he laid.

Soon the word 'Sir' at his door was made.

He said, 'Enter and disrobe and lay next to me.

We'll start the first test of your loyalty.'

She laid next to him,

frightened within.

He said, 'Relax. I'll give you a chance and be gentle to you,

as long as you respond kindly to the things I'm about to do.'

She lay there trying to calm herself down,

but relaxation was a hard thing to be found.

He said, 'Breath slowly. Fear taints the taste of your blood to me,

but other Vampires often prefer the wild taste, you see.'

Your blood. Those words made her shiver within,

but the thought of her beauty made her want to give in.

He reached and touched one of her breasts with his icy hand.

At first it felt evil, then the sensation turned grand.

He rubbed her nipple between his finger and thumb,

then softly there was a tune that he began to hum.

It was a song she'd never heard before,

but with every note, her sensuality did soar.

Slowly he moved his hand down her chest,

Gliding past her stomach down to her love nest.

He started touching that swollen spot down there,

the one that the Catholics say never to dare.

Gently he stroked it as she filled with lust,

then she joined with it, giving her hips a thrust.

Gently he kissed her disfigured lips,

rubbing ever faster her as she still moved her hips.

Then he went from her lips to her throat,

humming and kissing between every note.

Her body now no longer belonged to her,

between all the sensation, her eyes started to blur.

Then a sharp pain ran through her mind,

as she felt his fangs in her neck almost to the spine.

Still rubbing and rubbing, oh, so tenderly,

he was taking her to a place where she felt totally free.

She was getting closer and closer to that exploding brink,

then he stopped suddenly and said, 'I've had all I wish to drink.

Now get up and get out of my room,' he said.

Mildred's face turned so many shades of red.

'There's a room down the hall, just past the third door.

It's where you will sleep; there's nice hay on the floor.'

'Hay,' she said. 'You want me to sleep on hay? Why don't I get a bed?'

'It might be a possibility when you don't act like livestock,' he said.

'Livestock,' she yelled angrily at him.

He gave her a very evil grin.

'Beauty; remember that word? How you said it so sweetly to me?

It's looking more and more like it's something you'll never see.'

She ran to him and knelt at his feet and said, 'I'm... Sir, I'm sorry I yelled.'

Her mind was in a frenzy from everything that had transpired, and swelled.

She thought to herself, "Am I damned if I do, and damned if I don't?"

Wondering what was to come, where she had no say in her will's and her wont's.

He looked at her and said, 'Is it finally setting in,'

giving her another one of those shit-eating grins.

She said, 'Oh, yes, I'm starting to see.

My life has no choices that can be made by me.'

He said, 'That kind of reminds me of the woman you hate,

when she was locked up with Tally and had to deal with her fate.

Now she has a life growing within,

conceived in hate and surrounded by sin.

All of her pain was caused by what you did do.

Now I'm returning some of her pain back to you.

Go to your hay now, my wayward lost sheep.

I like my silence so don't make a peep.

Actually, I think I have a new rule that you will do:

Don't say a word unless I'm talking to you.

Now, I'll be going into town soon...

For the last time now, off to your room!'

Town. That word echoed in Mildred's mind when he said it.

He said, 'I have to go. Listen to my rules and try not to forget.'

Sadly, she walked down the hall to her cold and dark room.

She laid on the hay and wept fiercely as she was consumed by gloom.

Eventually, all that had transpired was taken away,

as she slept alone in the fetal position, all curled up on the hay.

Kian rode off in his carriage, steadily, into the night.

He saw the town from a few miles away with an unusual source of light.

When he got to the town every man, woman, and child was carrying a brightly lit torch.

He rode up to the jail where Tally and the judge were yelling 'You must find her,' as they both stood on the porch.

When he stopped the carriage they ran to him and said, 'Have you seen Mildred, Kian my friend?'

He answered, 'No. What is wrong?' The judge said, 'When I arrived home I found blood on her bed where she had last been.'

'Blood,' he said. 'Blood on her bed...

Oh, my God, I pray she's not dead.

Who do you believe her captor could be?

Do you think it's that bitch that's roaming free?

I bet it's her! She's seeking revenge!

Now it's time we must search the night and avenge.

I swear not to rest until Mildred's back in my arms,

now let's make a plan before she suffers more harm!'

'You're right!,' the Judge exclaimed. 'We need to make a plan.

We'll have this hunt with every woman child and man.

Tally, go get Sylvester Cunningham and his bloodhounds,

they'll find that bitch if she's anywhere around.'

Kian said, 'That's a great idea, judge, tracking her blood's scent.

The dogs will find traces of it everywhere she has went.

While you're using the dogs, I'll venture out on my own,

and when we find Mildred I'll take her to my home.

I'll have her live there with me,

until we become one, you see.'

The judge said, 'Yes, I believe that would be your best course of action.

Me knowing she is safe and with you would give me so much satisfaction.'

Kian said, 'Well, for now, I'll be on my way.

The longer we wait the further they'll stray.'

Kian rode off in his carriage as Tally mounted his horse.

The Judge yelled, 'Be safe,' and Kian said, 'Of course.'

Tally asked the judge before riding away,

'If Cunningham wants money what do I say?'

The judge said, 'Tell him "yes." I'll pay him his due

when Mildred is safe and the hunt is through.'

'Okay,' Tally said as he trotted quickly away.

He said, 'I'll be back by the first crack of day!'

As he rode the better part of the night

along an old trail with no others in sight,

up ahead he saw a man standing on the path he had to ride.

He reached and touched his revolver strapped on his side.

Undoing the flap that covered his sidearm,

he thought to himself, 'Could this person mean harm?'

Once he was close enough to be within ear shot,

he pulled back on the reigns and his horse slowed its trot.

He came almost to a complete standstill,

then he was overtaken by such a cold chill.

He drew his revolver and pointed it at the man up ahead.

The man yelled out, 'You can't kill me! I'm already dead!'

'Already dead? We'll just see about that,' Tally said,

as he fired off a round that soared past the man's head.

The man yelled out, 'You'll have to do much better than that!

My reflexes are much quicker than the world's fastest cat!'

Slowly the stranger started walking straight towards Tally.

He shot off another round and yelled, 'Are you with Mildred and Sally?'

The stranger flinched and the bullet whizzed by.

Laughing out loud, he said, 'That was a nice try.'

Furiously, Tally fired off every round he had left in his gun.

Walking up to him and his steed, the stranger said, 'Let's have some fun.'

As the stranger drew near, Tally burst out, 'Kian, is that you?

Oh, my God, Kian I almost shot you in two!

Why were you acting so strange when I called out to you?'

Kian replied, 'Because I have things I must do.'

'Things you must do what do you mean?'

Kian looked in his eyes and said, 'It's time you came clean!'

'Kian you're not making any sense. Are you okay?'

'Yes,' he replied, 'now let's do things my way.'

Softly, he said, 'Tally come down from your steed.

We have many things to discuss before I do my deed.'

His words were kind and removed all of Tally's fear.

He came down from his horse and stood by Kian, so near.

Kian said to him, 'Tally you're an evil man and have committed many crimes.

Now it is time for me to give you all of your fines.

You and the judge are one evil mess,

do you have anything that you wish to confess?'

'Confess,' Tally said. 'Whatever do you mean?'

Kian replied, 'I know your crimes from what I have seen.'

'Crimes,' Tally said. 'I'm a man of the law!'

Then Kian struck him, cracking his jaw.

Kian said, 'That's just a taste of what is to come.

You'll be like a lad at confession before I am done.'

In terrible pain, Tally yelled out, 'Fuck you!'

Kian said, 'Now that was the wrong thing to do.'

Taking tally's arm, Kian gave it a whack.

He let out a scream as the bones made a *crack.*

Kian said once again, 'Do you have anything to confess?

you have to come clean if you know what is best.'

'Confess,' Tally replied. 'What is it you wish to hear?

What kind of story will bring pleasure to your ear?

Do you want one made of the rumors in town?

Or do want one that's evil, vicious, and profound?'

Kian replied, 'Oh, we can make this simple and without the lies.'

Then he looked right at Tally and said, 'Look into my eyes.'

At first Tally tried so hard to fight Kian's will,

but, in a few seconds, his guts started to spill.

He was rambling his thoughts almost to obsession,

then Kian said, 'This is a piss-poor confession.

Now let me tell you about those you and the judge have given pain,

and as I tell the tales you'll feel their suffering in your favorite membrane.

There was this young girl named Kate.

She made the Judge's daughter very irate.

Mildred told her father about how this girl had wronged her.

Then the judge's emotions started to stir.

He wrote up a warrant for the young girl's arrest,

the charges were battery that the judge pressed.

In a mockery of a trial, there wasn't any chance

and she ended up in the jail with you in her pants.

She couldn't have been no more than eighteen.

The judge gave her six months with you and your scene.

Six months of hell dealt by your hands,

with no will of her own, just your commands.

Oh, Tally I know everything about you,

I know your lust and the things that you do.'

Tally started to speak and Kian said, 'Just be still.

Now it's time your every moment was my will.

Look deep in my eyes and connect with me,

and your path will be to show loyalty.

For if you betray me and the things I have said,

you'll wish over and over that you could be dead.

I am now your master, your will is my own,

and I will now kill the bitter seeds that you've grown.

Now get on your horse and ride back to town,

and if any one asks you broke your arm on the ground.

Tell them there was a snake you didn't see on the trail,

and your horse threw you and your arm hurts like hell.

I'll ride on up ahead to Sylvester's and get him and his hounds,

now get on your horse and start riding back to the town.'

Tally pulled on his reigns and his horse made a turn.

Getting back to town was now his largest concern.

Just as he was slowly trotting away.

Kian yelled out, 'Do mind what I say!'

Then the two of them rode out of each other's sight,

with one in pain and the other in delight,

delight of what was soon to come,

to those in town and the game he'd run.

Kian rode on to Sylvester's place,

all the while with a grin on his face.

When he got there, he gave a loud yell.

Sylvester came out and said, 'What the hell?'

Kian said, 'You're needed badly in town.

They want your help, so bring your hounds.

There's a young woman that's went missing today,

they need your help before the culprits get to far away.'

Sylvester said, 'Okay I'll hitch up my horses and bring the wagon around

My dogs have the noses to help them be found'

Kian asked, 'Why do you need a wagon?'

Sylvester replied, 'If the dogs run to town, their asses will be draggin.

I keep their cages ready to go on a wagon out back.'

Kian thought to himself, 'What a nice place to attack.'

He dismounted his horse and said, 'Let me lend you a hand,'

as his thoughts were unfolding exactly as planned.

He walked near the barn with Sylvester and, as they stood by the door,

he sunk his fangs in Sylvester's throat not wanting to wait anymore.

Then he clawed his wrist and dripped his blood in Sylvester's mouth

and said, 'Soon it will be daylight and we need to be

heading south.'

Sylvester fell to the ground when Kian let him go.

He lay there for a few minutes until Kian said, 'It's time for the show.'

They took the horses out back and hitched up the wagon,

then went to the hounds on the chains who's tails were not waggin.

They were growling and barking at Kian and their master.

Kian said, 'Get them controlled, we need to be a little faster.'

No matter how hard Sylvester did try,

the hounds stood their ground and stared him in the eye.

Kian yelled, 'Get out of the way! I'll handle this!'

He looked the hounds in their eyes and started to hiss.

At first it was quite an audible sound,

then it went so silent, it was no longer around.

The hounds started yelping and shaking their heads,

then laid on the ground as if they were dead.

Kian walked up to the male and put his hand on it's back,

then said to Sylvester, 'Now they're keyed to attack.'

They loaded the hounds into the cages and locked the pens,

and Kian said, 'It's time we went like the four winds.'

Sylvester started to speak and Kian gave him a glare

and said, 'You're now my minion. Don't even dare.

Just do what I say when we get back to the town,

or I have ways to see that you're no longer around.

Turn up your collar to conceal my bite.

I don't want my handiwork to be in anyone's sight.'

Sylvester couldn't help it and he spouted out, 'What have you done to me?'

Kian replied, 'I've made you a thing that will no longer be free.

You will thirst for blood and sleep in the day,

and your only will is to do what I say.'

Still weakened from Kian's bite and the oncoming transformation,

Sylvester couldn't focus his thoughts for further communication.

Kian yelled, 'Get on your wagon now, and let's go to town.

There's going to be lots of horror to be found.

Hopefully before this night is dead,

the streets of town will be covered in red.'

Kian mounted his horse and he and Sylvester rode south,

as all Sylvester could think was, 'Shut my mouth.'

After few hours they arrived in town,

They had driven their horses into the ground.

The judge walked up to Kian and he said,

'Your damn horses look almost dead.'

Kian said, 'I told Sylvester we needed to be here as fast as we can

so that we could do the search and I could find your daughter's hand.'

The judge said, 'Oh, I know how much she means to you,

and if we catch her captor there days will be through.'

'Yes, judge,' Kian replied, 'I'm sure your justice will suit the crime,

and a noose will fit the throat of the person that took what is mine.'

'A noose,' the judge said, 'that will be too swift for this offense.

Solitary for life sounds more like an appropriate sentence.'

Kian said, 'Whatever you decide will be just fine with me.

Now let's go to the house to track her and try to set her free.'

The Judge said, 'You sure you don't want to give the horses a rest?'

Kian replied, 'No, we need to get these hounds quickly to their test.'

The judge looked at Sylvester and said, 'Yes, you're right.

We'll run those dogs all through the night.'

Then Kian noticed Tally wasn't around,

and wondered where he could be found.

'Where's Tally, Judge? He needs to be in on this hunt.'

The judge said, 'At the doctor's in a subtle grunt.

It seems that he has broken his arm on his way back to town.

A snake spooked his horse and he fell on the ground.'

Kian said, 'I'll go check on him,

and then we'll be off like the wind.'

He walked to the doctor's office and found Tally hiding in the corner in a chair.

He said, 'Oh, Tally, come to me. It seems you've forgotten my words,' with his eyes in a glare.

Slowly Tally rose and walked to Kian, trembling all the way.

Then Kian said, 'Have you forget what I did say.'

'Tally,' he said, 'this is your night,

because my will you chose to fight.

Now get outside like all the rest,

so we can put those hounds to their test.'

Tally walked out the door with Kian following behind,

The judge said, 'Are you okay?' Tally said, 'I'm fine.

The doctor put my arm in a cast but I still have one good arm,

so let's go find your daughter before there's too much harm.'

Every one with horses mounted and they rode away into the night

to the blood trail left by Mildred from her fight.

They all got off their horses and walked up to the front door

where the blood droplets had dried on the floor.

Sylvester was still sitting on the wagon seat

and was starting to feel he wanted something to eat.

Kian yelled and said, 'Sylvester, get out those hounds!

Time is of the essence! My true love needs to be found!'

Sylvester got down and opened the cages the dogs were in,

they started barking and sniffing the wind.

He took them by their leads over to the front door,

they took in the scent that was left on the floor.

Then Kian made a silent hiss once again.

The dogs started growling and smelling the wind.

Quickly they ran around the house to the alley and back.

They stared at Tally and lunged to an attack.

Before anyone could do anything to stop the hounds,

Tally was flat on his back and pinned to the ground.

They went so quickly at his throat,

in a few ravenous bites it was all she wrote.

Tally laid there and bled out 'til his death.

The judge was so startled, he couldn't catch his breath.

Then the dogs calmed and started pawing at Tally.

It was as if there was something under his pants to see.

Kian undid his belt and opened them,

then pulled out a bloody neckerchief from within.

'Oh, my God! Oh, My God,' Kian yelled out.

'This belonged to Mildred,' over and over he did shout.

'It's not bad enough he did this evil deed.

Look at this stain, it's Tally's seed!

Judge, what kind of man was this that in which we laid trust?

Did you know of his obsessions? Tell me! You must!

Now all we have is a dead man on the ground,

and my fiancee Mildred might never be found.

Tell me! Tell me! Did you know of his obsessions?

I order you, Judge, make a confession!'

The judge started trembling and said, 'Yes, yes, I knew!

I knew of all the terrible things he could do...

Even in the jail, he would torment and rape

the poor ones I convicted that could not escape.'

'So you're just as guilty as this man of sin.'

The judge said, 'Kian, forgive me, my friend.'

'Friend? Friend! The fuck you say!

Get out of my sight! I'll be on my way.

Take that dead piece of trash and the others back to town.

Sylvester and I will see if there's anything left of Mildred to be found.

Saddle up all of you and get out of my sight,

if you're not gone in seconds, I'll end you this very night!'

The judge said, 'Can we use the wagon to take Tally back to town?'

Kian said, 'Put a noose on his neck and drag him on the ground.

He doesn't deserve a wagon or even a cemetery plot.

Scoundrels like him should be left out to rot.

Now go before I unstrap my sidearm!

I'm seeing red and willing to do harm!'

Quickly they threw a rope around Tally and drug him towards town,

as they rode away the judge yelled, 'I hope that she's found.'

When they were gone and far from sight,

Kian looked at Sylvester and shouted, 'What a wonderful night!'

Then he said, 'Load your hounds and follow me,

we've got a long ride and I have someone to see.'

They rode all the night and arrived at Kian's home just before dawn.

He opened the bedroom door to find Sally sleeping as she awoke with a yawn.

'Good morning Sally are you doing well?'

She replied with a grin, 'I've been as lonely as hell.

Hello Kian, my love, I've really missed you.'

'Sally, my love, I've so missed you too.

I have something special you might like to hear:

poor, poor, Tally's not with us any longer, my dear.

Because of his cruel and evilness, he's met his fate,

when his jugular veins were the first thing the hounds ate.

Oh, hounds, wait a second, I've forgot something I need to attend.

In my travels since I've been gone you could say I've made a new friend.'

He left the bedroom and found Sylvester in the parlor, sitting in a chair.

He said, 'Sylvester, it's time you rest,' and took his hand and led him to some stairs.

They went down into an old musty basement.

Kian said, 'This can be your home, or your encasement.

Follow all the rules and things I say,

or behind one of these walls will be where you stay.

I'll come get you when you're of need,

for a chat or an evil deed.

I'll be back tonight after sunset,

and I'll have some food for you to get.

Now go lie down within that crate by the wall,

and await my next bidding call.'

Sylvester did as he was told and Kian returned upstairs to Sally's room.

She jumped out of bed hugged and kissed him and said, 'I've had so much gloom.'

'Gloom? What gloom,' Kian asked with concern.

'Oh, it's Mildred, that bitch; makes my heart burn.'

'What do you mean? Didn't she do everything you said?'

'No, not at all,' said she, then Kian's face turned blood red.

He ran out of the room screaming, 'Mildred! Mildred! Mildred!'

He found her cowering in the corner of her room showing sensations of dread.

Quickly he grabbed her throat and lifted her off her feet,

looking her eye to eye he said, 'My friend down stairs needs to eat.'

He dropped her and grabbed her by one hand and drug her down below,

then he yelled, 'Sylvester, awake! I have a woman you might know.'

Sylvester arose quickly out of the crate,

as Mildred thought she'd met her final fate.

He threw her to Sylvester as easily as a child throws down a rag doll.

'Sylvester here's a snack for you. Drink this bitch, but don't take it all.

She's not getting off that easy. She'll either die by my

hand,

or be cursed to live forever with a mutilated face walking the land.

I told you to do everything Sally said, didn't I?

Now don't whimper or try to cry.

It is no use, compassion only comes from a beating heart,

and mine stopped beating almost at the very start...

the very start of my kind.

Weren't you curious of this name of mine?

Kian, in some tongues, means *ancient one*

but, as for Sylvester, you're the first to come.

Take her, Sylvester. Take her now,

You're instinctively driven to know how.'

Sylvester ran to her, grabbed her by the hair, and jerked her head to the side,

then lunged his newly-formed fangs quickly towards her throat wanting to fulfill the thirst burning inside.

Just at the point of piercing her flesh he stopped and said, 'I can't do this!'

Kian looked him in the eyes and let out an evil hiss.

Instantly Sylvester began to suck and suck, letting out voracious tones of pleasure as he fed.

Then, no sooner than he started, Kian jerked him away saying, 'I don't want her dead.'

Mildred began screaming louder than a young pig being castrated.

Sylvester stood there in thirst, hungry and frustrated.

Kian cupped his hand over Mildred's mouth to silence her

as he said, 'I'll take a nip.'

He ripped her blouse and buried his fangs slightly above her breast as he moved his hands up and down her hip.

Mildred stopped trying to yell and succumbed to Kian's touch as he drank her.

His finger hit that spot again and her emotions did stir.

Sylvester was watching as she moved in an erotic fashion,

remembering how long it had been since he'd felt any compassion.

He was enjoying toying with her and her blood's tainted taste.

As once again she found that erotic place.

Kian saw Sylvester's desire for her and said 'You want a woman, don't you?' as he repeated his words of choice.

'Yes. Yes, and I want a man,' Mildred said in a very soft voice.

Kian turned her to Sylvester and said, 'This is the man of your choice.'

He tossed her to Sylvester and said, 'Do with her what you will,

but if I come back later and she's dead, you also I will kill!'

As Kian was about to leave, Sylvester threw her on the floor,

and then he said, 'I'll do things to you you've never done before.'

As Kian was going up the stairs he heard the ripping of her dress,

and in an excited tone Mildred was saying, 'Yes! Oh, yes! Oh, yes!'

But before he reached the top stairs anger began to set in.

He thought, 'Why the hell should I let that bitch ever feel another orgasm again?

I brought her here to be Sally's servant until her days did end.'

He ran down the stairs and threw Sylvester away from behind her,

then the words of his earlier promise became quite a blur.

She realized what he'd done and why she was having sex,

understanding now his words can create for her a hex.

He said, 'As long as you're here you'll never ever have another man,

because you having pleasure isn't within any of my plans.'

Spitefully she said, 'It doesn't matter to me, this finger works quite well!'

Then he ran over to her and bit it all to hell.

The bones were showing and she was in agonizing pain.

Kian said, 'One more outburst from you, and you'll have no fingers to remain.

Kneel before my feet and show me now that you will obey.'

She did it instantly for she'd had too much pain for one day.

'Sylvester, take another drink and bite her where she'll know.

Come and do it fiercely, I love a good show.'

Kian said, 'If you scream when he bites, he'll bite you even harder again,

and each time you scream his teeth will find some new skin.'

Sylvester threw her to the ground again and sank his fangs

in the tenderest place.

She lay their with sheer horror upon her face,

yet she didn't make one single peep

for the pain she endured and sent her anger down deep.

It was now fuel to try and resist Sylvester's attacks,

more powerful than a dagger stuck in one's back.

She gathered her clothes, wrapped her finger, and draped what was left of her dress over herself.

Kian said, 'Go upstairs and start doing your chores, if you know what's good for your health.

Get some rest, Sylvester. I'll see you at sunset.

We have people in town we must make regret.'

Sylvester went back to his crate.

Mildred went upstairs and thought of her fate.

As she did the chores,

she checked all the windows and the doors.

They were still locked, like they have always been,

with just a few drafts from the cold wind.

That was the closest thing she could find to escaping

this living hell and her soul that they were continually raping.

Kian went to Sally's bedroom. She asked, 'What was all that sound?'

Kian replied, 'Oh, you mean like the howling? It was all the wolves around.

Would you like to have breakfast, Sally? You and the baby need to eat.'

'Oh, Kian, breakfast would be great! You are, oh, so

sweet.'

'Come on I'll take you to the dining room and then I'll go make something for you.'

'Kian, have I taken the time to thank you for all that you do?'

'Yes, in your eyes, I see a million thank you's and with every smile you give.

For the first time in years, you being in my life makes me feel like I actually live.

Come, let me help you up. Out of bed, the baby is really getting big now.'

Sally said 'I know it will be here soon and, when I get home, if I keep it, I'll explain it somehow.'

'Home,' Kian thought to himself. 'Why would she ever want to leave me?

Here she can live a peaceful life and be so free.

Home?' This was an option Kian had not considered. 'How dare she after all I've done?

No! No! No! how foolish of me to think I was the one.'

He dropped her back into the bed and ran into his library and locked the door.

Then his anger started and revolved from question to question, 'Is she my love or a whore?

Did she like what Tally was doing to her? Did she play me for a fool? Why did she flirt with me to begin with? Was it Mildred's fault?'

Over and over, his thoughts revolved fueling his rage making him question feelings, human feelings, when he was a Vampire with ice in his veins and his heart in a vault.

'After all these centuries why have I even thought I could live a life as humans do with love and compassion?

Mildred loved me and showed me affection. She did tend to bitch, but bitching is generally a woman's fashion.

Yeah, Mildred, I forced her to run through briars 'til her face was shredded because of Sally's pain.

Now I live with Sally and the thought of her leaving me drives me insane!'

Kian opened the door to the library and yelled out, 'MILDRED COME HERE!'

Sally went to his door and looked at him and said, 'What's going on my dear?'

'Sally, please just go away. I have things on my mind I need to work through.'

Sally asked, 'Oh, Kian, is it something I said or did do?'

Kian said, 'Just go away! I'm not safe to be around right now.

I have things I have to figure out somehow.'

Sally hung her head and returned to her bedroom

as Mildred showed up with eyes filled with gloom.

'Yes, master? Isn't that what you want me to call you?'

'No, just come in here. There's something I have to do.'

Mildred entered the room and Kian slammed the door and locked it tight.

Then Kian said, 'Do you remember that night?'

'What night are you speaking about, master?'

'The night your beauty met with disaster.

Do you remember running in the briars like a woman possessed?

Well there's something I must confess.

I mesmerized you into thinking you saw Sally in the briars.'

Mildred's eyes burned red like two flaming fires.

'So you're the one that caused me to mutilate my face?'

'Yes, and now I'm feeling remorse and disgrace,

which is a hard thing for me to do

after all that I've been through.'

'What you've been through!,' Mildred said with a shout.

'Looks like I am the one that has truly lost out!'

'Come to me Mildred! Come to me!

This will be painful but I'll set you free.'

Mildred walked to Kian. He ripped what little clothing was left off of her flesh,

then he bit and he clawed and bit and clawed her until her entire body was cut as fine as a screen door's mesh.

Screaming in agony and passing out from the pain, she was lifeless and limp, leaving Kian to his plan.

Once she had been prepared, Kian bit deep in his wrist and dripped and rubbed his blood over every inch of her body with his right hand.

He used so much of his own blood he, too, passed out.

Hours went by and he was awoke with a shout.

There in the library was Mildred, nude; her body, skin, and face we're once again sheer perfection.

Kian remembered their lost love and happy life and unusual connection.

She looked at him and said, 'Thank you for restoring my beauty to me.'

Kian looked at her and said only one word: *jealousy*.

Mildred thought for a second and realized what he meant:

jealousy had caused her and Sally's argument.

Then Kian opened the door and said, 'Go to her now.

Help her with the baby and get home somehow.'

Mildred said, 'But, Kian, what about us?'

Kian replied, 'That plan's turned to dust.

I am a Vampire. I must accept my place.

I'm not fit to bond with the human race.

So go back to your father and back to the town.

Don't let anyone know where I can be found.

There's a wagon outside, hitched and ready to go.

Take Sally with you and maybe a friendship can grow.

Go to her, be kind, ask forgiveness, and leave this place.'

Mildred went to Sally's room with a sad look on her face.

'Sally,' she said, 'can you be my friend?

Kian's given me a chance to start over again.'

Sally started to say, 'How,' but Mildred said, 'You don't want to know,

but Kian says that the two of us just have to go.'

Sally said, 'I believe I have a dress that will fit you.'

'Thank you so much and I'm sorry for what I did do.'

'Sorry? You don't have to be sorry, I believe you've been through enough.'

'You're probably right, but some of it's made me tough.

Anyway let's get to that wagon and go back to town.

I don't think we should be out here at night. There's bad things all around.'

Sally and Mildred walked to the main doorway.

Kian was there and said, 'I have something to say.

Thanks to the two of you, I've learned some new things.

Life's not only about love, beauty, and rings.'

At the same time, almost, they said, 'Will we see you again?'

'No, it's better this way. Now go, let your new lives begin.'

He opened the door and the light hurt their eyes,

and he slammed it shut; he'd said his good byes.

They rode into town in Sylvester's wagon

with the dogs in back, with their tails a-waggin.

But when the townspeople saw who they were,

it began to make some of them stir.

They ran and got the judge and said, 'Your daughter's back

and, to beat all, she's with the whore who caused the attack!'

The judge went out and saw them,

and then the questions did begin.

'Wait, someone yelled, 'isn't that Sylvester's wagon and his dogs in back?'

'And why is your daughter with the one who attacked?'

'Your daughter, wasn't she all marred and scarred all over the place?

Now look at her! She's beautiful without a mark on her face!'

'The other woman, she's pregnant! Who's seed is her spawn?'

The crowd continued to carry on.

Then it happened: someone yelled, 'They're witches!

How else do you account for miraculous switches?

Burn them! Burn them before they witch the whole town!'

Then they were grabbed and pulled to the ground.

They were kicked and spat on, then took to the jail.

They were locked within as people chanted, 'You'll rot in Hell!'

The judge went to his new jailer whose name was Toby

and said, 'Let my daughter and that other woman free.'

Toby said, 'I'm sorry, I can't do that. They've corrupted your mind.

These two witches will be burned in due time.'

'Burned,' the judge said. 'You're not burning my daughter or the other one!'

'Sorry, judge, it's already scheduled for the rising sun.'

'Well, at least can I talk to my daughter to see if I can prove her innocence?'

'No, judge, the miraculous healing of her scars leaves her no defense.

The pregnant one is surely carrying Satan's seed.

So that's the way it is, indeed.'

The judge grabbed the jailer. They wrestled on the ground.

A shot rang out, heard by many in town.

Some people ran in the jail to see the judge lying dead.

Toby said, 'He tried to take my gun, but it went off instead.'

Sally and Mildred heard the shot but had no idea the extent of that,

so behind the bars to be burned at dawn is where they

both sat.

Mildred said to Sally, 'I'm sorry for getting you into all of this.'

Sally said, 'It will be okay,' and reached through the bars and called her 'Sis.'

Hand in hand they stood for several hours thinking the town had went mad,

for in just a few hours they knew what to come would be worse than bad.

They could hear the sound of armfuls of wood being dropped around each stake.

With every clunk and thud they realized that there would be no escape.

Sally asked Mildred, 'Do you believe in God?'

She looked her in the eyes and gave a small nod.

She said, 'Before yesterday, I didn't believe in any power higher than my own,

but to look at me now and see there are so many new things that have been shown.'

Sally said, 'Then let us pray, not for God to save the day,

but for him to guide us and show us the way:

the way to salvation and the way to redemption,

and to cleanse our souls without any exemption.'

'Sins,' Mildred said, 'before now I didn't believe in that also,

but now after all that has happened it's a concept so easy to swallow.

I guess that *karma* thing so many speak of

is what fits me, just like a glove.

I've seen so much torture and so much pain from what

Tally did in this jail.

He had made it hellish a place for his prisoners that weren't allowed to pay bail.

He and my father did so many cruel deeds,

now I am left to face their own seeds.'

Sally said to her, 'Don't be so hard on yourself. It's not your fault,'

as tears streamed down Mildred's face that tasted like salt.

Mildred said, 'In a way you might be right.

Let's change the subject for the rest of the night.

We only have a few hours before dawn.

Let's talk about happier things,' as she gave a yawn.

They went on chit-chatting through the night

about their lives and things of delight.

Then entered Toby back to their cell

and said, 'Its time you witches went back to Hell!'

He put a black bag over their heads and bound their wrists tight.

Neither of them put up a fight.

He and another walked them to their stake,

as Mildred and Sally muttered, 'There's been a mistake.'

The crowed started chanting, 'Shut up you witches!'

along with the words 'Burn those bitches!'

Toby put their tied hands high over their heads on a nail driven there.

Now even louder the crowd's chanting did flare.

Mildred asked, 'Where is my father? Doesn't he have

anything to say?'

Toby said, 'You're out of luck, witch. He died yesterday.'

Then he said, 'Now pour the coal oil and give me a match,

I have two witches I need to dispatch!'

He took the matches and lit each stake afire.

The coal oil *woofed* and fed the crowd's desire.

Neither woman made a sound as they were consumed by the flames.

After the fire had burned out they were buried in graves without names.

Several days went by and Kian came to town.

He asked if the women had been around.

In the pub a man said, 'You mean those two witches we burned?'

Kian looked at him with dreadful concern.

'Witches? Witches? What do you mean?

There's wasn't anything about them that was unclean.'

The man looked at him and started to laugh.

Kian hooked his thumb in his throat as if it were a gaff.

'What did you do with their bodies? Tell me before I rip out your veins!'

The man said, 'I'll take you to the place where we buried their remains.'

Kian retracted his thumb from the wound and handed the man a towel from the bar,

then he said, 'Don't try to run. I promise you won't get very far.

Cover your throat and let's be on our way.

If you don't, I'll end you right where you stay.'

Kian walked out the door with the stranger following behind.

Then said, 'We'll take my buggy there, if you don't mind.'

The man started to speak as if he had been given a choice.

Kian said, 'Silent fool!' in a loud, demanding voice.

They climbed onto the buggy and headed out of town

to go to the unmarked graves where his lost friends could be found.

Kian said, 'Do not speak, just point along the way.'

The man's face turned pale and showed signs of gray.

He was thinking to himself, 'What specter have I found,'

as he pointed every turn to those beneath the ground.

They came upon a clearing with dead trees, bushes and vines.

It was killed from the sulfur from a nearby coal mine.

The man pointed to fresh earth over near a large, dead tree,

then he leaped and began to run, trying to be free.

Kian screamed, 'Stop! Don't take another step, for it will be your last!'

The man picked up a stone and towards Kian he did cast.

Kian caught the stone and crushed it in his hand,

and looked at his victim and said, 'What a foolish plan.'

The man began to run again, but he met Kian, face-to-face.

Kian grabbed his neck and said, 'It's time you're erased.'

He opened his mouth, his fangs gleamed in the sunlight

just before they pierced the throat of the man filled with fright.

Kian bit and sucked his throat until the man was spent,

but this was not enough for the anger he needed to vent.

He walked over to the graves and grabbed earth in each hand,

then he looked up and cursed God saying, 'Is this your master plan?'

He laid upon the graves staring high up in the sky,

and the only words he could say were, 'Why? Oh, why? Oh, why?'

After several hours he rode back into town.

He took the stranger's body and threw it on the ground.

People rushed from far away to see what he'd done.

Little did they know there was much, much more to come.

He sprang off the buggy and started his revenge,

for the lives of two he loved now he must avenge.

He ripped off heads and tore out hearts from anyone that was near.

So many gun shots rang out, it deafened one of his ears.

He was shot so many times without any effect,

as he killed each one that he did select.

After several hours his rage began to slowly subside.

The only thing left was the dead and those that chose to hide.

He climbed onto his buggy and screamed, 'You all have one concern, for each and every night or day I will make my return!'

That town became desolate and empty overnight.

There was not a soul that wanted to live there in fright.

Kian kept going to that town every night and day

in hopes to find one foolish soul on which he might prey.

After he did his search of every building and street,

you could hear him whistling for those he loved so sweet.

Natasha said, 'One lonely night I lost my way and drifted into his town,

and in the moonlight he took my soul as my throat he found.'

As I lay on the ground and with almost my last breath, .

I uttered, 'Please help me, I'm afraid of death.'

Kian scoffed 'Death death is far better than where I live.

Eternal damnation is all I can give.'

'Please, please, I beg of you,

I don't want my time on this earth to be through.'

Kian stood and thought as I was drifting away.

I could see that tunnel of lights, just as they say.

Then the sweetest taste I've ever had

brought me back to this plane. I was so glad.

My energy came back and I looked at him.

I asked him his name and he was gone like the wind.

There I stood under the moonlight,

with my mind confused and the taste of delight.

I felt the puncture wounds he'd left on my neck,

but there weren't any other injuries I could detect.

I wandered over and over, all through the town,

but there wasn't a single person there to be found.

I went in the general store to find something to eat;

I had a craving hunger for red bloody meat.

I found a can of beans and opened them with a knife,

then I ate them and was never sicker in my life.

A little while later the sun started to rise.

It seemed so hot and it hurt my eyes.

I went into the pub and laid behind the bar.

I knew with the sun's effect; I couldn't get very far.

I fell into a restful sleep and drifted away.

I awoke in the darkness; it was no longer day.

I still had that starving hunger deep within.

I went to the general store to try it again.

Each and every can I tried

made me so sick down deep inside.

Then I heard the sound of a buggy and horse near.

I was trapped between the emotions of happiness and fear.

I went outside to have a look-see,

and there Kian was, staring at me.

I started to speak and he said, 'Woman, be still!'

His words were so cold, they gave me a chill.

He said, 'Stay here, I have things to do.

When I'm finished I'll come back for you.'

A few minutes elapsed and he was back.

I said, 'What have you done to me from your attack?'

'Attack? That would be more like me ripping out your heart.

Let's just say that was a kiss from me to depart.'

I asked, 'Where's all the people that live in this town?'

He said, 'Well most of them are scattered all around.

If you notice in the road up ahead,

they left so fast they didn't bury their dead.

Yes the crows and vultures the next day had a feast.

It's horrifying what happens when humans unleash a beast.'

'A beast? What kind of beast do you speak of?'

'Oh, one that's been wounded, then spurred by lost love.

It's so hard to guess the actions of the brokenhearted...

Now get in my buggy it's time we departed.

As we ride back to my home along the way,

I'll let you know if I want to hear what you have say.'

We rode through the night and arrived at his place.

He showed not any emotion on his entire face.

'Follow me,' he said as we went in the door.

I saw that there were things scattered all on the floor.

Paintings, books and furniture were all ripped apart.

I thought, 'I'd better be silent, if I am smart.'

He walked me into the parlor and said, 'Find some place to sit.

There's something you need that I must go get.

I'll be back in a few hours you'll be okay in here.

Just remember the sun is now something you must fear.'

I couldn't help it, I yelled out, 'What have you done to me?'

'I've done exactly what you asked, can't you see?

You said, "Don't let me die," so I didn't. Now you've joined my realm

where the thirst for blood and eternal life, pain and suffering are at the helm.'

'No! No,' I screamed. 'It can't be true!

I don't believe in Vampires and what they can do!'

'Belief, hmm... That's an interesting topic for me.

At one point of my life I thought it was the only way to be free.

But as I've learned from the centuries and so many mistakes,

belief is a process that only leads one to heartbreaks.'

I said to him, 'Wait, if you're a Vampire how were you in the sunlight?

Shouldn't you have been out prowling late in the night?'

'Good question, woman. I see you've heard some of the lore,

but I find the sunlight something that I adore,

although you will never be able to gaze on it again,

unless you want your eyes to burst in flames from within.'

'You know, you keep calling me *woman.* I do have a name.'

'Well, *woman,* at the moment it's not needed in this game.

I'll be back soon, I don't have to go far away,

and, after I'm back, you can have more to say.'

He left me sitting and waiting for him, all alone.

I decided to get brave and inspect his huge home.

I went room to room and the whole place was a mess,

I'd never seen so much destruction, I must confess.

I heard something in the basement so I went down the stairs.

There was a man sitting in a crate saying, 'Nobody cares.'

I looked at him and said, 'Are you okay?'

He jumped out of the crate and ran my way.

He grabbed me by the hair and went to bite my throat!

I felt as helpless as a newly born goat.

Then, just before he sank his fangs in my neck,

there was something about me that he did detect.

He yelled out, 'Oh, no! You're just like me!

Will that bastard ever feed me?'

I thought, 'Feed me? Oh, my God, *that's* where he went.'

This put my mind in a moral argument.

Can I do it? Can I take another's life so that I may live?

Most of my life, compassion is all I did give.

I looked at the man who had came from the crate,

he was shaking and nervous and seemed so irate.

I said, 'Can I help you? Is there something you need?'

He answered, 'Yes, bitch, there is! I need to feed!'

'Well, you can have some of my blood. Maybe just a taste...'

He said, 'No, it won't work. It will just be a waste.'

We talked for a few moments then I heard a door,

along with a woman screaming like I'd never heard before.

I started to go up the stairs and the man said, 'Me first!'

He pushed me to the floor, he was crazed by his thirst.

I got up and then went slowly up the stairs.

Kian was holding a woman with long, golden hair.

Sylvester ran toward her to take the first bite.

Kian said, 'Wait your turn; you'll have some tonight.

Woman, come here. It's time that you feed

and you accept the curse of my seed.'

I walked over to the woman who was hysterical now.

Kian looked in her eyes and calmed her somehow.

Then he said, 'My friend here needs a drink.

Now, surrender your neck; you don't have to think.'

I went to her and felt the freshness of her sweet-smelling skin

and could almost taste her blood boiling from within.

Kian said, 'That's adrenalin; it sweetens the taste.

Now feed, woman; there's no time to waste.'

I paused and looked at Kian, I could not take the bite.

He cut her neck with his fingernail and it smelled like delight.

He took the tip of his nail and dripped a drop on my tongue,

and I lunged for her neck—my first bite had begun.

I was sucking and drinking from her jugular vein.

The pleasure was so erotic, it nearly drove me insane.

Maddened by hunger and with lustful thinking,

all the while I continued sucking and drinking.

'Stop, woman! Stop, I Say!

Sylvester needs to also be fed today.'

Kian had to pull my hair and pluck my fangs out of her neck

before I had drank her to the last speck.

He threw her to the corner and Sylvester pounced on her like a cat.

He tore her throat out with his fangs while drinking as happily he sat.

Kian said, 'You know what to do with her when you're through...'

'Yes, master, I know and it will be your will that I do.'

'Woman, come with me. Let's go to the library and speak.'

'Yes, that would be nice... You know, I'm not feeling weak;

not weak at all since I've *fed,* as you say.

Will I have to do that every day?'

'No, not every day, but often, my dear.'

I hoped I could accept it and remove my moral fear.

We went into the library and sat as best we could.

It seemed in a rage all of the furniture had became splintered wood.

'What happened here, may I ask?'

Kian said, 'No, asking is only a single task.

I'll ask the questions and you answer me.

I've been out of touch with the world, can't you see?'

Natasha said, 'May I ask just one question of you, will you grant me that?

Then, after you answer, about current events we will chat.'

He said, 'Alright. So, what's on your mind?'

choose what you like we'll see what we find.

She said, 'Where do you put the bodies so they cannot be found?'

'Sylvester takes them to town and dumps them onto the ground.

Each and every past resident I find and kill from that town

is added to the pile of corpses from what they left lying around.

It's a kind of mark from me,

that no one from there will ever be free.

Okay, my turn. Catch me up on current events going on.'

She said, 'Well, basically it's the same old thing: people killing people from dusk till dawn.'

'I like the way you think, woman. Death seems to be the only thing humans know,

and will always be the only thing that makes their heart beat so slow.

Killing, now that's another story. Everything kills in some fashion:

for food or shelter and political or religious action.

I watched a preying mantis eat a grasshopper one day.

With every nibble he sucked its life away.

This was long before I became what I am,

and I truly didn't understand.

It's all just one giant, consuming wheel.

From the happiest or saddest life death is the same deal.

You're born to live and destined to die.

There are no reasons to wonder why.

Just make the best of what you can

as you walk upon this land.

Do the best in all that you do;

remember there is only one of you.

But if you can touch another's heart,

this is where the pain can depart.

Sorry, woman, I got a little carried away.'

'No, no, go on. It was poetry that you say,

He said, 'No, there's other things to discuss: things I've thought of for years,

things I've needed to do but I couldn't overcome my own fears.'

'What ever would you be afraid of, Kian? You're a Vampire and immortal.'

'Well, to tell you the truth, I'm afraid of Satan's portal.

The gates of Hell, that place of no return,

where forever in torture you sit and burn.'

'The Devil, she said, 'don't make me laugh. That's just a story they made up to control mankind.'

He replied, 'Well, I believe I have a story of my own that may change your very mind.

I've never told anyone this before, so you will be my first.

At one time I was a religious man, before I became cursed.

I was there at the time of the Crucifixion, where Jesus hung on nails.

This is an actual account I witnessed, not made-up fairy tales.

As I stood in the crowd, I saw him take his last breath,

just before the Spear of Destiny showed it was his death.

The Centurion laid the spear on the ground,

so he could help Jesus to be lowered down.

Satan was there for the event, yet at that time I didn't know,

but later on his trickery had began to show.

He had taken some of the wood from the cross where Jesus hung,

and fashioned it into a cross using his nails and silver tongue.

He gave it to a man and said, "Wear this around your neck in Jesus' name.

Show the world you believe in what he stood for and don't have any shame."

The man thanked Satan for the gift and put it around his neck,

then Satan cursed the cross that supposedly signified respect.

He cursed it so as long as a single one was worn, Christ could never return.

The only way to break the curse was for the original to be burned.

The first man with the cross withered and died one day;

it was the power of the curse that sucked his life away.

After several owners' death from the cross being passed on,

they brought it to our religious sect for they feared something was wrong.

We were basically early priests with a faith that was very old,

but when a man with the cross came, we listened to the stories he told.

We believed in good and also evil too,

so it wasn't hard to accept what the cross could do.

We took the cross from the man and said "Leave us to our prayers,"

as we walked to the alter, slowly up the stairs.

We lay the cross in a water bowl that we had previously blessed,

when in the door a man walked and said, "I have something to confess."

Then the cross began to spin in the bowl,

and the man screamed, "I confess! I'm here for all your souls!"

The cross burst into flames and the water turned blood red!

The man said, "Thee shalt have no lamb, now drink of his blood instead."

We all ran to the bowl and drank the blood deep down our throat.

We had became Satan's blood-thirsty minions, and now were trapped in his moat.

Cursed to walk the earth with thirst for blood from

mankind,

trapped eternally between two realms that we would never find.

As Satan turned around and started walking out the door,

he said, "Thy cross has been destroyed, yet they've already made many more!"

We barricaded ourselves in our monastery in Jerusalem. But we couldn't eat.

Everything that went in our throat and down to our belly soon landed at our feet.

We went through terrible convulsions and so much pain,

we all thought, at some point, we'd go insane.

The people in town that we were an inspiration for

started to wonder why we had barred each window and door.

Days went by... We chewed on wood... We bit our own flesh...

Yet, none of this gave our new thirst a single bit of rest.

Then, it happened. The curiosity got the best of the people in town.

They took axes to our doors and knocked them down.

Oh, this was such a terrible course of action,

because in their blood came our satisfaction.

We fought it so hard at first,

but then we all gave in to the thirst.

That first taste of human blood was Heaven's delight,

but then we were forever Damned from the curse of the first bite.

We fed and fought our way out of the monastery. There were nine of us.

We grabbed some camels and took off, leaving a trail of dust.

No one followed us. We wandered from town to town,

leaving trails of the dead laying on the ground.

Eventually, we all decided it would be better to go our separate way.

There were too many bodies we left behind to stay.

Over the years, we traveled and tried to put things in place,

things that could actually have helped the human race.

We made Vampires into leaders of countries to fight our wars.

They made sound decisions without guilt-ridden horrors.

But the ones we made that weren't from the first bite

could only be active after it was night.

Most of all the lore you hear

is true about us, my dear.

Some things we made up to enhance our position,

leaving mankind to have even more superstition.

So, woman, that's it. I've unleashed all my sin,

and told you how my unholy origin did begin.

Do you have anything you want to say

before I go to my place to lay?'

'Yes, I have one question about the things you do:

The townspeople—why have they so enraged you?'

'I'll take you tonight and give you the answer you ask,

then you will know why I've made their death my task.

For now, go rest, and at dark we'll be gone.

I have some things I must ponder upon.'

He led me to the bedroom where Sally had been.

There wasn't one thing out of place when I went within.

I noticed when he entered, his nostrils did flare.

I looked in his eyes and they were filled with glare.

My senses were heightened and I said, 'I can smell your friend.'

For a mere second, his heart ached within.

Then he said, 'Rest now and I'll come and get you.

There are several things we have to do.'

I laid on the bed and then fell asleep. In the blink of an eye,

when Kian came in and said, 'Woman, now is the time that we must fly.

We'll get to the town awhile before dawn breaks through.

I have some things I want you to do.'

We rode off in a hurry into the dark night,

yet I could see fine as if it were daylight.

My hearing and sense of smell were also enhanced.

I was so amazed at how a predator could be so advanced.

Kian drove the buggy without saying a word.

We ended up in a desolate place with few sounds to be heard.

he said, 'Come with me

I have something for you to see.'

He helped me down from the buggy and said, 'Walk over here.

I'll show you what happens to things you hold dear.'

We walked over to two mounds of earth. He plunged his arm down below.

There was a bit of remorse on his face that did show.

He pulled Mildred's skull out of the ground, still with charred flesh on her face,

then looked at me and said, 'This is a smell my mind can't erase.

This was Mildred; over there is Sally. They were two of my friends.

Now their burnt smell calls me from the four winds.

The townspeople burned them both as witches at the stake

and, for this, they'll pay for there sinful mistake.

Take this scent deep in your mind,

and kill any person where this scent you do find.

There were men, women and children all at the fire.

These are the ones I want you to kill with desire.

Each and every one that put my loved ones in the ground,

drop off their bodies to that pile in the town.

Now there's one last thing you must do for me:

grab the rope out of the buggy,

and tie me to this dead tree.

Grab the coal oil, too, and bring it here,'

as he held Mildred's skull, oh, so near.

Natasha tied him to the tree and doused him with the oil.

He said, 'I'm ready to join them in the soil.

Now throw a match and just let me be,

and continue to kill to avenge us three.'

I threw the match, then he burst into flames.

I rode away and heard him scream both of their names.

Over, and over, he screamed them again.

I felt I'd lost my only friend.

Okay," she said, "the town is now so near,

I can smell the blood of those living in fear.

Look, here's the sign for this pitiful town,

you'll see why I say this when they know I'm around."

She gave the reigns a whip and the horses started to speed.

She said, "I ride in quite quickly to do my deeds.

Every night they try a new place or town to hide from me,

even those that have left this town will never be free.

But those that have left and tried to escape my power,

met their fate when I said it was "their hour."

Raphael awoke from his dream blistered and burned,

and he was sorry his human feelings had returned.

He ran to the house to find some shade

from the mistake that he had made.

He took a look at the clock to see how long he'd been in the sun.

It was only five or six minutes that his burn had come from.

Then he thought to himself, "In five or six minutes I had such a long dream."

Then he looked in the mirror and let out a scream.

His face and neck were burned almost to black.

Then he wondered how long before Ingrid would come back.

He knew that she had the power to remove all this pain,

but the thought "At what cost?" tormented his brain.

He began to consider options he could do to relieve the pain,

or perhaps even escape from Ingrid's degrading game.

"I'm human now and no one can stop me,

if I have to die to set myself free."

He went into the bathroom and got a razor blade

to carry out the decision that he had made.

Just as he walked in the room to free himself,

the suit of armor said, "That's bad for your health."

Then he found himself inside of it;

it was a very uncomfortable fit.

The pressure of the suit inflamed his pain.

Ingrid's voice said, "You're still in my game."

She said, "I can see everything in my home

and, no matter where I'm at, my voice can roam.

So just wait for us and we'll be back soon

and, if you're a good boy, I'll give you more room."

Anna and Ingrid ended up at Tristan's for ice cream.

Ingrid looked at him and said, "What a dream."

Anna said, "Mother, are you okay?

A moment ago it seemed you drifted away."

She said, "Oh, I had to take care of our house guest.

When we get back home you'll see what I thought best."

She had a smile upon her face

with a hint of evil and a little grace.

"Mother," Anna said, "how long will it be

before my full powers are here to see?"

Ingrid acted like she didn't hear what was said

as Tristan came near and her face blushed so red.

"Hello, ladies. It's nice to see you here again,"

Tristan said with soft words and a small grin.

"So, my favorite customers, what will it be?"

Anna said, "Make it frozen yogurt for me."

Ingrid said, "Make mine a surprise,"

as she gave him a wink with one of her eyes.

Tristan said, "I'll be back in a jiffy."

Ingrid thought to herself, "And he looks so spiffy."

"Mother," Anna said, "I asked you a question about my powers."

Ingrid replied, "This isn't the time, the day, or the hour.

I'll have that discussion with you when the time is right.

Sweet things are all I care to talk about tonight."

"That must be nice," Anna spouted out.

"All I have is loneliness and a world filled with doubt.

Mom, you know my life's far less than serene.

Sometimes I'm so lonely I just want to scream."

"Well Anna, part of that is you have to go outside the door.

You can't find a man all cooped up and pacing the floor

And those romance novels you read don't do anything

except show the happiness other relationships bring.

My child, you have to decide what you want and plot your course

or, even if you find a man in these times, it will end in divorce.

Oh, I yearn for the olden days,

when love was love and play was play.

And all a man had to worry about was when to take it out,

and not wear a silly condom because of diseases or doubt.

Yes, Anna, when it comes to humans, it seems

they have cursed most of the sensual dreams.

Speaking of sensual dreams, where's Tristan with our surprise?"

He said, "I'm right here," and it lit up her eyes.

"Yogurt for you, my dear Anna Marie,

and Ingrid I whipped you up some tutti frutti."

Ingrid said, "Thank you so much for the delicious treat.

Won't you join us and also have something to eat?"

Tristan replied, "I'm sorry, I can't join you.

Today's ordering day, I have so much to do."

Just as Tristan had went away.

Ingrid thought, "What day is today?"

Then she realized as she tasted her sweets,

that it had been several days since Raphael had something to eat.

Then Ingrid's voice rang out in the house again.

It said, "What would you like to eat my little friend?"

Raphael was hesitant to answer her question.

She said, "If you don't answer I'll make a suggestion."

Then he thought if he left it for her to decide

that his stomach was in for a hell of a ride.

So he said, "Can I have something Chinese?"

She replied, "Yes, if when I'm home you're ready to please."

"Please you? How can I do that with this terrible sun burn?"

Ingrid said, "When we get home just let it be my concern.

Now take off that armor and get in the tub,

and pay mind to the places you need to scrub.

Anna and I will be coming home soon.

Now go wait for my return in the bathroom."

Anna said, "Mom, you didn't hear a thing I did say.

Once again it seemed like you drifted away."

"Yes, Anna, I did. I was talking to Raphael again.

I released him from that suit of armor that I put him in."

Anna giggled and said, "You put him in that?

That's even better than when he was a black cat."

"Well what is worse, Anna, is he has a terrible sun burn,

and he was going to kill himself, so he needed to learn.

Like I've told you before, Vampires are quite a prideful lot and they don't know how to react when they're put on the spot.

Having stripped away Raphael's immortality,

and not letting him be able to go free,

makes this part of the game so much fun.

Now eat up, we have to run."

Ingrid finished her dish and yelled. "Tristan, goodbye.

I'm sorry, but Anna and I must now go fly."

He walked out and met them at the door

and said, "You know where to come when you want some more."

Ingrid gently touched Tristan's hand,

wanting to feel the love that was so grand.

But when she did she got a strange sensation

and looked at Anna without hesitation.

Then she said, "Come, hurry, we need to go home."

Tristan looked at her and said, "Must you roam?"

She snapped out a "Yes!" and then bolted out the door,

then got in the car with Anna and said, "We won't be back anymore."

Anna said, "Okay, Mom, this whole day you've been wigging me out.

Would you care to explain what's going on and please don't shout?"

Ingrid said, "Well, up until I touched Tristan's hand,

the whole day had been going so grand.

I have Raphael just where I want,

and stopped him from doing his stupid stunt.

Everything was going kind of serene,

until I felt Tristan's hand, then I wanted to scream.

I thought that I knew him from long ago,

and the memories I had, set my heart aglow.

But when I touched his hand,

I realized he wasn't the same man.

There's something evil and powerful inside that shell,

almost as if it were born from the bowels of Hell.

Now start the car and let's get out of here,

and this is a place we'll never to return to, my dear."

"Mother, don't you think that you're overreacting to this?"

She said, "No. Pain and suffering is on that entity's list.

Now let's go home, I need to take a break

and, mark my words, his place is a mistake.

Stay clear of it and of *Tristan's Treats*,

for he has some powers few can defeat."

Tristan came out the door as they drove away

and yelled, "Be sure and come back another day!"

The sound of his voice made Ingrid shudder and have fears,

which was something she hadn't felt in a great many years.

When they got home Ingrid went to Raphael in his bath,

and she asked him, "What do you think of my wrath?"

"Ma'am," he replied, "I know you're in charge now,

and if I'm loyal to you, you might release me somehow."

She grabbed his arm and he screamed in pain,

and she said, "If you're nice this can go down the drain."

"Nice," he asked. "What does this *niceness* entail?"

She slapped his neck and he let out a wail.

She said, "Isn't it funny how you've avoided the sun all these years,

and just a few moments enjoying it can land you in tears?

Now it's time you decided: *naughty* or *nice.*

I can make your burn hotter, or cool you like ice.

It's funny how, now that your human feelings are back,

that the things that were masked can now be an attack.

You will now have to piss and take a crap like the rest,

and to go without food will cause you duress.

So, basically, my newborn man,

you're at the will of all my commands.

So, from now on, your will is my own,

or I'll give you new pains that haven't yet shown.

So, Raphael, are you ready to make a pact,

or would you like a hint of a heart attack?"

"Yes," Raphael said, "I'll do what you wish."

She put her hand in the water and made a small *swish.*

As she stirred the water around in the tub he was in,

the pain ended and pleasure started to begin.

She reached down between his legs and found his cock,

and started stroking it gently until it was hard as a rock.

She smiled at him and said, "I'm ready to play,

and you'd better do your best to please me, my way."

She pulled him out of the tub and he was dripping wet,

then said, "Give me some sex that I'll never forget."

He took off her clothes and kissed her white breasts,

and she said, "This is the first of your many tests."

He asked her, "Do you like it done from the rear?"

She said, "If I don't like something, I'll tell you, my dear."

She bent and grabbed the sink and he entered her from behind

and, as he was pumping, she said. "That's almost divine."

She could see her lovely face in front of her in the mirror,

and could see Raphael fucking her so hard from the rear.

Moaning and groaning, they began to bond as one.

"Together, together," Ingrid said, "let both of us cum."

The sound of her voice made Raphael's pleasure multiply and gestate,

and he came before her and she screamed, "I told you to wait!

Now use that damn tongue you keep wagging at me,

and finish my orgasm or more pain you will see."

Raphael lay on the floor and Ingrid dropped her pussy on his face,

and he started licking as she said, "Now I believe you're in the right place."

She was rocking back and forth so hard, like a woman insane,

Raphael wondered if his nose bone would be driven into his brain.

Then she started screaming, "Yes! Yes! Oh, yes!

You are definitely going to pass this test!"

Her muscles went tense and she let out a gasp

and, between her thighs, Raphael's face was still clasped.

She sat there quivering a moment, then got up on her feet

and looked at Raphael and said, "Let's get something to eat."

She gave him a kiss and put on her clothes, then Raphael did too.

Out of the bathroom they went and she called, "Anna, where are you?"

Anna replied, "I'm here in the living room.

All the noise you were making filled me with gloom."

"Oh, Anna," Ingrid said, "I'm sorry I haven't thought about you.

Is there anything you'd wish for Raphael to do?"

Anna said, "No way! I'll never have sex with that beast.

I'd rather have a hot tub of water and candles for my sexual feast.

I'm not like you, Mom. I can't just do it without a connection.

The sexual partner I choose must show love and affection."

"Anna, you are not seeing exactly what I am doing.

It's my sexual partners that are getting the screwing.

To take a man and make him perform on command

is one of the worst things a woman can do to a man.

Even more, like in Raphael's case where I have taken his powers,

makes every time we have sex a curse, whether it's minutes or hours.

Isn't that right, Raphael? Please do tell Anna Marie

just how you feel about sex with me."

"No, I won't, because you'll punish me with pain."

"There, Anna, you see how I can torment his brain?"

"But Mother, what is the reason you keep him around?"

"Anna, you'll see in due time the answers to be found.

"Raphael?", about dinner, do you know how to cook?"

He just stood there and gave Ingrid a look.

Then he said, "Cook? I haven't cooked in hundreds of years."

Ingrid said, "Then I guess you need some practice, my dear.

Go in the kitchen and you'll find anything you need

to make us the meal you wish to feed.

But, don't be skimpy, I have a big appetite

and my beef, bloody rare, is total delight.

Anna and I will just sit and watch some TV 'til your done.

Now, go and create something that's tasty and fun.

Anna, it's been seven years, are there any great, new movies to see?

She answered, "I've almost been torn away from movies since your ship ship sank in the sea.

Ironically it's been a Vampire movie named *Twilight* that

I've watched on TV.

It's filled with suspense, action, horror, and love."

Ingrid said, "Oh, that's what Raphael was speaking of:

how they had glamorized Vampires and made some seem like a weak goat.

Nosferatu or Dracula where always my favorites when they ripped out a throat."

"Seriously, Mom, I don't know how something without a heart beating

would be capable of love or even a kind greeting.

Raphael's showed me that all Vampires can't be trusted at all

because eternal life and blood is their only true call.

Anyway, what do you want to watch on TV?"

Ingrid said, "Do you have any channels that would be humorous to me?

I could use a good laugh today,

and take some of this fear away.

Tristan's touch is still on my mind,

and I have so many answers to find.

But for right now I need a laugh

and after dinner I'll take a bath.

But I haven't decided yet if I've had my fill of pleasure,

so later on Raphael again might be put to my measure."

"Mom, do me a favor and don't talk about sex.

All it does is remind me of my ex."

Ingrid said, "Tommy? You still have feelings for that piece of shit?"

"Mom, he was my first, the one they say you never forget."

"Well, as a sorceress, after time you'll have many a new form,

and because of that you'll have many new first loves to be born.

Anyway what do we want to watch on TV?"

Anna said, "I'm not in the mood and I need to pee."

She went and locked herself into the bathroom

because she was feeling down and so filled with gloom.

Right now she felt more alone than when her mother was away.

She was depressed from the sexual games her mom likes to play.

For a second she thought she would give herself that release

that wracked a woman's body and created such peace.

But then she remembered that her mother could see and hear everything.

Now not only was Raphael trapped in her mother's invasive ring.

She came out of the bathroom and said, "I'm going to town,

and I don't want your prying ears and eyes around.

You and Raphael can do anything you want while I'm not here,

and I hope that he fucks you 'til you smile ear to ear.

But for right now, I'm tired of your sexual game.

I'm going to town before I go insane."

"Anna," Ingrid said, but she didn't reply.

Anna ran out the door as she yelled, "Goodbye!"

She drove through the vines and started to town,

wondering where some happiness could be found.

Putting all fear aside, she went to Tristan's place

because he was one of the few that could put a smile on her face.

She walked in the door and he said, "Welcome back, dear."

The tone of his voice showed her no fear.

He said, "Sit down and I'll be right with you.

I have a few things that I need to attend to."

After a few moments he came to her table,

and asked, "Would you like some ice cream or to hear a fable?"

"A fable?" Anna thought, "what a strange thing to say,"

but she ordered ice cream and the thought melted away.

Tristan came back with her ice cream in a golden dish

and said, "For you, Anna Marie, you can make a wish.

You do believe in wishes, Anna, don't you?"

She said, "Lately I believe in much more than I used to.

But seriously, for the last few days

it seems my life has went array."

Tristan said, "Oh, I'm sorry to hear, my dear.

Maybe a wish can bring you some cheer."

She took a bite of her ice cream

and drifted away, warm and serene.

When she awoke she was in the back room,

tied to a table with sensations of doom.

The light was dim and the air had a foul smell,

then Tristan entered and said, "Welcome to Hell.

Do you know why your friend Ingrid didn't come back

to my shop full of treats and place where I attack?

It's because her and I have crossed paths many a time,

and you can say that the outcomes were less than divine.

But she always managed to escape my grip,

and, with a few words, she made a slip.

But now she's back and I have you as bait.

When she finds out she'll be so irate.

But, wherein the problem lies,

is she can't hear your thoughts or even your cries.

So the only way she'll know you're here

is when you don't return, my dear."

Anna started to talk and Tristan screamed, "Don't waste
your breath!,

for if you anger me, I'll give you a living death.

I know all about your mom's Vampire friend,

that she's holding him captive and condemned.

She believes it's fun to use him as a toy.

Well, I have plans to end her joy.

Sorceresses, too, can be mesmerized,

and all their powers can be brought down to size.

Remember that ice cream that was sweet as sin?

Well it had some of my blood within.

Now part of you belongs to me,

and I will not let you ever go free.

So lay there and wait while I lock up my store,

and then we'll begin with a little horror.

I'll show you things you've never seen,

and you'll be too frightened to even scream."

Tristan returned and said, "Now let's start our game,

and hopefully you won't go insane."

As he laid his hand on her forehead,

she started seeing people that were dead.

Some of them whole, and some torn to shreds,

vision after vision, they were all dead.

Anna blinked her eyes trying to make them go away,

but Tristan was implanting them in her mind to stay.

Anna yelled out, "What about that wish,"

and Tristan was standing alone as she left with a *swish.*

It's funny how things work out, you see,

especially when it comes to supernatural powers that be.

Anna had transported herself to the far side of town,

alone in an alley with no one around.

She walked to a store and said, "Can I use the phone?

I need to call my mother to take me back home."

The owner said, "Oh, my child, I can take you home,

this is a bad side of town for a youngster to roam."

He said to his clerk, "Please watch this place."

His generosity put a smile on Anna's face.

But, before they could leave, the store got a call,

it was Ingrid and she said, "Trust no one at all.

I'll be there very soon to pick you up, my dear.

Make sure to stay in a place with lots of people near."

Anna walked out of the store onto the street

and got evil looks from the people she'd greet.

Now the thing with Tristan began to sink in,

that, all along, he wasn't her friend.

Then she wondered how she had made her getaway.

Were her latent powers growing stronger each day?

Almost instantly her mother was standing by her side.

Anna said, "How did you get here that fast? Who gave you a ride?"

"Well you should be able to answer that question, my dear.

The answer for me is the same for how you got here.

But for me it was guided and directed to one place."

She said, "You're lucky you went here," with a concerned look on her face.

"Now take my hand and I'll take us back home,

and I hope you learned a lesson about leaving alone."

Anna said, "What about the car? It's parked by Tristan's place."

Ingrid said, "Don't worry about that," with a smile on her face.

In the blink of an eye they were back at their home.

Ingrid said, "now please don't ever go out alone"

Anna saw the car in the driveway.

Ingrid said, "Let's go in, it's been a long day."

She said to, Anna, "Everything we do comes with a price.

It drains our energy and makes us feel not so nice."

Anna said, "What about Tristan, Mother? What should we do?"

She said, "Yes, he's definitely a problem that needs tending to.

But not today, I'm totally drained."

Anna said, "Me, too. I feel almost insane."

Ingrid said, "Then I believe it's early to bed

so we can rest our weary heads.

Then when tomorrow starts anew,

we have some interesting tasks to do.

Raphael," Ingrid yelled, "come be by my side."

Then they went in her room as he swallowed his pride.

Anna went in the bathroom, combed her hair, and brushed her teeth,

then went to bed and hid under the covers, clutching a pillow beneath.

This was a trick she would do as a kid when she was afraid.

It was to block out the evil thoughts that left her feeling dismayed.

After all of the turmoil of the day and the powers they had used

left them feeling tired and somewhat confused,

they both drifted into a deep sleep needed to reclaim their power.

When Raphael noticed Ingrid's weakness he thought,
"This is the hour."

He got out of bed, went in the study and closed each door,

and scanned her library from the top to the floor.

He hoped there would be some kind of text

that could prevent anything that could come next.

Over the centuries Ingrid had collected quite a few books,

some were for knowledge and some just for looks.

She had each one sectioned off on each shelf,

from the birth of a child and how to amass great wealth.

Supernatural was the section Raphael went to right away,

hoping to free himself from where he stay.

There were books on witches, demons, zombies and
wizards,

also some on how to break spells using the tongues of
lizards.

The spells and curses area is where he concentrated his
thought,

hoping to break the bonding that for days he had fought.

He read and he read until he drifted asleep,

after not finding any answers to keep.

Then he awoke shaking from the dream he was in.

Refocused his eyes and started reading again.

There were some books with only illustrations,

and foreign languages that caused him frustrations.

There wasn't anything his reading did yield

that could provide him with any type of a shield.

So he put all the books back to where they had been,

and went back to Ingrid's bed and climbed within.

She looked at him and said, "Raphael, how was your quest?

Do you think I'd leave something for you to escape house arrest?

Besides my powers don't come from a book."

He glared at her angrily then lay there and shook.

For now it has seemed to be

that he has no way to possibly get free.

Because of his greed he was now Ingrid's pet,

and this was a lesson he would never forget.

She rolled over and went back to sleep,

and he fell out, too, and slept so deep.

As they both lie there warm and serene,

they were awakened by a scream.

Ingrid called to Anna, "What is it, my child?"

She ran to her room and her mind went wild.

For standing right in the middle of Anna's bedroom space,

was Tristan with an evil smile on his Devilish face.

He said, "Hello, Ingrid, or shall I call you 'Kathleen,'

or any of the other names that I have seen."

His eyes were glowing intensely with red,

and he was holding Anna by the hair on her head.

Ingrid said, "Let go of her hair!"

He smiled even wider and gave her a glare.

He said, "I know you recognize this face,

but truthfully I'm not of the human race.

Before I sucked the life out of this man,

in order to complete my devilish plan,

I gained all his thoughts and knowledge of you,

from the first time you kissed until you were through.

Funny how you and he could have spent all that time

without you saying a word of your powers like mine."

"Powers like mine" peaked her curiosity,

she said, "You're not like me, you're an atrocity."

"Atrocity," he said, "I'll have you know

I have more power than you ever can show."

He blinked his eyes and became a devilish beast,

and roared, "I'll rip out your daughter's throat just for a feast!"

Then Anna screamed and pulled away,

she jumped out of bed and behind her mother she stay.

The beast lunged at Ingrid to make an attack,

she snapped her fingers and he lay flat on his back.

Twisting and squirming, trying to get back on his feet,

Ingrid said, "Oh, you're not that hard to defeat.

I know you've followed me from town to town,

all of those years I knew you were around.

Lurking in the shadows for that one day,

that you believed I'd be yours to slay.

Now that you're there, flat on your back,

I believe you didn't think out your attack.

Then the beast said, "Anna, Anna Marie,

the blood that you drank can set me free.

Now use your powers as I command!"

Her mother said, "No," as she touched Anna's hand.

Anna fell to the floor in a deep peaceful sleep.

Ingrid said to the beast, "She's not yours to keep.

This battle is only between me and you.

Are there any more tricks you wish to do?

Don't you realize I let you into my home for this fight

because I'm tired of your spying and dreams of delight:

the delight to take my one last breath

and have me die a torturous death,

giving you dominion over mankind,

leaving some a hopeless world to find.

But all these years I've been watching you, too,

and awaiting for your plan to come through.

Now, after centuries of preparation,

how do you like your plan's gestation?

Since you killed Tristan to try and get me,

then I guess Tristan forever you'll always be,

At least until his body gets old and goes to the grave...

All you shape shifters are always too brave.

Do you want me to say something fancy or just blink my eyes

before I transform you for your treachery and lies?

Whoever taught you enough sorcery to make you take this chance,

trust me, I can destroy them with one simple glance.

The best thing about what I'm going to do to you now

is after it's over you won't remember anything anyhow.

She blinked her eyes at the shape shifter on the floor

and bound the devilish beast from using it's powers anymore.

This caused the beast to transform to Tristan's original body and age,

and cursed him to live till he expired upon her stage.

Then she walked over to the old man,

and leaned over and took Tristan's hand.

"Let me help you up, it seems you've fallen down,"

as he looked at the unfamiliar place around.

Anna woke up also and stood on her feet,

and her first words were, "I need something sweet."

"Sweet," Ingrid said, "that works right in my plan,

Let's go into town with this gentle, old man."

Looking at the clock, Anna said, "But, Ingrid, it's three AM."

She said, "Tristan has the keys, I know he'll let us in."

"But mother, what about-" Ingrid said, "Shh, my dear,

Tristan isn't the same since he fell on his ear.

He took a bad dive and had a hard fall,

and, unfortunately, he remembers nothing at all.

Tristan, I'm your friend and so's Anna Marie,

and we'll take you back home if we can eat free."

"Eat for free? Where do I live, in a grocery store?"

"No, Tristan, you own an ice cream parlor that's worth a lot more.

Well, anyway, to us girls who love our sweets,

our favorite hang-out is *Tristan's Treats*."

Ingrid yelled, "Raphael, come here, my dear,

I know you've been listening with those big ears.

I'll make up for the dinner you cooked that we didn't eat.

We're going into town to have something sweet."

Raphael said, "You mean you're taking me out of this place?"

This was the first time he actually had a smile on his face.

Ingrid said, "Yes, we'll take you to town,

but you'd better behave or there's pain to be found."

They all got in the car and headed for Tristan's place.

Raphael still had that big smile upon his face.

When they got to the door Tristan fumbled with his keys.

Ingrid said, "Let me try them," and opened the door with such ease.

Once again Tristan was in an unfamiliar place,

and his total confusion put a smile on Ingrid's face.

"Anna, why don't you go help Tristan remember his way around?

I'll stay here with Raphael for his big night on the town."

Tristan looked at Anna and said, "For some reason I feel tired and weak."

She replied, "Well, you could have a concussion," so tender and meek.

It seemed to Anna, once again,

that Tristan was a true friend.

Her mother had cleansed the evil away

and Anna's tender friend was back to stay.

Anna thought, "It's funny when you look at *evil* and *devil* as a word,

when you turn the letters around *live* and *lived* become what's heard."

Anna then said, "Well, Tristan, let's get to those treats.

Everyone's waiting for something to eat.

Let's just do hand-dipped; it's too early for a shake.

Hey, Ingrid and Raphael, what kind will you take?"

Ingrid replied, "Make mine the kind called Rocky Road,

which emulates life and the trials we behold."

Anna called out, "Raphael, so what will it be for you?"

He said, "I'd like something sweet, holding things I can chew."

She said, "That sounds like butter pecan to me.

I know you'll love it! Just wait and see!"

She came out with three bowls full and sat down,

then she passed the ice cream to the others around.

Ingrid said, "So, Anna, what was your choice?"

She answered, "Black walnut and vanilla," with such glee in her voice.

Ingrid said, "Tristan, my friend, it's been a very long night.

Go to your room in the back and, when we're done, we'll lock the door tight."

Tristan said, "Thank you," and went to his room,

then Ingrid said, "Anna, you forgot all the spoons."

She laughed and said, "How silly of me...

I'll be back in a jiffy."

She came back with three spoons and they all dove in.

Raphael said, "I like this," with a heartfelt grin.

Then he said, "It's been such a long time

that on any real foods I could dine."

Ingrid asked him, "So is it better than the blood you eat?"

He said in reply, "Blood can be bitter or sweet.

You see when you drink of a human being,

it holds all the pleasures or torments they've seen.

It's almost as if you're tasting their soul with every drop,

that's why sometimes a Vampire can't stop.

And, as you know, we have to feed.

It's not out of pleasure, or even greed.

It's definitely a curse that has been bestowed on you,

but the immortal life part seems like a blessing, too.

I guess basically what happens is a paradox,

when you lose your compassion but stop all the clocks.

Until now, my need to feed has made me look at humans
as if they were cattle,

but, now that I'm human again, the deeds I've done are
making my mind rattle."

Ingrid stopped him and said, "Yes, and the longer that
you're human, the more you will see.

Some of the thoughts and visions your mind keeps will

become sheer agony.

At some point, if I don't help you with the pain inside your brain,

the tormented lives of those you've killed will drive you insane...

Now let's eat up and get out of here, there's something I wish to do.

I want to drive to the top of Colin's Point and watch the new dawn break through."

They got in the car and drove to the highest point in town,

then got out and walked to some rocks and sat down.

They were all facing the East with anticipation,

for the sun to glisten off the dew with its loving sensation.

Then, just as the sun started to peak,

Raphael tightened up his cheeks.

He tried his best not to cry

as the sun arose in the sky.

But the beauty of the sunrise took him away,

back to the home where he used to stay

with his lovely wife and his children.

Then, like a dam that had broke, his tears did begin.

Ingrid then did glance his way

and he expected her to have something smart to say,

but she leaned over and took his hand

and said, "These are the qualities that makes a man.

Don't hold back, let it all go,

or the pain will continue to grow.

That's the problem that human beings make:
they tuck things inside until their hearts break.
Now that you have a pulsing heart,
and your emotions have began to start,
I'll try my best to comfort you
if you continue what I say to do."
She wiped the tears from Raphael's face
and said, "I believe you've found your place.
Now be kind, compassionate, and a gentleman
and we won't have further problems at hand."
Raphael tried his best to gain back his composure,
but now he must face many years and find closure.
Closure for all the sins he did create,
sins for the ones he sent to their fate.
Now he was believing what Ingrid said
about how his deeds would leave him in dread.
Anna looked at Ingrid and said, "Okay,
isn't it time we start this new day?
How about breakfast? I could use some eggs and coffee."
Ingrid said, "That sounds kind of fabulous to me."
Raphael just sat there looking at the ground,
consumed by the thoughts that his mind did resound.
Ingrid said, "Come on, Raphael, let's get in the car.
I know where there's a restaurant that's not very far."
They all loaded up and then drove away,
with the sun in the rear view mirror and Raphael in dismay.

When they got back to the city, Ingrid said, "Let's go here.

You can have your breakfast with a bottle of beer.

I admit that's a strange way to start one's day,

but there are those ones that need it to keep their shakes away.

There's another topic about human beings and their senseless addictions,

they can stop anything they do with heartfelt convictions.

It's not like they're Vampires and they'll die without alcohol or a drug.

These are basically escapes used to sweep life under a rug.

I've seen person after person say I just *can't* quit.

If they used 'I choose not to,' it would be the best fit.

Anyway let's go in this place,

and see if the food puts a smile on Raphael's face."

Looking at Raphael, Ingrid gave him a grin.

Yet he was still dealing with his turmoil within.

They all walked in through the front door,

almost instantly a platter of food hit the floor.

The waitress immediately started cleaning her mess.

Some of the food had splattered upon her dress.

She looked over at the three of them and said, "Grab a seat.

I'll be over with a menu for what we have here to eat."

Then she scurried through the door to the kitchen,

and said, "I need the same order and don't even start bitchin."

The cook looked at her with a glare.

She just looked back without a care.

Then she went back to the man at his table who's order hit the floor.

The man said, "Just cancel my order," as he headed for the door.

Then she yelled out, "Billy, you can cancel that number three,"

then walked over to Ingrid's table and said, "What will it be?"

Ingrid said, "Maybe a menu would be a great start

unless, like your other customer, we can depart."

She looked at Ingrid and said, "How silly of me.

I'll be back with those menus in a jiffy.

How about coffee? Would you like some to start?"

Raphael asked, "Where's the restroom? I need to depart."

The waitress said, "Over by the kitchen door, the first one on the right."

Ingrid and Anna both said that coffee would be alright.

Raphael went into the bathroom,

then gazed in the mirror and was flooded by gloom.

But it wasn't because of what Ingrid had done to him,

it was his life of torturing others and sin after sin.

Visions of his victims started flashing through his mind,

then there was a knock on the door and Ingrid said, "Let's dine."

That brought him back to the current reality he was in.

He went back to the table and said, "Let the eating begin."

Anna laughed and said, "We're still waiting for the menu.

It's seems like our waitress doesn't know what to do."

The waitress came back with their coffee

and said, "Because of my mistake you can have it for free."

Raphael asked, "Does that also go for a hot cup of tea?"

She replied, "Of course it does, all the drinks are on me.

So are you all hungry with a big appetite?"

Anna said, "Yes, we've been up all night."

"I'll give you time to look at the menus and I'll be back soon.

I'll bring you your napkins forks, knives and your spoons."

"Spoons," Ingrid said, "shouldn't those have came with the coffee?"

"Oh, my God," the waitress said. "How silly of me."

Raphael looked at her and said, "Hey, everyone makes a mistake now and then."

Ingrid looked at Raphael as the waitress left to go get their things with a grin.

"That was an unusual comment, Raphael, that came from you.

It seems your human emotions are beginning to shine through."

"Yes," he said, "they're definitely coming back to me,

and with many of them, there's so much pain to see."

Ingrid said, "Yes, just like I warned you that they would,

and they'll be bouncing back from sensations of pain to feeling good.

But even with the good, it can cause you such pain,

for the loving things that you've lost can drive you insane.

You'll have visions and flashes of things that used to be.

The common terminology is called PTSD.

They associate it mainly with those that have been in war,

yet it can possess the minds of anyone that has had trauma or horror.

The torment is buried deep in the subconscious mind,

and each and every moment there's triggers to find."

The waitress returned and said, "Are you ready to order your food?"

Ingrid said, "We're in a conversation, don't be so rude.

Just leave the utensils and I'll call when we're ready," she said to her.

Anna asked, "Could you please bring me some artificial sweetener?"

Ingrid continued her conversation with Raphael's full attention,

he wanted to learn how to put his memories into a suspension.

Ingrid said to him, "I could clear your mind and make your slate clean,

and you won't have any more past memories to be seen.

But I believe it's best you learn things from them,

even if there's so much pain they hold within.

After all, your memories that now are beginning to gestate,

aren't even as painful as those people had that you sent to their fate.

And their loved ones that found them after your feast?

Have you given one thought to *their* pains, at least?"

That statement compounded Raphael's mixed emotions,

and began to even further all of his painful notions.

He just sat there and hung his head

for the survivors of the ones that he left dead.

Then he looked at Ingrid after he sorted his thoughts,

and said, "I used to get so much pleasure as they all fought. I found it exciting to take their last breath.

But now I realize how they found salvation in death.

As I had to be stealthy and sly in the night,

they no longer had any life or worries to fight.

Immortality without emotions or any loving sensation,

doesn't appear to a Vampire as any kind of frustration.

Yet, now that you've removed that veil from me,

I know that I was the one that wasn't free.

It's strange how power can corrupt your mind,

and make the cruelest situations feel so divine.

Seriously, now I feel lonely and weak,

and I want God to forgive me for killing the meek."

Ingrid said, "Raphael, you've come a long way.

There might not be any more games that we have to play."

Anna said, "Yes, Mother, this is a new side of him,"

then took a sip of her coffee with a slight grin.

Ingrid called, "Waitress, we're ready to order, please come to our table.

Try and bring us some more coffee and his tea if you're able."

The waitress said, "Tea, tea...

How silly of me."

Anna said, "Oh, now you forgot that too?

Is there anything correctly that you can do?"

The waitress looked at Anna and gave her a glare.

Ingrid looked at the waitress and gave her a stare.

Raphael said, "Come on, let's all be nice."

Ingrid snapped at him, "We don't need your advice!"

The waitress came with her order pad and said, "Alright..."

Ingrid said, "Wow, Anna, she knows how to write!"

Anna looked at the waitress and said, "What is your name?"

The waitress replied, "It's Sarah Jane."

Anna said, "I thought you looked familiar to me.

Weren't we in college together in biology?

You were the one that sat in the back and fucked with me.

Now I see you've really excelled with your college degree.

That's why when we entered you dropped that plate,

you were ashamed for me to see where you've landed in fate.

Isn't karma such a wonderful thing?

It can make a poor man rich or destroy a King."

Sarah Jane just looked at her with nothing to say,

realizing this was such a terrible day.

She stuttered out the words, "Have you decided what you want to eat?"

Ingrid said, "Yes, dear. I'll have pancakes, buttery and

sweet,

I'd like them drenched in butter with sugar and cinnamon."

Raphael said, "I'll just take two eggs, over easy, with some bacon."

Anna Marie said, "I'd like an omelet with everything,

and a couple of hot biscuits, if it's not too much to bring.

Seriously Sarah Jane I'd hate to see you drop another plate..."

Sarah left the table feeling so Irate.

She went into the kitchen and the cook said, "What's up with those three?"

Sarah Jane answered, "They're tormenting me."

He said, "Really, you don't have to put up with that shit.

I'll go give them a piece of my mind they won't forget."

He walked out of the kitchen with his spatula in hand,

ready to do something Sarah Jane would think grand.

He looked at the three of them and said, "Is there a problem here?"

Ingrid looked at him and said, "No, no, my dear."

Then he said, "Well, they say the customer's always right,

but I won't let you and my waitress fight.

So if you don't like the service you can get the fuck out of here."

Ingrid said, "I'd prefer you didn't cuss at me, dear."

The cook waved his spatula and said, "Why not, you bitch?"

She gave him a grin and his attitude did switch.

Then she said, "Why don't you go back to the kitchen

and reserve the waitress for all of your bitchin?

You'll never again say a kind word to Sarah Jane.

Everything you say will cause her emotional pain.

Do you understand what I've said to you?"

He said, "Yes, ma'am. I'm sorry, I have cooking to do."

He went back to the grill and started making their food.

Sarah Jane said, "What happened?" He said, "You're too fucking rude.

Now get your little, scrawny ass

out to the tables and make some cash.

And the next customer that walks out because of you,

your employment in this restaurant will be all through."

She walked right up to his face

and said, "I don't need this place."

He said, "Don't let the door hit you on the ass,

you useless bitch. You have no class.

Now get the fuck out of here,"

as he swiftly kicked her in the rear.

She ran out the front door with tears on her face,

saying over and over, "I don't need this place!"

Anna looked at Ingrid with a big smile,

and said, "I've hated that bitch for such a long while.

It's amazing how you can punish people so easily,

for all the pains and torment they've given to me."

Raphael asked, "Do you think that's right

for your mother to take care of your fights?"

Ingrid said, "Raphael, who are you to question me and the things I do?

The answer to that question is held within you.

Think back how you played your game with Anna Marie,

wanting to control her forever and not set her free,

because of my fortune and your greed,

trying to make her one of your seed.

But now you see the tables have turned

and, because of the things that you had yearned,

you have became a prisoner to me.

We'll decide in time if I set you free."

The cook came to the table with their plates.

Ingrid said, "It's now time that we ate."

To her surprise, Raphael bowed his head,

and these are the words that he said:

"Thank you, God, for your peace and your love.

Thank you for creating the Heavens above.

Thank you for this food that we'll eat.

Thank you for life's lessons, both bitter and sweet."

Anna said, "Thank you, God," then, "Amen."

Then the three of them started to dig in.

Ingrid called to the cook and said, "These pancakes are great!"

Anna said, "This omelet really does rate."

Raphael sat silent and said not a word.

He'd already said all he wanted heard.

The cook came out and said, "Would anyone like some more coffee?"

Ingrid and Anna said "Yes" and Raphael said, "I'll have a little more tea."

They ate and they drank until they had their fill,

then Anna called out, "Bring us the bill!"

The cook came to the table and said, "This one's on me

for how badly my waitress treated you three."

Ingrid said, "Thank you so much, that was so kind,

and those were the best pancakes I've had in such a long time."

They all stood up from the table to go home.

The cook said, "Come back again, if you're out to roam."

Ingrid said, "Oh, yes, we'll be back again."

As they left the restaurant, the cook had a grin.

When they got out to the car Ingrid said, "Raphael why don't you drive?"

Raphael said, "Do you want to get home alive?

I've never driven one of these mechanical things;

they're not needed when you can manifest wings."

Ingrid said, "Well, now that you're a human being,

it's time that you caught up with the modern scene.

Don't worry, I won't let you crash.

Now get behind the wheel and hit the gas."

Raphael got in and behind the wheel.

He hit the gas and the tires made a squeal.

He ran through a red light and almost had a wreck.

There were blue lights in the rear view mirror and he said, "What the heck?

I don't have a license to show to that cop!"

Ingrid said, "Just pull over to the curb and stop."

The officer got out of his car and walked up to them,

and said, "What's the big hurry that you're all in?

Let me see your license and registration."

Raphael looked at Ingrid with total frustration.

She was sitting next to Raphael in front seat,

and she said, "Raphael, isn't the officer sweet?"

She took the registration out of the dash,

and said, "Your license is in your side pocket with all of your cash."

He pulled out a license with lots of money

and the officer said, "Are you trying to bribe me?"

Raphael said, "Oh, no, I just needed to separate my license from my cash,"

as Ingrid handed the officer the registration from the dash.

The officer said, "Well, your license and registration look in order,"

and said, "I'll let you off with a warning but no more reckless disorder."

He walked back to his car and then pulled away,

and Ingrid said, "Let's go somewhere and play."

Raphael said, "I thought you wanted to go back home..."

She said, "It's a beautiful spring day, let's the three of us roam."

Anna said, "So where do you want to go?"

She said, "Somewhere exhilarating that puts on a great show."

Anna said, "I know what you have on your mind:

the amusement park with the rides and exhibits to find."

Raphael said, "The amusement park? The one with roller coasters and Ferris wheels?"

"Yes," Ingrid said, "I want to spend the whole day there and see if it gives you any squeals."

Raphael said, "I've never rode on any of those things before."

Ingrid said, "They can be fun or fill you with horror.

Also there are so many things there fun to eat,

from polish sausage to cotton candy, so sweet.

Actually I know of an old trick the carnies do:

they fry lots of onions to bring hunger to you.

They say there's something about the smell of fried onions that makes you hungry,

then you'll want any type of food that you see.

Kind of like how they serve salted peanuts in a bar for free,

and the salt dries you out and makes you thirsty.

There's so many tricks made by mankind,

just so they can squeak out of you another dime.

Reciprocity has always been my favorite psychological tool,

they make you think you're getting something for nothing as a general rule.

Like, 'You look so good in that car you're in,

I'll talk to my boss and see if we can slash the price, my

friend.'

Or a man takes a woman out for dinner and a movie,

then drives her back home when she's feeling groovy.

He'll get out and walk her to the door,

expecting her to put out like a whore.

Most of the time the man's wishes take place

because the woman thinks she's been treated with grace.

And the only return she can give to him for his nice deeds

is to welcome him in and let him plant his seeds."

Anna said, "Wow, Mother, that's what Tommy did to me!

So, it wasn't love after all I see..."

"Yes, Anna, it's so hard to separate

whether it's love or lust when you go on a date."

They arrived at the amusement park and parked the car.

Ingrid said, "Hollywood parking, we don't have to walk far."

Anna said, "Okay, Mom, did you make us this parking
place near the concession stand?"

Ingrid said, "Yes, I did. Isn't my manipulation so grand?"

Anna said, "You know, sometimes, I wish you'd just let
things be

and whatever happens to us will just come free.

It's not nice to get everything you want, and your way,
every day,

sometimes life's tribulations have so much to say.

Like when you were gone those seven years,

as I lived alone with a heart full of tears,

I learned a lot of things for myself

and none of them hurt my health.

I believe some of them actually made be stronger inside,

even though there were those times that were a rough ride."

"Ride? Ride! What a great idea Anna Marie!

Now let's go and let our childishness run free!"

Ingrid got out of the car and took Raphael by the hand

and said, "Now let's go enjoy my plan.

You have a pocket full of money that we can spend,

now let's go let your new sensations begin."

Raphael said, "A pocket full of money... You said you can't create money for personal gain."

She said, "That came from the cookie jar in the cabinet that sits over the sink drain."

Raphael thought that he caught Ingrid in a lie,

she just looked at him and said, "That was a nice try.

Now let's go to the ticket booth and get the bracelets for every ride

and hopefully, Raphael, before we're finished, you'll find your child deep inside."

They got their bracelets and went through the front gate.

Ingrid was so anxious for the fun to gestate.

She said, "Raphael, do you want to pick, or is it up to me?"

He said, "It's all your choice," in a voice so softly.

Ingrid said, "Let's start with the roller coaster, okay?"

Raphael said, "We'll do whatever you say."

The afternoon sun was so hot and so bright

that Raphael thought of his sunburn and looked at Ingrid in fright.

He said, "Won't the sun burn me and leave me in pain?"

Ingrid said, "Don't worry, let's get on with the game."

She said, "I will shield your skin from the sunlight,

now let's go have some sensations of delight."

Anna Marie said, "I'll just go my own way

and leave the two of you kids to go play."

Anna left them and started to vanish in the crowd.

As she was leaving, Ingrid yelled, "Be careful!" out loud.

She looked at Raphael and said, ""You never know

what kind of sickos you can find at these shows.

This is a place where the misfits can hide,

and plot evil schemes as you take a ride.

Years ago clowns were loved by all,

now their place in humanity is very small.

It's strange how things can fall from grace

and become a fear to the human race.

Well, speaking of fear, let's get in line for the roller coaster ride.

I can't wait to see how it makes you feel inside."

They walked to the roller coaster and the man lifted the bar and locked them in.

In just a few moments, it took off into the wind.

Twisting and turning and going up and down,

Raphael just sat there and did not make a sound.

Ingrid looked at the safety bar where he had his hands

and, after the ride was over, she said, "Wasn't that grand?"

The whole ride she flailed her arms and twisted her feet,

as Raphael sat white-knuckled and glued to the seat.

She looked at him after the ride was done

and said, "Wasn't that ride so much fun?

Come on, let's get in line and do it again!"

He said, "Once is enough," with a tight chin.

"Okay be a party-pooper... We'll go try something else new.

Maybe the kiddy rides would be the best fit for you?

Funny how once you could fly, so discrete,

and that ride we just rode had you glued to your seat."

"How did you know I was afraid? What gave me away?"

"It was your white knuckles on the bar and your face looked like clay."

"Okay I give up. What does 'white knuckles' mean?"

She said, "It's when you're clenching something so tight there's no blood to be seen."

"Okay," he said, "are there any more unusual quirks that show fear?"

She said, "When you have them, I'll tell you, my dear.

Besides if I tell them all to you before the sensation,

you'll be nervous and won't enjoy the revelation."

"Enjoy? How can a person enjoy fear?"

"That's a strange question coming from you, my dear.

You enjoyed people's fear for centuries, time after time, my friend.

Do you see it differently now that you're seeing this end?"

"I see your point... So now what ride's the next deal?"

She said, "Let's try something that will make you squeal."

They walked over to the Sky Diver and got in line.

She said, "You'll find this ride, oh, so divine."

The carny opened the door and locked them in.

She and he waited for the ride to begin.

Ingrid grabbed the steering wheel and said hold onto your seat

and hope you don't throw up that food you did eat.

This baby really goes fast as it spins

and turning the wheel lets you soar in the wind."

The ride started slowly and Ingrid made the cage spin

as Raphael thought, "What has she gotten me in?"

Once again she was happy and screaming in delight

as Raphael's face showed horrible fright.

When the ride was over and Raphael climbed out, he was dizzy

and he asked, "Do you have any more of these fucked up rides for me?"

Ingrid said, "No, those two are the best they have here.

The rest of the rides are much more calm, my dear."

They went from ride to ride as Ingrid cheered with glee,

as Raphael started to think, "Oh, no, poor me."

Ingrid said, "I sense you're not having any fun.

Let's go find Anna and then we shall run."

They walked all over looking for Anna Marie,

but she wasn't anywhere in the carnival to see.

Then Ingrid said, "Let's go back to the car, I can sense that she's there."

They walked out of the park and found Anna sleeping in the back seat, without a care.

"Anna," Ingrid said, "wake up, my dear.

Why are you in the car sleeping here?"

Anna rubbed her eyes and said, "I wasn't having any fun all alone,

so I figured I'd wait here until you were ready to go home."

"But, Anna, I thought you said you wanted to go your own way..."

She said, "Yes, I did, that's why you've found me here where I lay."

Ingrid said, "Wow, you're really a buzz kill.

I thought you'd come here and enjoy the thrill.

Okay, Raphael, it's time get back behind the wheel,

this didn't turn out to be such a fine deal."

Anna said, "Mother, are you just going to bitch?

And letting him drive? We could end up in a ditch."

Ingrid glared at Anna and said, "Just lay in that seat,

I don't want to hear any words that aren't very sweet."

Anna said, "You know, I'm getting really tired of you,

and your always telling me what to say or do."

Ingrid said, "Young lady, you'd better bite your tongue,"

and looked at Raphael and said, "It's time to run."

He started the car and backed out of the space.

Ingrid looked in the back seat with a strange look on her face.

She looked at Raphael and said, "Oh my, Anna's gone."

He didn't say a word because she might think it was wrong.

Ingrid said, "I guess she'll show up sometime tonight...

I hate it when the two of us fight."

Raphael thought to himself, "I'd leave, too, if you treated me that way..."

Ingrid said, "I can still hear your thoughts, you'd better watch what you say."

Then Raphael thought he could never get free

as long as Ingrid knew everything he thought and could see.

It brought him such anger he wanted to yell,

because being with this sorceress was a living hell.

She looked at him and said, "'A living hell' is right."

He said, "Don't take it out on me because you had a fight.

I've done everything I could to do things your way

and tried my best to have fun with you today.

Now I am trapped between you and Anna Marie,

along with my own life pains now that I see.

So just let it rest and I'll drive us back home,

and I won't have any more thoughts where your mind can roam."

Ingrid said, "That will be fine,"

and he tried his best to clear his mind.

She said, "Just watch the road and keep your mouth shut,

and don't put us in a ditch or stuck in a rut."

He said, "Why does it matter? You can fix any mistakes."

She said, "Well, every spell I cast has energy it takes.

Some spells are easy like waving your hand,

and others take so much energy, the pain I can't stand."

Raphael said, "You mean you can actually cast a spell that can kill you?"

She said, "That's a question I'll never answer, no matter what you do."

He got out of the fairgrounds and pointed the car towards home

and tried his best to not let his mind roam.

With both hands on the wheel, he gave the road full attention,

just like a drunk driving on a suspension.

When they got home, the ring of vines were gone away.

He said, "Is this a new game you're wanting to play?"

She said, "No, I believe that you have evolved a lot today,

and you won't be trying to get away.

Even if you did where would you go?"

He thought to himself and said, "I don't really know."

When they walked in, there sat Anna Marie,

right in the middle of the study.

She looked at her mother with a stern face

and said, "I am starting to accept my place.

I have magical powers just like you,

and if I hold on to your apron strings they'll never come

through.

So either you let me have some space of my own,

or I'll leave and come back after my powers have fully shown."

"Anna," Ingrid said, "what I'm doing is best for you."

Anna replied, "By telling me what to do or not do?"

Raphael just sat there as the two of them talked.

Then he said, "I'll go cook," and away he walked.

Anna and Ingrid both said at the same time,

"Yes, it's kind of late, it would be nice to dine."

Then they both looked each other in the face,

and they both smiled with a hint of grace.

Anna said, "I'm sorry, but sometimes you frustrate me."

Ingrid said, "I'm sorry, too, for not letting you be."

Then she said, "It has been so long ago

that my own powers did begin to grow,

I had forgotten what it was like between me and my lover,

when all of our powers we did discover.

We were like two kids trying to top the other,

with every new power that we did uncover.

We thought we were the strongest powers on Earth,

until we were taught our true worth:

the one that controls the fire known as Hell,

that burns forever as a molten well,

came to us one day and said, 'You look so sweet,

and you think your powers no one can defeat.

That's a pretty bold thing for you to say,

for on this rock things are done my way.'

He raised his hand and threw a lightning bolt,

which caused my lover to revolt.

I tried to throw a spell his way,

he swung his arm and on my back I lay.

My lover ran and wrapped his arms around him.

He let out a laugh and had an evil grin.

My lover yelled, 'I can't break away,'

and the Devil said, 'He's mine to stay.

But this one is not worthy of Hell,

I'll give him dominion over his own well.

He'll be trapped between Hell and Earth.

There his pomposity can have some worth.

You'll never see him another day,

for in the Underworld he will stay.

And, woman, now let's see as for you,

bow to me or you'll go somewhere too.'

In an instant my lover was gone away.

It took everything I had to kneel that day.

But I swore vengeance if we ever met again,

even if it was a battle I could not win.

So, Anna, you see my child

what can happen if your powers go wild.

Never think you're more than what you are,

and you will possess an ultimate power.

Just use your abilities for good for you and mankind,

and there won't be any problems that you'll find."

Anna looked at Ingrid and bowed her head

and apologized for the words she said.

Her mother said, "Anna, it's okay.

Just remember what I had to say."

Raphael came in and said, "Dinner is done,"

and off to the kitchen, away they did run.

He said, "I'm not real used to these modern devices to cook.

When you had a wood fire you could always look.

So the meat might be a little burnt on one side."

They both had a grin that they tried to hide.

He said, "Yeah, go ahead and laugh at me,

I'm not cut out to be a butler, you see."

Ingrid said, "Raphael, it's okay, now let's eat,"

and actually her words seemed almost sweet.

They ate the meal then Ingrid said, "How about wine?"

Raphael said, "Yes, Ingrid, some wine would be fine."

"Anna, would you like to have a glass with Raphael and me?"

She said, "No, I'll go see if there's something on TV.

If you need me I'll be resting in my room.

The story you told me has filled me with gloom.

I didn't realize, in life, how much you have lost,

and that your lover payed an ultimate cost."

Ingrid said, "It's not a pleasant story I like to tell,

and any thought of the Devil makes me madder than hell.

So, go ahead to your room and bed to lay,

and we'll never discuss that another day.

Good night, my child, I'll see you in the morn.

Hopefully the new day will have better thoughts to be born."

Raphael said, "What was that story you told Anna Marie?"

She said, "It's only a story for her and me.

Right now let's concentrate on the wine,

and thank you for cooking what we dined."

"Thank you," he thought to himself, "that's a change of pace."

Ingrid just looked at him with a smile on her face.

Then he said, "Don't you have any orders for me?"

She said, "No, tonight you and I can be free."

"Free," he said, "you mean I could just walk out that door?"

She said, "Yes. Either that, or you could fuck me like a whore."

Then she asked Raphael, "How have your new sensations been?

Like chewing food or sucking in wind?

Or feeling the beat of a pulsing heart?

Or having emotions you wish would depart?"

He said, "They all seem the same to me.

Even though it's been centuries,

I guess it's like they say about riding a bicycle: you never forget.

I like having the sensations back, but there's things I'll always regret.

You know, 'regret'—that's a really big word

and, to a Vampire, it's kind of absurd.

We just act on impulse, without thought,

and never have memories that should be forgot.

Now that I'm human, you can already see

how much my past does torture me."

Ingrid said, "And, like I said, the torture will grow stronger each day

unless you learn coping skills, or I take the pain away."

"'Coping skills,'" he said, "okay, what does that mean?"

She said, "To replace bad memories with thoughts so serene."

"'Serene thoughts?' My only serene thoughts have been stolen from me,

back when the female Vampire killed my family."

Ingrid said, "So, your maker was a female?

I'm all ears now, so please do tell."

"Her name was Natasha and she was made from Kian, a pure blood and very old.

Kian knew the true origin of the Vampires and to Natasha, the story he told."

"The true origin of Vampires?" Ingrid said. "Now you have my total attention.

I've read tons of lore about their origin in awe and suspension.

But now, after all these years and a glass of wine,

I'm about to have the true answer to find."

Raphael drank up his glass and filled it again,

and said, "I don't know where exactly to begin."

Ingrid said with a curious look on her face,

"Raphael, it's simple, just cut to the chase."

He thought for a second and said, "You didn't hear this from me,

but it was Satan himself that brought the Vampires to be."

"Satan," she yelled, and yelled "Satan" again,

"Now this changes the whole game I've been playin'.

I've crossed paths with many Vampires over the years,

and if I knew what you said, then they'd suffer for my tears.

Satan and I have a huge score that is undone.

From this night forth, the Vampires better run!

I'm not talking the weak ones that just take a drop,

I'll concentrate my wrath to those right on the top.

Raphael, what else can you tell me

about the original Vampires that be?"

He said, "I only know what my maker said

about the original ones they called the *undead.*

he said they can walk in the light of day,

and don't live by the rules the rest of us play.

They've made paupers into kings and sent kings and rulers to the grave,

and one day they plan for all of humanity to be enslaved."

She said, "Enslaved how? How do they plan to do this?"

"Supposedly the religions are on the top of their list.

It's easy to get humans to do anything you see,

if they think you have a faith that can set them free.

Individually they're very powerful, more than I could ever be,

but as a group, all together, they almost have totality."

"Totality," she said, "what do you mean by that word?"

He said, "They almost have the power of Satan, or so I have heard."

"So, Raphael, you're saying if I try to kill them,

it's best one-on-one for a battle to begin?"

"Yes," he said as he gulped down his wine.

Then he said, "May I be excused? I don't feel very fine."

She said, "Yes, you can, go to my bed.

I won't be able to sleep with these thoughts in my head.

Never did I think that when I trapped you as my guest,

that you would give me the answer to my ultimate quest.

Thank you, Raphael, you've settled our debt,

and anything you've done I will forget.

So go. Go sleep soft and get your rest,

as I sit and plan my greatest conquest.

In the morning I'll have a chat with you and Anna Marie,

and try to resolve any of your animosities.

You're welcome to stay here as long as you like and look after her.

That is, if you can settle your differences, and both of you concur.

Goodnight, I'll see you in the morning and we'll see how things go.

I have to think out how I'm going to deal with this new show."

Then Raphael left and went to her bed,

as Ingrid was already running her plan through her head.

She poured a glass of wine and said, "Let the battle begin,"

then drank it all down and started to grin.

She went to her study and looked at the world map,

and sat in a chair with her hands in her lap.

She laced her fingers together and said, "Where do you be?"

and eight points on the map started glowing brightly.

When the morning came she would be on a plane

to seek out the closest Vampire and discover his name.

She just sat there and at the map she did stare,

then drank another wine and passed out in her chair.

She woke in the morning with Anna touching her arm.

She said, "You're up early, did you set an alarm?"

Anna said, "No, I felt something was bothering me,

so I decided to walk around the house and see what I see."

Ingrid said, "You must have felt my anger and rage,

because my life has been turned to a new page.

It's a continuation from long ago

and I'll be leaving, I want you to know.

Raphael and I have settled our score,

and you don't have to be afraid anymore.

I asked him if he would stay here with you,

and what he said, was he'd be glad to.

This isn't up for discussion, I must go away."

Anna said, "Don't I get anything to say?"

"No, you're on your own. Do the best that you may.

Try to keep your ill feelings for Raphael at bay.

Forget what he did when he was a Vampire,

I have to leave it's almost the hour."

"Mother, where are you going? Please, tell me."

"It's not your concern and don't follow me.

I'm going to do battle with things you can't face,

not only for vengeance, but for the human race."

"Mom, now your starting to scare me...

What kind of battle will this be?"

She said, "One that I should have done ages ago,

but I didn't have the information I needed to know.

Now I'm armed with a direction in sight,

and the creatures I deal with are in for a hell of a fight.

Raphael," Ingrid yelled, "it's time to awake!

And be nice Anna, he's fixed his mistakes."

Raphael entered the room and said, "Have you talked to her?"

Ingrid said, "Yes, but her emotions yet stir.

Seriously the only way that she'll accept you,

is if you apologize for the things you did do."

Raphael looked Anna straight in the eyes

and said, "I am sorry. I apologize."

She said, "Mother, how do we know he's not lying,"

then Raphael fell to his knees and began crying.

Anna said, "How do I know he's not just putting on a show?"

Ingrid said, "I guess when I leave, in due time, you will know.

It doesn't matter if he tries to do something to you

now that some of your powers have began to show through.

If you feel like he's trying to do something bad to you,

you can wish yourself to another place like you already do.

Now I'll leave you both here in the study while I go pack.

I'll send a card now and then, because I don't know when I'll be back.

Both of you promise me to try to get along well

and, when I get back, I'll have stories to tell."

They both said, "We'll try as best as we can."

Ingrid said, "That sounds like the best plan."

Anna asked, "So, where are you going to go?"

Ingrid said, "Again, I don't want you to know."

Then she left for her room to gather her things,

and when she came back she said, "Let's see what life brings."

Raphael and Anna walked her to the door

and, in a flash, she was no more.

Ingrid appeared at the airport and flew to Salt Lake City.

She was all dolled up and looking so very pretty.

When she got off the plane there,

so many men gave her a stare.

She was dressed to the hilt or more dressed to kill,

and her vengeance was totally controlling her will.

But she knew that she had to play her cards right,

until the day her and the Vampire began their fight.

She checked into a hotel, flaunting her diamond rings,

and with every move she made her hips swing.

The bellboy said, "Ma'am can I take your bags for you?"

She said, "Yes that would be such a kind thing to do."

He rode in the elevator with her up to her room and opened the door.

She said, "Wow, this place is wonderful and has service galore."

As he stood there in her room awaiting a tip,

she put a hundred dollar bill in his hand and, boy, did he flip,

stuttering out, "Oh, thank you, ma'am, for this."

She said, "Great service is on the top of my list."

He said, "Ma'am, do you mind if I ask your name?"

She said, "No, not at all. It's Ingrid Fontaine."

Well, thank you, Mrs. Fontaine. If there's anything else you need just tell the desk clerk you want Kevin Steed."

"Thank you, Kevin. Hey, does this place have a bar?

I need a few drinks; I've traveled so far."

He said, "Yes, it has a bar and a restaurant, too,

and, as far as their cooking, it should please you.

Personally I believe it's the best food in town."

She said, "Thank you, maybe later you can show me around."

He said, "Mrs. Fontaine, you're way out of my league, ma'am."

She said, "You seem so nice, let me make the plan.

I have plenty of money that can be used,

but I need a guide so I don't get confused."

Kevin piped up, "Well, Ingrid, I'm definitely your man;

I know this city like the back of my hand."

She said, "What time do you get off? I'll be in the bar."

He said, "At ten pm." She said, "That's not very far,

it's already nine forty-five.

I'll go have a few drinks to feel more alive.

Well, for now, goodbye, my friend.

I'll be in a booth when you come in.

They do have booths in the bar, right?"

He said, "Yes, it's kind of a secret but it's open all night."

She said, "An all-night bar in Salt Lake City? Isn't that a sin?

You'd think the Mormons would say something," as Kevin did grin.

He said, "Well, there are some places here in town

where the influence of the church isn't around."

"Okay, Kevin, my newfound friend, I'll see you in a few."

As he walked out the door, he said, "Yes ma'am, see you."

She threw the suitcase on the floor

and in a few seconds was out the door.

Then she remembered she forgot to ask where the bar was located.

A man held the elevator door and patiently waited.

She said, "Excuse me, can you tell me where's the bar's at?"

He said, "The basement floor," as he smiled and tipped his hat.

She said, "Wow, everyone here seems to be so well-mannered and nice."

The man said, "That's because you don't know the cat from the mice."

She thought, "My, what a strange thing to say,"

as the elevator opened and he walked away.

The man had gotten off at the fourth floor,

she pushed the button for the basement and waited for the door.

When the door opened, she saw Kevin on that floor.

He said, "Ingrid, forgive me, but I couldn't wait any more.

I punched out early and said I had something to do

because I wanted to spend some of my tip on you."

She said, "Save your money; all the drinks are on me.

Now let's go find a private corner to be."

She noticed that the entire bar was lit up with black lights.

In places it glowed and others is it was dark as night.

She looked at Kevin and said, "What's the deal with the lighting?"

Then she said, "This atmosphere isn't that inviting."

He said, "We have customers that like it, they say."

Ingrid asked, "What type of people would like it this way?"

Kevin just looked at her and didn't say a word,

because he didn't want his answer to be heard.

He just said, "Ingrid, here there's some things we don't say,

and you're much better off if you keep it that way."

She said, "Kevin, in the elevator, a man said a strange thing to me,

something about 'cats and mice,' you see."

Once again, Kevin's lips were sewn tight,

and he looked at Ingrid with a little fright.

She knew he was hiding answers from her,

so she invaded his mind and the answers did stir.

That's an advantage about being a sorceress you can invade a mind:

you can hear words that no one else could ever find.

It's much more invasive than the Vampire thing,

when they mesmerize you to answer anything.

As she sat with Kevin and read his mind,

getting the answers she wished to find,

she was gently rubbing him on the thigh,

and all he could think was, "My, oh, my."

She kept rubbing and rubbing, and reading his mind,

trying to get pieces of the puzzle she needed to find.

He got excited and said, "What are you trying to do?"

She grabbed his erection and said, "Oh, my. You'll do."

She said, "Drink up and let's go to my room to play."

He was so surprised he didn't know what to say.

When they got to her room she threw him on the bed.

She said, "Kevin, lay back, and I'll give you some head."

Ingrid always wanted to be the one in charge,

and loved the feel of a penis in her mouth, getting so large.

After reading his thoughts she knew this was her best plan

to get anything from the young man.

She thought, "All you have to is suck a little dick,

and a man becomes your lollipop stick.

They'll do anything you ask for a little head,

as they lay on their back, in delight, on the bed."

Kevin was moaning and said, "You're gonna make me cum,"

and then Ingrid started to hum.

The sensation took him over the top,

and into to her mouth his cum did pop.

She said, "Yummy," as she swallowed the last drop.

He was shaking and said, "That's where most women stop."

She said, "Well, an amateur is a woman that won't swallow cum, but pros like me like to get the whole job done.

So Kevin, have you ever given a woman head?"

He looked at her and his face turned red.

She said, "Okay, Kevin, I can understand,

but before the night's over, you'll be a new man."

Over and over and over again,

they made love 'til the new day did begin.

When Kevin left her room he was a totally drained,

as he went to the elevator with his cock in such pain.

Ingrid thought to herself, "Well, I've had time to play.

Now it's time to start my day.

I'll see how much bait I can leave around town

so the beast I seek can easily be found."

She thought antique stores would be a great place to start,

they're places a person can save things forever without a beating heart.

They can accumulate things over the years

that, in the long run, their worth will be dear.

She started with the small ones and worked her way to the top,

to some of the most expensive and exotic shops.

This task took her several days,

and it actually started seeming like play.

She would go in and ask questions only an elder would know

because she, herself, had seen many centuries go.

She, herself, had amassed all her wealth,

from the items she stored upon her shelf.

So, when it came to antiques, she knew quite a lot,

from all the centuries and lives she had fought.

But when she had searched every shop in town to no avail,

she wondered where she would find the Vampire under his veil.

She knew if she got close to him,

she could feel Satan's power within.

That was a power she'd never forget,

the one that has left her so long in regret.

So she took a break from her quest,

and decided to have some rest.

She went back to the hotel bar and had a few drinks,

as she sat alone and tried to think.

A man sat down with her and handed her a note,

and this is the message that someone wrote:

"I can smell the scent of a brother on you.

You'd better be careful what you do."

Before she could do anything the man was away

as she analyzed the note and what it did say.

Then she realized that Raphael was only twice removed from a pure blood,

and his smell was on her from when she made him her stud.

Kian's blood was what the pure blood sensed from Raphael

now not leaving her with any defense and stuck with his smell.

She was hoping she could use stealth in this fight,

but she might as well just glow in the night.

Now that the Vampire played his hand,

it was her turn to outwit this man.

Well, calling it a *man* was a far mistake.

The only thing he warranted was a wooden stake

driven in it's heart so deep

to release some of the pain that she keep.

Anyway, she just continued to drink,

and tried to relax so she could think.

Kevin walked into the bar and said, "Hey, look at you.

Do you mind if I join you for a drink or two?"

She said, "Sure, sit down; they'll be on me.

I could use some company."

Kevin said, "You mean like that one night?"

Ingrid said, "No. You've had your delight?"

He said, "You mean we can't do that any more?"

She said, "What do you think, that I'm a whore?"

This was a different side of her he did see,

and he said, "You sure you want my company?"

She said, "I'm sorry, it's been a long day.

Don't take offense to what I did say."

Kevin said, "It's okay, I have a strong chin."

When he said that, Ingrid did grin.

She said, "Look, you put a smile on my face.

Maybe there's hope for the human race..."

Kevin thought, "What a strange thing to say,"

then he said, "Ingrid, are you okay?"

She said, "Like I said: it's been a long day.

They have a pool table; would you like to play?"

Kevin said, "I'm not very good at pool,

and I never play a woman, as a rule.

It's bad enough when I don't win,

but when a woman beats me, it really sets in."

She said, "Come on, a game will be fun,

and I promise not to make a run."

He said, "Okay," and they went to the table.

She racked the balls and said, "Break away, Mable."

Kevin chuckled and broke the rack,

the sound of the cue made a *crack*.

Ingrid said, "Sounds like you broke your stick.

Good thing you didn't break with your dick."

Kevin said, "Wow, tonight you're just full of them."

She said, "A hundred bucks, Kevin, if you can win."

He said, "You know I'm not that good at this."

She said, "Maybe some incentive will help you not miss."

They played the game down to the eight ball,

and, "In the right corner pocket," Kevin did call.

He dropped the ball in just like a champ would do,

then Ingrid said, "See? I'm proud of you."

She handed him the money with a big smile.

Then she said, "Let's go sit for a while."

They sat and had childish chit-chat.

They talked about this, and talked about that.

Then Ingrid said, "Well, it's getting late Kevin,

I need to get my beauty sleep and be gone by seven.

Kevin said, "Ingrid, I've never seen a woman in my life more beautiful than you."

She said, "Thank you for being my friend and the kind words, too,

but for now I must go retire.

I liked the way you sat that table on fire.

Goodnight, Kevin, I'll see you again.

After all, you're my only friend."

She left the bar to go to her room,

and thought, "Was that letter supposed to make me feel doom?"

She got In the elevator and went to her floor,

went in her room and then locked the door.

She lay on her bed and said, "What a night,"

and thought, "Was that note supposed to give me a fright?"

She closed her eyes and slowly drifted far away

without a care for the Vampire knowing where she stay.

Then, before she knew it, it was dawn.

She stretched out her arms and let out a yawn.

Then she said, "What a wonderful sleep,

I wonder what new adventures this day shall keep..."

She went and showered and brushed her teeth and her hair,

then she stood in front of the mirror with a blank stare.

She got so caught up with her own reflection,

for a moment her and reality had no connection.

Then there came a knock at her door and she opened it.

The waiter said, "This is a breakfast you'll never forget."

"Breakfast? Breakfast? I didn't order anything to eat."

He said, "Then you must have an admirer that thinks you're sweet.

Because, after all, this came with a card,

and putting two and two together isn't that hard."

"A card," she asked. "Where's it at? Give it to me.

It has more answers that I must see."

He thought, "What a strange thing to say,"

then gave her the card as he walked away.

He closed the door, almost slamming it,

in disgust for the tip he didn't get.

Kevin had told almost everyone that worked in the hotel

about his huge tip and how she'd fucked him like hell.

That's another place a man goes astray:

when they boast about a woman in whose bed they did lay.

It seems to always get back to them,

and any further advances they will condemn.

When it comes to sex there's no secrets on hand,

well, as far as secrets on the lips of the man.

Ingrid took the card and opened it in sheer anticipation,

hoping for her it would hold some new revelation.

But inside was just a sketch of a cat and a mouse

and the words, "Be careful, you live in my house."

She thought, "Oh, yeah, there's a new gal in town,

one that can turn this game completely around."

Then she ate some food and thought, "This is great,"

as she had a sample from almost every plate.

She put on her clothes and thought, "I'll start my day

and, maybe by nightfall, my admirer will play."

"Oops," she thought, "nightfall, how silly of me...

The Vampire I'm looking for has twenty-four hours to roam free.

He could be in a boutique or a store that I'm in

and the only way I'd know is to catch scent of him.

So the days will be long, and the nights will be, too,

until I finish this task I came here to do.

And I know trying to defeat him might be harder than hell;

I'll have to be more cunning and use my best spell,

one that can't drain my energy

and leave me as helpless as I can be.

But I have been totally helpless just that one time,

and there will never be any more kneeling for me to find."

Even the thought of that spurred her desire

to conquer the Vampire connected to fire.

She put her clothes on and went down to the bar for a

drink.

The waitress came to her booth and said, "It's a bit early, don't you think?"

Ingrid said, "Are you going to take my order, or talk about time?

I need a few drinks to calm down my mind."

The waitress said, "I'm sorry, I didn't mean to offend you."

Ingrid said, "Yeah, don't worry, I'll forgive you.

It's that just lately I have a lot on my mind,

and there's someone here that I must find."

The waitress said, "Really? Who is this person you seek?"

Ingrid said, "He's a Vampire that lives like a sheik."

After the waitress heard what she did say,

she said, "I'll be back with your drink," and scurried away.

Ingrid then knew that she had a clue about the Vampire on her list.

The waitress came back with her drink and Ingrid said, "Sit down. I insist."

The waitress said, "No, I can't. I have things I must do."

Ingrid said, "Sit down, this isn't a request, I'm demanding you."

The waitress sat down from no will of her own.

Ingrid looked in her eyes and into her mind she did roam.

She saw a man that had died from a Vampire attack,

lying in an alley, motionless and flat on his back.

Then she felt the emotions the waitress had attached to the man

and realized that a Vampire had ended their engagement

plan.

She dove further back in her mind and saw the attack

by a tall handsome man all dressed in black.

She felt the emotion the waitress felt as the Vampire took his life,

and had to disconnect from her mind because it cut like a knife.

When the waitress came back from Ingrid reading her mind,

Ingrid said, "Thank you, and let the bartender know he makes drinks that are fine."

The waitress stood up and then walked away,

as Ingrid thought, "I get new pieces of the puzzle each day."

She just sat back and drank her Long Island iced tea,

and yelled to the waitress, "Keep them coming to me."

She drank so many that she was three sheets to the wind,

and a stranger sat down and said, "You look like you need a friend."

Slurring her words she said, "Who the hell are you?"

He said, "I'm a Vampire with another clue.

Since you didn't take the hints and you're still in this town,

my maker says if you're not gone by dawn, you'll be no longer around."

She blinked her eyes and was sober and talking plainly,

and said, "Tell your maker I don't want any more choir boys to see.

Now go and tell your master I'll be easy to find if he wants me, and not to send any more messages through his choir boys, weak as a flea."

The Vampire stood up and hissed and said, "You'd better watch who you're talking to."

Ingrid said, "Don't show me those fangs or they'll be on my necklace after I'm through."

Then she laughed in his face and said, "Just go away

and tell your maker, when he wishes, I'll be ready to play."

The Vampire stepped from the booth and left with a hiss,

as Ingrid thought, "Now I'll be on top of his list."

Kevin walked in a little later and asked, "May I sit down?"

She said, "Why should I let you, after you smearing my name all around?"

Then he thought to himself, "That was a stupid thing to do."

She said, "Yes, it was. You should have kept it private, between me a you."

He looked at Ingrid and said, "What did you say to me?"

She said, "Just go away, for you and I will no longer be."

He started to say something and she said, "Don't you beg."

He walked away like a dog with its tail between its legs.

Then she sat quietly biding her time

for when the pure blood decided to dine.

She left the bar and went out into town

and secretly observed all of those around,

trying to find that one man out of place

that was the one who had fallen from grace.

She thought about contacting Anna on the telephone,

but didn't want anyone to be able to track her home.

For who only knows where these Vampires are?

They could tap the phones or drive by in a car.

She thought, "The best thing, right now, for Raphael and Anna Marie

is to absolutely not have a single contact from me."

She completely detached from their world because she thought it was wise.

She even blocked her telepathic powers there to prevent their demise.

Ingrid didn't want a thing that could trace anyone to her home,

then she went on her way and the town she did roam.

As she walked she started playing a game in her mind as she passed every street.

She was using her imagination to think of the place they would meet.

It ranged anywhere from a club or a toy store,

or in the seat of a movie with the screen filled with horror.

Many scenarios she ran through her mind

but, hour after hour, he was nowhere to find.

Then she realized she was doing the wrong thing, searching around.

She needed to sit in one place and let her own self be found.

Ingrid went to the Jade coffee shop and she sat down,

and looked at the people all around.

She ordered coffee as she sat there alone,

and there was a smell that chilled her to the bone.

A gentleman walked up and said, "I believe you're looking for me.

I decided not to send any more 'choir boys' for you to see."

Ingrid said, "Well, hello! How the hell do you do?

I've been here several days looking for you."

The pure blood said, "Yes, and so I've been told.

Don't you believe looking for me is something that's bold?"

She said, "So you think I'm as simple as swatting a fly with your hand?

There's much more to me than you understand."

The elder said, "Now you've peaked my curiosity...

Maybe there's things, after all, that you can teach me."

Ingrid said, "The only thing I want to teach you is the feel of a stake."

The pure blood snarled and said, "Woman, don't make a mistake.

I don't exactly know who or what you are,

but I will not let you go too far.

So, learn how to be polite and bite your lip,

or into your throat my fangs I'll slip.

You'll either die or be reborn that day,

the decision is all in the game I play."

Ingrid sat there a moment and studied his face,

he had kind, blue eyes and without a hair out of place.

He looked at her and said, "Tell me about you, if you will, please," as his words came out so tender with ease.

She said, "Well, I'm a redhead, all through and through;

five-eight and feisty like no one you've knew.

But, my friend, I'm sorry to say,

I can't be mesmerized by what you say."

Then he said, "Bitch, let's cut to the chase:

why have you come here and invaded my space?"

She answered, "Well, for a trip I was long overdue,

and I figured, while on vacation, I'd drop by and kill you."

He said, "I don't know if you're crazy, or just a whore,

but one more outburst like that and you'll be no more.

Kill *me?* Kill *me?* Are you just insane?

You'll be a true treat when your last drop I drain."

Ingrid said, "Are we just going to sit here and have a battle of wit?

Or do you want to go on with the game and see really who's fit."

"Okay," he said, "but one thing before we begin:

I like the names of those whose lives I do end."

"My name, well, it's Ingrid. Well, at least that for right now.

In return do I have to pry your name off your lips somehow?"

He said, "I go by Zohar." Ingrid said "What an unusual name.

Now that we're introduced, can we continue the game?"

Zohar said, "Whats your hurry? Are you that anxious to die?"

Ingrid said, "No, I've been here too long. I need to fly.

There's seven more of you out there somewhere,

and, one by one, they will all face the wrath that I bear."

"Seven more? Ingrid, someone's been telling tales out of school.

The origin of us pure bloods and our numbers aren't talked about as a rule."

"Origin? You're funny. I heard that you all made a pact with the Devil, himself."

He said, "You're misinformed, there was no pact on our shelf.

The Devil just cursed us all for what we tried to do to one of his spells,

leaving us to live forever without emotion and a taste for blood that continually swells.

You wouldn't understand how it is to live for thousands of years,

killing person after person to survive without regret or tears."

Ingrid said, "You'd be surprised the things I can understand,

now can we get back to the situation at hand?"

As she said that, the Vampire was looking her straight in her eyes,

he saw she had no fear of him and might be more than he realized.

He said, "Okay, let's drink some more coffee and chit-chat a while.

Is there really a hurry for two people like us," he said with a smile.

She replied, almost with a giggle, "I have all the time I'll ever need."

He said, "Let's have more fresh-ground coffee; it's my favorite bean seed."

He called out to the waitress and she brought back two cups right away.

Zohar looked at Ingrid and said, "It's such a fabulous day.

You'd think after over two thousand years of seeing the sun rise and it fall

that, at some point, you would get so bored and tired of it all.

But every new day I see something beautiful and dear,

whether it's a bright new color or some music I hear."

The two adversaries sat and talked almost about everything,

forgetting for a few moments that he'd have to step in the ring.

Then Zohar said, "Since you have no fear of death,

where do we go when we take our last breath?"

Ingrid said, "For most people, it's either Heaven or Hell,

and for those undecided there's an intermediate well."

He said, "You mean an Underworld? There's one that does exist?

I always thought the story of an Underworld was just a childish thing on a list."

She said, "No, sorry to tell you it does exist between Earth and Hell,

and the people that stay there pain and sufferings swell.

They can't feel hot, nor neither cold,

or remember a day their life did behold.

They all walk around like zombies without sight, hearing, or taste.

They can't talk, yell, or scream so there's no sounds that they waste.

But even in the Underworld there's exceptions for certain people and the rules there.

You can end up in a special cavern, craving earthly things with your senses, finding them nowhere.

I happen to know a couple female Vampires and a boy named Tommy down below.

If you would like to join them—trust me, it's no bother—I'll help you go."

He said, "No. On that offer, I believe I will pass,"

as he asked the waitress for some water in a glass.

The waitress came back with the glass of water and he drank it all down.

Then he said, "That's an advantage of being a pure blood: all the sensations can still be found.

We can eat food, shit, shave, and shower,

and never have to mind the sun or the hour

because it cannot turn us to dust.

True bloods can feel love or just fuck for lust.

We can walk in a church and kiss a cross,

and cross a flowing stream without any power loss.

Garlic tastes so Fucking great!

Around a neck or on my plate!,

We love to see our face in the mirror,

for vanity is a sin we hold so dear.

As far as wooden stakes, like you said before,

you can stab our chest with a whole Fucking wood door!

We can transform into all living things any day or hour,

and the fears of mankind just strengthens our power."

Ingrid said, "Are you finished talking all about you?

I'm getting bored. Let's get on with this Shit we must do!"

The Vampire rose to make his attack,

then Ingrid tapped him on the back.

He said, "What is this trickery?"

She said, "There's a lot more of it to see."

He spun around to attack her again

and, when he looked, she was gone like the wind.

She had shrouded herself with an invisible cloak,

and said to him, "You see I'm no Fucking joke!"

He flailed his arms wildly trying to get hold of her somehow,

as she said to him, "Zohar, who's in charge of you now?

In the list of things that can't harm you, that you so proudly boast,

you didn't mention anything about having a toast."

Then, on their table, appeared a golden goblet,

filled to the top with Ingrid's blood that she had let.

She reappeared and said, "Now drink of me,

and from this curse I will set you free.

If you drink of it freely I'll let you live,

because, without your curse, I feel you have something to give.

But if you won't drink of the goblet freely, of course,

I'll make you drink of it simply with force."

He said, "Force? Ha, ha! Don't make me laugh!

You are the one that shall feel my wrath!

I'll rip you to shreds after I drain your last drop,

and the whole time I'm drinking, you'll beg me to stop."

Ingrid said, "You can't say I didn't give you a chance,"

as she stood there in a vigilant stance.

She said, "You look thirsty. Why don't you have a drink?"

The goblet was in his hand before he could think.

"How does it smell? Why don't you give it a whiff?"

He raised it to his nose and took a sniff.

Then she said, "Be a good boy and drink it all down.

You'll find it the best blood that you've ever found.

But this now will be the last blood you taste.

Sarcastically she said, it's a pity that you'll be erased."

After he drank it, with the last words he did make,

he yelled, "The other pure bloods won't be so easy to take!"

He fell to the ground as she walked away,

and next to his body the goblet did lay.

She stayed in Salt Lake City and watched for his obituary with it's note.

When she read it, her thought was, "He was a rich fucking old goat."

It seemed that he was quite a prominent man,

owning lots of property and buildings so grand.

It said that he was an only child and survived by none,

and when and where the funeral would be done.

"The funeral," Ingrid thought, "I love to wear black. It looks great on me.

I wonder if any other pure bloods will be there to see their old buddy..."

This was a wish Ingrid hoped to manifest.

It would make it simpler to finish her test.

But the funeral went on with just humans there

as the stench of his ashes drifted in the air.

No instructions were made for the event of his death,

no life insurance for when he had took his last breath.

So they figured cremating him would be okay,

but now his companies were in total decay.

Ingrid left the funeral at Memory Grove to go back to the hotel.

As she rode in a taxi she still remembered the pure bloods smell.

Along the way she watched the sun go over the *Oquirrh* mountains and set.

and this was an evening she wouldn't forget.

When back at the hotel she took the elevator down

to the bar that sat below the ground.

Just when the elevator doors opened, someone yelled, "Our guest has arrived!

Come on in, baby, and pray you get out alive!"

She tried to run back into the elevator and make an escape,

because going to the bar now seemed like a mistake.

The bar was packed wall-to-wall as they drug Ingrid in,

and the Vampires started chanting, "You killed our friend!"

She twisted and turned and tried every spell,

but they continued to attack her, she screamed louder than hell!

They tied her to a post and all gathered 'round.

A Vampire said, "What do we do with this witch that we've found?

She's the one that has taken our maker away from us!"

A female Vampire yelled, "Let's burn the bitch and grind her bones into dust!"

"Burn the bitch! Burn the bitch!" became all the Vampires' chant.

The manager of the club said, "This place is all wood," as they continued their rant

A Vampire said, "Let's take her out in the country,

where there's not a soul to see.

Then we'll burn this evil bitch alive,

because fire's one thing a sorceress can't survive.

Someone take the delivery truck to the back door,

and we will load in this Fucking whore.

Then drive out of town and head due east

and we'll be waiting for this hot feast."

They untied Ingrid and threw her in the back of a panel truck, and all she could think was, "What the fuck?

Why didn't any of my spells take effect,

and they were able to do things I object?"

She heard the truck start and felt it going up the ramp to level ground,

then she started feeling some of her energy to come back around.

She thought to herself, "After all this time and I didn't know

that below the Earth's crust, my powers cannot show."

Then she sat back and rested during the ride,

for when they reached where they were going, they'd find a surprise inside.

Every once in a while, she pounded on the walls and screamed, "Let me out!"

The Vamps in the front seat yelled, "It doesn't do any good to shout."

They drove for a while and met up with the rest

at the location they chose to be best.

They opened the truck and threw her on the ground,

and they took turns kicking her around.

She got on her knees and tried to crawl away,

and a Vampire said, "Do you want to play?"

He hiked up her dress and mounted her from behind.

As he started rocking, he said, "I think she don't mind."

A Vampire said, "Maybe you need to stick it in the other part..."

The one fucking Ingrid said, "That's where I began to start."

Another one walked in front of her face and said, "You know what to do."

She shook her head, "No!" He hit her and she started sucking him too.

She blocked any senses or pain or emotions she felt,

because she was preparing for their hand to be dealt.

A Vampire said, "When you two boys are done, bring her to me,

and we'll tie her up to this dead, old, oak tree."

He said, "The rest of the crew are gathering wood for the fire!"

He exclaimed that sentence with so much desire.

He said, "Okay, that's enough! Bring that whore to me!

It's time to get on with this ceremony."

He took Ingrid and bound her up tight

as they dropped logs and limbs at her feet to ignite.

It wasn't long and she was surrounded in a ring of dry wood,

about one-third of the height that she stood.

She begged and pleaded and put on a great show,

as internally her powers continued to grow.

The Vampires encircled her in a small ring.

Someone said, "Throw on the gas and let's all of us sing!"

One of them said, "What, 'Ring of Fire' by Johnny Cash?"

Another said, "'Burn the witch' has much more class."

They started chanting "Burn the witch!" again,

and then they thew a match under her chin.

Just as the fire ignited, Ingrid forced the flames down

and it spread in a backlash to the Vampires around.

She intensified the flames, causing even the air to burn.

The Vampires were caught with nowhere to turn.

Then as they were all burning alive in the night,

she yelled, "I'm more than a witch for you to fight!"

She waited for sunrise before she left,

just to make sure none of them escaped death.

After the sun came up, it even destroyed the charred bones that were there,

as she thought to herself, "Vampires had better beware."

Then she drove the delivery truck back to her hotel and took a shower

and was on a plane home in less than an hour.

On the flight back she wondered how many of Zohar's clan she did kill,

and as she reminisced on the trip back, the whole thing kind of gave her a chill.

She thought, "For a moment there, I was almost done.

It's a good thing to know where my powers will not run.

This is a secret I'll never give away,

because it could be the end of me one day."

She got to the airport and called Anna Marie

and said, "I'm at the airport; come and get me."

Anna said, "Can't you just will yourself back home?"

She said, "I have no energy left from where I have roamed."

Anna said, "Okay, we'll come and get you."

Ingrid said, "Okay, I'll be in the lobby by Gate Two."

As she was walking with her luggage to find a seat,

she looked at the world map for the others to defeat.

Only seven places lit up and it gave her a smile,

and she thought, "I'm going to be traveling quite a few miles."

Anna and Raphael arrived at the airport and went in,

and found Ingrid sitting asleep in a chair with her suitcase under her chin.

Anna said, "Wow, that trip really did take a lot out of you."

Ingrid exclaimed, "If only you knew!"

Anna said, "So, tell me: where did you go?"

Ingrid said, "I'm sorry, but there's just things you can't know."

She looked at Raphael and said, "I see you didn't kill each other."

Raphael just smiled as Anna said, "Mother!"

Raphael said, "Actually, we had a great time,

and Anna Marie has a brilliant mind.

We have had some very interesting chats,

from the birth of Christ to Egypt's connection with cats."

Anna said, "Truthfully, Mother, Raphael can be lots of fun."

Ingrid said, "I'm glad you like him, hun."

Ingrid implied, "Or has it became more than just 'like' between you two?"

Anna replied, "We didn't do anything, Mother. I'm nothing like you!"

Ingrid smiled at Raphael and said, "Then he's still all mine!"

Raphael sat there speechless with no words he could find.

Ingrid said, "Okay, off to the car. It's time that we roam

because, in a few days, I'll be leaving home."

Anna said, "You're leaving that soon again?"

Ingrid said, "Yes, dear. I must sail like the wind.

I have many places to go and things that I must do,

and I'm truthful sorry for having to leave you.

But this quest I am on isn't one of desire.

It's to prevent the earth from becoming a huge ball of fire.

All in all, I have seven trips I must take,

and in any of them I can meet death if I make a mistake.

Anna Marie, that's all I can tell you.

Now, let's hurry home; I have things to attend to."

They walked out of the terminal and got in the car to go home,

and Ingrid asked Anna, "Have any more of your powers shown?"

She said, "I can do a few more new tricks,

like bending spoons with my mind or setting fire to sticks."

Ingrid said, "Before you know it, you'll be more powerful than me."

Anna said, "Mother, I believe that day I'll never see."

Ingrid said, "Anna, the first rule is never have a grain of doubt,

because it can destroy the mountain peaks from which you shout.

Simply said, a grain of doubt can destroy a mountain of faith, dear,

so to become one with your powers, you have to conquer your fear.

Magic is something natural; it flows in everything,

and when you connect to it, the powers of the universe sing."

"Sing, Mother? What do you mean by that? Please, tell me."

She said, "Well, everything in reality is a little off key,

but when you connect to the source and it begins to align,

then there's infinite possibilities and powers to find."

Raphael was driving and listening to their conversation,

and what Ingrid said didn't need any translation.

He understood what she was referring to,

and thought, "Magic, some day, I could even do.

Because, after all, you can do anything in this life you care to do,

as long as you never give anyone power or dominion over you.

As it's said: 'Believe in what you believe and it will come true,

believe in what others believe and they will consume you.'

Raphael said, "Now that I'm human again and free from that curse,

and my minds not controlled by that longing thirst.

I know that when it comes between 'good and bad',

that it's all just a form of projection.

Because, if you don't know the future outcome, there's no absolute connection.

For something bad today that landed you in tears

could save the world in a thousand years.

But so many humans are only worried about now.

If we're to ever find clarity we need to think of the future somehow.

I thought, even when I was an immortal fiend,

I never cared about the future scene.

I just lived one day at a time,

just like those living with less years than mine.

Ingrid has let me turn over a new leaf,

and it has strengthened my forms of belief.

Just like when someone does almost die,

they come out of the experience and think, 'Now, God, I'll try.'

All of their days or years before that near death event,

God's name was never on their lips or thoughts that were spent.

Speaking of spending words, in life you have only so many to say,

and they can bring people close or push loved ones away.

Words have power and energy

and, each one you use, it never comes free.

Some people live to just babble on,

and when they die, they'll always be gone.

Others that instill new thoughts and new plans

into the hearts or the minds of man

will always be known for what they said,

long after their obituary has been read."

A horn honked and Anna said, "Raphael, are you okay? You're not driving very cautious today."

He said, "Anna, I'm sorry. I was lost in a deep thought for a bit."

She said, "I thought it was something, because of the car you almost hit."

The rest of the way home he cleared his mind and watched the road.

They got to the house, and Ingrid said, "Can you take my load?"

He said, "Sure, I'll get your luggage. You both go on in."

Ingrid said, "Would you care to join me for wine in the den?"

Raphael said, "Sure, that will be fine. Do you want this suitcase in your room?"

She said, "Actually, no. Throw the whole thing in the trash, it holds memories of doom."

Raphael had learned not to question what she say,

so he put the suitcase out for garbage day.

The garbage men were in for a surprise if they opened it;

the clothes Ingrid wore were stunning and always a beautiful fit.

He went back in the house and joined her in the den for wine.

She poured him a glass and walked to the piano and said, "Do you mind?"

He placed his drink on top of it and opened the keys and tapped on them

and said, "Is there something you'd like?" She said, "Make me soar like the wind."

He started to play and she smiled as he tapped on every note.

She said, "Raphael, that's a beautiful song. I can't place the era it was wrote."

He said, "It's one of mine, you see;

all Vampires generally have a hobby.

We all need some kind of release for living so long,

some find it in music, and some in song."

Ingrid said, "I never thought much about that,

but when all you can do is kill, have sex, or chat;

I guess you'd have to have something to take you away

from the dismal lives in which you stay."

He said, "Yes, when I play I can see all the colors around,

that in the night are hard to be found.

Personally I always yearned for the sun,

and for centuries I knew that it would never come.

But you've broken my curse and set me free,

and now there's so much more beauty to see.

I believe there's not a Vampire who's heart doesn't break,

for one day filled with the colors, that daylight does make.

I believe most humans that suffer a Vampire's bite,

it's definitely a curse to have to live in the night."

Ingrid said, "Enough about Vampires. I had a terrible fright, and I still have seven more that I must fight."

He said, "Seven?," in a curious way.

She said, "Yes, I dispatched one the other day."

He said, "It's none of my business, but are you hunting them down?"

She said, "Yes, until I kill the last pure blood around.

Raphael, this is something you must never tell Anna Marie,

not even if something happens to me.

If I should go and never come back,

you'll know I died from a Vampire attack.

Just try your best to help Anna have a good life,

and try to guide her away from things that will cause strife.

But as you've noticed she can have a mind of her own,

just understand this and leave her alone.

She will come back to her senses in time,

and then you should take her out to dance and dine.

If she should start to date again, check the man out

and make sure he's true, without any doubt.

If you have to even run a background check

to see if there's things she should object."

Raphael said, "You're asking a lot of me."

She said, "What, do you want me to give you money?

Actually I think I should give you an account..."

"Do you have any suggestions for the amount?"

She said, "How does five hundred thousand dollars sound?

That should last you 'til I get back in town.

Consider it me paying you to watch Anna Marie,

and for you to make sure she that she lives happy and free."

She said, "Tomorrow we'll go to the bank and set up your account.

Are you satisfied with that amount?"

He said, "Yes, Ingrid, it's much more than fair,

and with that amount we can go anywhere."

Ingrid said, "I'll give you some locations to never go,

if you and her travel, that you'll need to know.

But never tell Anna Marie that these are the places I'll be.

If she traveled to them looking for me it could end in tragedy."

He said, "Yes, Ingrid, I know you've taken on a dangerous plan.

And you'll be traveling from land to land.

Just be careful and come back home,

I wouldn't want to see Anna end up alone."

Ingrid said, "You know, you and I have came a long way

from when we met that very first day."

Then he asked, "Do you think you can ever forgive Tommy, Lyra, and Lenore?"

She said, "Right now, I don't want to think any more.

But there may be a time when they can fall in my grace,

but for right now they're in the best place.

Even you and Anna, I'm always worried about when I'm away,

and I try my best not to give them any clues to lead them your way.

Raphael, right now, I'd like to go to bed.

If you care to join me, I won't mess with your head.

But if you know how to cuddle I could use your arms wrapped around me,

and give me some tenderness that will set my mind free."

They went to her bed and held each other tight.

She gave him a warm kiss and told him "Goodnight."

As Ingrid slowly relaxed and drifted away,

she started dreaming of the past few days.

In her mind, she thought, "How hubris of me,

I almost fell prey to my pride and vanity.

I'll have to not be so arrogant in the future with the Vampires I meet,

and keep all of my powers and my actions much more discrete."

Those were the last things her mind had to say,

then she relaxed and drifted away.

The morning came and they all did their usual things.

Ingrid yelled, "Let's be on our way! I need new dresses and rings!"

They loaded into the car and drove into town.

Ingrid said, "Let's go to the cheapest shop around."

Anna said, "Mother, that's not like you... Are you okay?"

Ingrid said, "Yes, I just feel like shopping cheap today."

"Cheap," Anna thought. That was a word she'd never used,

and hearing Ingrid say it now left Anna confused.

Anna said, "Aren't you planning to go on another trip," almost with doubt.

Ingrid replied, "Yes, and I want something that won't make me stand out."

"Wow," Anna said, "now that's a new twist.

Normally being noticed is on the top of your list."

Raphael parked the car in front of a resale shop.

Anna said, "You're kidding. This is where we will stop?

Mother, you're really going bargain basement today?

I'm curious about your trip and where you plan to stay."

Ingrid said to her, "Don't worry your poor mind.

Now let's go in and see what we can find."

They all went into the store and looked around,

and Ingrid called, "Come look at this dress I have found!"

Anna and Raphael walked over to the aisle where she was at.

Ingrid was holding a summer dress and said, "Do you think it will make me look fat?"

Anna asked, "Don't you think it looks kind of plain?

Mother, are you sure you haven't went insane?"

Ingrid said to Anna, "Heavens, dear, no. Not at all.

I just have to dress my part for this adventure's call."

Anna just said, "Whatever. I'm going to look at each DVD

and see if I can find any movies that can give some laughter to me."

Ingrid said to Anna, "Are sure you're okay?"

She replied, "Not really. I worry about you when you're away."

"Well. thanks for your concerns, Anna. I'm glad I'm on your mind.

I wish I could tell you more about the specters I find.

But, if I did, I know out of your concern for my safety,

that you would come and stand right next to me.

Seriously, I'm pleased with you more and more every hour,

but you're not even close to being in control of your power.

When I'm finished with my tasks, I will start training you

and help you control your sorcery that comes through.

But, as for now, I have so many things on my plate,

if I don't give them my full attention, they could lead to my fate."

Anna said, "Mom, you're scaring me again..."

Ingrid gave her a simple grin

and she said, "Don't worry, Anna. I try my best every day

to conquer these tasks and come home to stay.

Until then will you and Raphael try to get along,

for I don't know how many days or weeks I'll be gone.

But after each task I'll return to you

to let you know that my mission is through.

I have seven left that I must go attend,

so you know after each one I'll be leaving again."

"Mom, why won't you just give me one clue?"

She said, "Because I don't want any harm to come to you."

Ingrid thought for a moment and said, "Raphael knows my

plan,

and if I never come back, you and he can make a stand.

Because if I fail in what I must do,

the fate of the world will be left up to you two.

Now let me finish shopping, my time is so thin.

I need inconspicuous clothes that I must dress in."

She continued to shop, throwing things into her cart,

as Anna went to the DVDs with a heavy heart.

Raphael went with her and stood by her side

and noticed she had tears she wanted to hide.

He put his arms around her and held her near,

and said, "Don't worry about your mother, my dear.

I'm sure she has plenty of tricks up her sleeve,

and she won't be easy for anyone to deceive.

So just worry about us and what you want to do

until the day your mother comes back to you.

Seriously, if she needs us, she has her telepathic power,

and she can contact us any week, day, or hour."

Anna said to Raphael, "Yes, you're right."

It relieved the tears she was trying to fight.

She showed Raphael a movie and said, "This one is fun."

He read the title; it was *What Dreams May Come*.

She said, "This is such a great movie;

it touches on how the afterlife can be."

"Afterlife," he said, "that sounds interesting now that I'm no longer undead.

That's a whole new concept that I need to work into my head."

She grabbed her movie and they all went to the checkout line,

and Ingrid said, "I wonder if they have any mood rings to find."

Anna said, "Those were a fad long ago."

Ingrid said, "Yes, Anna, I know."

Ingrid took off her rings and said, "Anna, open your hand.

The place that I'm going, I can't look wealthy or grand.

You can have all of these rings of mine for you to wear,"

as she touched Anna's cheek and stroked her hair.

Anna looked at her and said, "Are you coming back home to me?

When people generally give away their priceless possessions, it means they'll no longer be."

"Priceless, Anna? There's only one priceless thing I ever did see:

it was the day of your birth and when you came out of me.

Yes, I have jewelry and treasures galore,

yet you are the one thing that I truly adore.

Now, let's pay for this stuff and get in the car.

The bank's up the road, not very far.

When we get there, Anna, I'd like you to make an account

with Raphael's name on it, with 500K as the amount.

I'm leaving him some money for you to play,

so you and he can do things while I'm away.

I didn't want Raphael to ask you for cash anymore, Anna

Marie,

because if he has some of his own, you can do things more freely.

Having to ask for money makes one feel grave,

and if you give them some they feel like a slave.

But then, on the other hand, if you just give some to someone in need,

and in passing one day you mentioned the kind deed.

They will normally take a bold look at you

then will lash out 'I didn't ask you to!'

So, like I say about the whole money thing,

how it torments the paupers and corrupts the king.

Just realize we never own anything on this Earth,

and love and compassion are the things with true worth."

Anna looked at her and said, "The love and compassion thing again?

When in my life will those sensations begin?"

"Anna," Ingrid said, "they'll be there one day to see,

generally after all of your searching has ceased to be.

In all of my years, I've had only one true lover, my dear,

and most of the men since just fucked me out of fear.

Almost every woman has a burning flame

that they wish they could find a man to tame.

But some of them don't know how to just be passive,

and accept the pleasures from minute to massive.

For me the pleasure I get out of most men

isn't as good as one of my fingers plunged within.

For once you've been with that ultimate man,

it's best to lie back and just take things in hand."

"Mother, quit. I don't want to hear any more."

Then Anna went silent and looked down at the floor.

Then Ingrid said, "Oh, yes, that's it! You think it's a sin

to touch yourself and delve your fingers within.

You really did listen to what that priest had to say

as he looked and lusted over you every day."

Anna said, "What priest are you referring to again?"

All Ingrid could do was return a big grin...

"Mother, can we just go to the bank, please?

I don't like it when it seems like you tease."

Ingrid said, "Yes, we can, but I have one last thing to say:

you really should try to experiment one day.

Just light some candles and draw a hot bath,

and let your tips of your fingers find the right path."

"Yes, yes, Mother; maybe I'll try it one day,

but for now let's be on our way."

They all went out of the store and drove to the bank down the street.

Ingrid said, "After we're finished, let's get something to eat."

They created his account and Raphael said, "Thank you, Ingrid, for the money."

Ingrid said, "You don't have to thank *me;* it all belongs to Anna Marie."

They went back to the car to drive away,

and it had started to snow earlier that day.

Raphael looked at Anna with a tear in his eye

and thought to himself, "How now the time does fly."

Ingrid said, "Well, it's really starting to look like January."

Anna said, "Raphael, driving in the snow can be scary."

Then she said, "Do you mind if I drive," with a look of concern.

Ingrid said, "If he doesn't drive, how will he learn?

This car has front wheel drive, it will do good in the snow.

Now get behind the wheel, Raphael, it's time we must go."

Raphael was a little hesitant to get behind the wheel.

Ingrid touched his hand and said, "It's not a big deal.

By the time we have ate and are ready to leave town,

there will be much more snow on the ground.

Cars are in the worst danger when there's just a few flakes,

and if you run into black ice, never push on the brakes.

Just let off the gas and keep your tires straight,

many that didn't do this were sent to their fate."

"Fate," Anna said, "I'm starving to death here."

Ingrid asked, "Would you like ice cream, my dear?"

She said, "I can handle ice cream when it's above fifty degrees,

but to eat some today would make me continue to freeze."

Ingrid said, "Well, we're caught between breakfast and lunch...

Do you know any places that serve a good brunch?"

Anna said, "There's a new place they opened last year,

and actually it's up ahead on this road quite near."

She said, "The name of it's FOOD 24/7.

All of their dishes taste like heaven.

You can have any dish you want at any time,

and their deserts are so divine."

Ingrid said, "Sounds like a great place for us to stop.

Let's park the car and in we'll pop."

Raphael found a parking place.

They got out and ran in with smiles on their face.

Shivering a bit, Raphael exclaimed, "It's so cold outside!"

Ingrid said, "It's because of your pulsing heart and the blood inside.

Before you weren't cold or warm blooded inside,

but now you have the elements from which you must hide.

After we eat, we'll get new clothes for your back,

and please don't pick everything in black."

As they sat at their table the waitress came and said, "Would you like coffee to start?"

Ingrid said, "Bring us a pot, please, our friend here needs to warm up his heart."

She said, "I'll be right back; do you need sugar or cream?"

Anna said, "Yes, we'll take both," so kind and serene.

Then she looked at her mother and said, "If you see anyone I know,

no matter what they've done, just let it go."

Ingrid asked, "Are you getting a premonition, Anna dear?"

Anna said, "No, I just don't want any trouble here."

Ingrid said, "Okay, from now on, I'll just tend to the things I have to do,

and I'll let you settle any difference with those that have wronged you."

"Thank you, Mother. That's a big relief.

I don't need anymore things that can cause grief.

I believe sometimes you can overdo it with the punishments you dish out."

Ingrid looked at her and said, "Are you trying to make me feel doubt?"

Anna said, "No, I want to live by what you said about the snow to Raphael today:

how will I ever learn to deal with my own battles if you keep taking them away?"

Ingrid said, "I know, but they say a mother knows best..."

"Well, you're not the mother I used to know with your test after test.

We got along much better when you were Kathleen,

and you were old and kind with no powers to be seen.

Now that you have this new face and body that's fine,

you've invaded my space too much and crossed that thin line.

Trust me I'm not down-playing what you have done

but, from now on, I'd like my own life to run."

Ingrid said, "Do you feel better now that you have that off your mind?"

Anna said, "Yes, I feel much better and now. I'm fine."

Raphael just sat there taking it all in,

and witnessed a new relationship start to begin.

Anna said, "Mother, in your journeys, I wish you the best.

From what you've shared, they'll be your ultimate test."

The waitress came with the coffee and they held their cups up.

Raphael said, "I can't wait to taste my first steaming cup."

The waitress thought that was something strange to say,

then said, "I'll be back for your orders," as she walked away.

Ingrid said, "You've never had coffee? You've been deprived.

Isn't it so grand to be back alive?"

Raphael said, "Yes, I relish it more and more each day I live,

and I notice all of the beautiful things that living can give.

Back before I was bitten, life was so hard and bleak.

My only salvation was when my wife kissed me on the cheek."

Anna said, "Your wife? You were married? Did you have any kids?"

He looked down at the table as he closed his eyelids.

Then she noticed that he had tears in his eyes trying to drop,

and decided this was a conversation that she needed to stop.

Ingrid called to the waitress and said, "I believe were ready for you, hun."

She came to the table and said, "Will the bill be individual, or all written as one?"

"Just one," Anna said, "and I'll take number one: eggs toast and ham."

The waitress then said, "What will it be for your handsome man?"

Anna said, "We're not together; we are all just friends here."

In her voice was a faint touch of cheer.

"Sir, have you made up your mind? What will your order be?"

Raphael looked up and said, "I'm not very hungry."

Ingrid said, "Raphael, order something or I'll pick for you.

I'm sure I can find you a taste that will be brand new."

He said, "Okay, why don't you do that, please, for me?"

She looked at the menu and said, "Give him a number three."

Ingrid said, "I'm partial to your number five;

it looks like something to make me feel alive."

The waitress then said, "Would you like any side orders to eat?"

Ingrid said, "How's the chocolate pie? I'd like something sweet."

The waitress said jokingly, "How can you keep your figure with so much to eat?"

Ingrid replied, "It's a magical secret that I keep discrete."

The waitress walked a way with a smile,

as she said, "I'll be back in a little while."

Then Ingrid said, "Magic, Anna, speaking that subject it reminds me:

never get caught below the earth's crust, or your powers

might not be.

After all these years, I learned on my last trip,

there is even a place where I could slip.

Please remember, Anna, everything I just said

because, if you lose your powers, you can end up dead."

As they sat and waited, the snow outside kept coming down

and it covered everything that was around.

Ingrid looked out the window and said, "The snow has so much grace,

and it makes the earth look like a heavenly place.

With all the whiteness that looks so pristine,

there's nothing more beautiful than a wintery scene."

The waitress came back with three steaming plates

and said, "Here's your feast that's ready to be ate."

She said, "Here's your ham and eggs," to Anna Marie,

then said, "For the man of the table, we have BLT.

And for the spicy red head, it's Reubens today,"

then she let out a giggle as she walked away.

Like before, Raphael chose to say a prayer before his meal,

but this time is was a shorter sweet deal.

He said, "Thank you, God, for your love and this life,

and for letting me now live in a world without strife."

Then he took a bite from his BLT,

and looked at Ingrid and said, "This is tasty."

She said, "If you want total delight,

try my sandwich, you can have a bite."

She handed him her Reuben and he tasted it

and said, "Now that's a taste no one can forget."

Then Ingrid said, "Keep it. I'll trade you for a BLT."

Raphael said, "Sure, that will be fine with me."

Anna said, "Your orders make mine seem like a waste."

Raphael said, "Would you like mine, or maybe a taste?"

She said, "No, it's okay. I'll just order those another day.

Now let's all of us munch away."

Raphael ate his all down and then licked his plate,

then Ingrid said, "That's bad manners at the present date."

He said, "Oh, I'm sorry. Please forgive me, I didn't know,"

and his face took on an embarrassed, red glow.

Ingrid said, "Ah, don't worry about it. It's not a big deal.

If you were at my table at home, I'd know you enjoyed the meal."

They drank some more coffee and chit-chatted a while.

The waitress came back with a big smile.

She said, "Hello. Was everything okay?"

Raphael said, "Yes, the best I've ate in many a day."

She looked at Ingrid and said, "How 'bout that chocolate pie?"

Ingrid said, "Yes, I'm ready," with a gleam in her eye.

Raphael said, "Chocolate? Can I have a slice, too?"

The waitress looked and Anna and said, "Anything for you?"

She asked, "Do you have any cherry cheesecake?"

The waitress said, "Actually, we have one our cook did just make.

I'll be back in a flash with the desserts for you three."

Ingrid said, "I believe, this time, Anna, you chose better than me."

Before she left, Ingrid said, "Bring an extra cheesecake for this man."

The waitress said okay, then left as Ingrid said, "Now you're in for some flavor so grand."

They got their desserts and Raphael said, "I don't know where to start."

Ingrid said, "Chocolate has always held a high place in my heart."

Anna said, "I'm sure it does because of the endorphins it can release,

and I'm actually surprised you didn't ask for more than one piece."

Raphael said, "Okay, now you have me, you two.

What do these endorphins do to you?"

Ingrid said, "It releases the same chemicals as intercourse."

Anna said, "That's why I said she ordered it, of course."

Ingrid said, "You know, I'm not a big slut like you make me out to be."

Anna replied, "Since you've been back as 'Ingrid' you've had more cock than I ever did see."

Ingrid said, "Well if you didn't try to live your life in a fairy tale,

you might find it easier to give up some tail.

Maybe on the way home we should buy you a dildo,

and see if using it makes you want the real show."

Anna said, "That's enough, let's eat our dessert!

Because if this continues someone's feelings will be hurt."

Ingrid said, "Yes, and they won't be mine,"

then handed Raphael his spoon and said, "Let us dine."

Raphael tried the cheesecake and said, "This is great!

I can't wait to see how the chocolate will rate."

Ingrid said, "It's best to eat them one at a time

so that your taste buds have time to align."

Anna said, "Yes, that's some great advice,"

as she was finishing the last bite of her slice.

Ingrid was finished almost as fast as Anna Marie.

Raphael said, "This chocolate is so savory."

Then Ingrid asked him, "Which one of them tastes the best?"

With a smile on his face Raphael said, "I didn't know there'd be a test."

He said, "I really don't know," with his hand on his waist,

"but they were both definitely a wonderful taste."

They tipped the waitress, payed the bill, then went to the car and got in.

With a big smile Raphael asked, "Can we come here again?

This was much better that that other place, the other day.

You know, the one with the waitress Ingrid ran away?"

Ingrid chuckled and said, "When I leave on my trip, you and Anna Marie will be able to investigate any place here in town as you roam free."

Anna said, "Yes, Mother, seriously, that sounds so great;

and if any men bother me, I can say Raphael's my date."

Raphael started the car and turned on the wipers to clear the snow.

Ingrid said, "Everyone buckle up, and away we go."

He pulled onto the street and sat in a fearful perch.

Ingrid said, "You drive like an old lady on her way to church."

She said, "Just sit back and I'll cover your ass.

No matter what happens I won't let us crash.

But don't rely on me, Raphael, this is your time to learn.

I want you and Anna to be able to go out without any concern."

He was still a bit nervous as he drove in the snow

but, when they got home, his heart started to glow.

They got out of the car and he had a big smile on his face.

Ingrid said, "Soon 'behind the wheel' won't seem like an unusual place."

As they started to the door Ingrid said, "We forgot Raphael's new clothes!"

She only remembered when she seen his red nose.

"Anna, do you mind going with Raphael back to town?

I feel like I need to go inside and lie down."

Raphael said, "We can do it another day.

I'll go inside and find a warm place to stay."

Ingrid said, "The warmest place is next to me."

Anna said, "Mother, will you just let him be?"

Ingrid said, "Raphael now has total free will.

He can be with me or light a fire for his chill.

Even if he wants to leave alone when I'm away,

I don't want you to have anything to say.

I know as a Vampire I made him my pet

but, like I said, I've forgiven him without any regret."

Raphael said, "Thank you, Ingrid, for setting me free

and relieving that terrible curse from me."

Anna said, "I'm out of here. I'm going to bed

before you make him feel guilty and he gives you head."

"Guilty," Raphael asked. "There's not an ounce of guilt in my mind.

I'm just enjoying this new life your mother helped me to find."

Anna said, "I think I'll just go to my room and watch my movie,

and I recommend it as something for you both to see.

I don't want to know where he goes or what you two do.

I'll fall asleep after my movie is through."

She left for her room and Ingrid said, "I need a shower. Would you wash my back, please?

In a hot sexual stance with a big smile as a tease?"

He said, "Now that my emotions are back, I don't know if I can make love without a connection."

She said, "Your choice is your own; I can handle rejection."

Ingrid dropped off her clothes right where she stood and said, "I'm going that way.

Think it over and come join me, if you care to play."

He watched her and that perfect body walk to the bathroom.

It gave him an erection and a mind filled with gloom.

Not from what she had done to him before when they had sex,

but his long lost feelings of love he had for his ex.

So he stood in turmoil thinking, "What should I do,"

then went to the shower and said, "Can I join you?"

She said, "Yes, take your clothes off and join me."

He stepped in the shower with a huge erection for her to see.

She said, "It looks like you're interested. Let's just be tender and let be what be."

She took a sponge and washed his whole body,

then she said, "It's your turn to wash me."

As he gently moved the sponge over her curves and her mounds,

they kissed tongue to tongue and made loving sounds.

They both rinsed off and she fell to her knees,

and looked up at him as if saying, "Please."

Then she took his penis deep in her mouth and grabbed his ass.

He let out some moans and took several gasps.

It wasn't long before he was totally spent,

and she sucked out his cum and down her throat it went.

She stood up with a smile and gave him a kiss

and said, "See? I can be tender or so full of bliss."

They got out the shower dried off and went to her bed.

She said, "Thank you," and those were the last words that were said.

When Raphael and Anna awoke, Ingrid was nowhere to be.

She had already began her next journey.

They were a little shocked that she left them that way.

They looked at each other with almost nothing to say.

She was now on a plane for Brooklyn Heights,

with the seventh Vampire in her sights.

She glanced through a book about the Jehovah Witness,

hoping the knowledge would give her mind fitness.

She knew by the locations of the pure bloods on the map and where they lit up,

they were all in places with religious denominations they could contort and corrupt.

All religions tell you how to live and what happens at your fate, with assurance,

weekly people pay ten percent for their afterlife insurance.

The plane landed and she gathered her luggage and went to a coffee shop.

There was a particular smell there that she knew, and it beckoned her to stop.

She walked to the counter and said, "I came here because of the smell of your unusual brand."

The man behind the counter said, "Oh, yes, you want the Brimstone. It's our best and the sales are so grand."

"Brimstone," she asked. "So what's the secret ingredient that makes every one want to stop?"

He said, "The water comes from a shallow well with high sulfur content and, each day, they almost drink us out of every drop."

Ingrid said, "Well, I believe I'll have to pass on that brand; sulfur isn't very good for my constitution.

So what else do you have that you could suggest for a tasty substitution?"

He said, "Well, we have several brands of coffee with chocolate in it."

She said, "How about white chocolate? Right now, I think it would be the perfect fit."

He said, "One white coffee. Would you like chocolate whipped cream on that?"

She said, "Oh, heavens, no, I'm watching my calories. I don't want to get fat.

It's bad enough to have the chocolate in the coffee,

but you know how a woman's cravings can be."

He said, "Yeah, look at me, I'm a walking billboard for a diet plan."

She smiled at him and said, "Oh, you're not that big of a man."

He went and got her coffee and said, "That will be three seventy-five."

She reached in her pocket and down deep she did dive.

It was pennies and nickles and dimes that she started to count out to pay.

He felt sorry for her and said, "Why don't we make this a free one today?"

She said, "Are you sure? I don't want you to think I'm a bum, oh, dear me."

He said, "I don't." She said, "Thanks," and walked away sipping her coffee.

With the coffee in one hand and her bag in the other,

she imagined the things that she would discover.

Then she thought, "If they sell that Brimstone Coffee all around town,

the scent of the pure blood will be so hard to be found.

The smell of sulfur will be on so many I meet,

as camouflage for the one I wish to defeat.

I can already tell this one's a little more wise,

and he won't be as quick to drop his disguise.

This adventure might take me a while to complete,"

she thought over and over as she walked down the street.

She went into a hotel and said, "I don't have any money,

but my husband's supposed to send some to me.

Can I stay here," she asked the clerk kindly, "for a few nights?"

He said, "The homeless shelter is down the road; you'll see the lights."

She took her bag and went out the door as she cussed at the man.

Everything was working, just as she'd planned.

She went to the shelter and said, "I need a place to stay."

A lady said, "What kind of misfortune has sent you our way?"

"Well, I lived with a very abusive man,

so I gathered my things and away I ran.

I had just enough money for a plane here."

The lady said, "Oh, bless you, my dear.

Have you eaten anything? We're about to serve the evening meal."

Ingrid said, "My hunger isn't the most important deal."

The lady said, "Don't worry, we'll find a place here for you.

But we have rules, you have to watch what you do.

Right now, go in the cafeteria and get something to eat,

and we'll make sure you don't have to live on the street.

By the way, my name is Charlotte. What's your name, lady?"

She said, "I'm Kathleen, but all my friends call me Katie."

"Okay, Katie, after you've had something to eat, just relax and try to clear your head,

and I'll brief you on the rules then take you to your bed."

She said, "Ma'am that is so gracious of you.

Without your kindness, I don't know what I'd do."

Charlotte said, "Well, it's not me as much as the church that owns this place."

Katie said, "You mean the Jehovah's?" and Charlotte said, "Yes," with a smile on her face,

"you know of the Jehovah's?" Katie said, "Just a little bit

but, from what I've heard, they seem like a kind outfit."

Charlotte said, "Well, actually, you're lucky. Normally, we're packed,

but one of or flock went away and hasn't came back."

At the risk of not asking too much at the start,

she went to the cafeteria and Charlotte did depart.

As she sat and ate potato soup, she thought, "This trip

might have much more to give.

I can learn how those that are less fortunate live."

Potato soup was a new taste,

and she ate every drop without any to waste.

The role she was playing had to be played to the tee,

if she was to conquer the pure blood and leave there safely.

A lady at the table sitting next to her said, "So where are you from hun?"

She said, "From a battered life and a man that made me run."

The other woman said, "Men! Oh, my God, what they can do to you...

Don't worry friend, you did the best thing you could do.

This place is top-notch compared to other places in town,

and you can trust me, I've been all around.

And as far as mistakes one can make with their life,

all my past memories cut my heart like a knife.

Well, enough about that. Would you like more to eat?

I'll take your bowl with me." Ingrid said, "That would be, sweet."

The lady came back to the table and sat both of their bowls down

and said to Ingrid, "I have a feeling you'll fun to be around."

She said, "I don't know how much fun I'll be,

but it feels so nice to finally be free."

"You got that shit straight," the lady burst out.

"A person can't live a life filled with pain and doubt,

wondering where there old man's out at night

or if he's with another bitch or in a bar fight,

wondering if he'll even come home

and, if he does, will he leave you alone?

You don't know how many drunk men I've let crawl all over me

because I was in a situation where I couldn't get free.

After so much time, your body just becomes a shell

and, if you lay there and let them fuck you, they don't beat you or yell."

Ingrid said, "Yeah, I know. I know exactly what you mean,

it's starts out nice then turns to a shitty scene.

Bastards! They're useless! I'm done with all men!

If I was younger now, there'd be a convent I was in.

You know when I was young I considered being a nun,

but the lust in my loins seemed like so much more fun

until you realize that you live with a prick,

and there isn't a place he hasn't stuck his dick.

You know, even when he did, I didn't really mind

until I learned he'd told his friends about our private time.

They'd come by when he wasn't around,

hoping I would give them what he had found.

One day one of his friends told me everything he had said.

I was so pissed I took him to our bed.

I let him do me any way he wanted to,

I think I was the wildest woman he ever did screw.

Yes, I got my revenge before I ran out our door,

and now he can find someone else to be his whore."

"That a girl," the lady said as she extended her hand.

Ingrid shook it and the lady said, "I'm Marie Ann,

but all my friends here just call me BJ.

I guess you know how I got that nickname to stay."

She gave Ingrid a smile and said, "I really like you.

Hopefully we can find fun things we can do."

Ingrid said, "Well, I'm Kathleen, but my friends call me Katie or Kate.

Now I need to find Charlotte because it's getting late.

I've had a really long, tiring day,

and I need a place for my head to lay."

BJ said, "Alright, I'll see you again."

Ingrid said, "Thanks for being a friend."

She walked out of the cafeteria looking for Charlotte,

hoping the stories she told she wouldn't live to regret.

She knew living her role was like telling a lie,

it's harder to keep it going the longer you try.

And at some point you have to remember so many things you said,

that you get confused with all the thoughts in your head.

Then, with a slip of the tongue, you let the cat out of the bag,

and then anything you say after that sends up a red flag.

Charlotte noticed her and walked her way

and said, "Did you make any friends?" Ingrid said, "I met

BJ."

Charlotte gave her kind of a look about what she said,

and thought to herself, "Our queen of head."

Then she said, "Grab your bag and come with me upstairs, the women have a floor of their own.

We think it's best so the men here leave you alone.

The men are on the first floor,

And after ten pm we lock their door.

We do the same thing with the women's floor too.

And never come back with any alcohol in you.

No drugs here, either. Do you understand?"

Ingrid said, "I don't do any of those things, ma'am.

Trust me I'll be on my best behavior

and this place is really my savior."

Charlotte said, "We have to fingerprint you and test your blood DNA. Here, it's a law."

Now this was a topic that almost dropped Ingrid's jaw.

"The church and the state want to make sure we're not harboring fugitives

that are hiding out here and taking advantage of what kindness God gives.

So, come to my office tomorrow and we'll do the tests, and fill out the forms."

Ingrid thought to herself, "A DNA test? Is that really the norm,"

but she said, "It's nice that you run such a safe place

and the church does so much for the human race.

It seems like God has sent me here to such a nice place,"

As she grinned and showed Charlotte a big smile on her face.

"Can you take me to my bed, please? I'm really sleepy."

They went through the door and Charlotte said, "Your cot's thirty three.

You'll find on it everything you need. Now go get comfortable and have a good night.

I'll be making my rounds later after ten pm. That's when I lock the doors tight."

She went to her bed and she lay down and thought,

"With fingerprints, DNA, and blood tests, I could be caught."

She'd never taken any of these tests before.

She got up and paced on the floor,

wondering what to do about them. Then she thought it might be best

to go ahead and take each and every one of the tests.

She knew they would find things they never saw before

and this might be a way to bring the pure blood to her door.

Thinking, "When all the tests are done and come back, if they don't say a thing,

the first part of my trap would now be starting to spring,"

she knew she'd be watched every where she did go,

from what the results of the tests would show.

So she quit pacing the floor and she lay down,

then she heard other people around.

They were all coming to their cots to go to bed,

as she drifted off to sleep without a care in her head.

The morning came and she was the first one to rise.

She stretched her arms and rubbed her eyes.

She looked at her watch and it said six thirty.

She crawled out of bed and felt kind of dirty.

The ladies' showers were right on her floor.

She took her bag with her through the door.

She got undressed and stood under a shower.

As she was standing there, with her face to the wall,

someone touched her back and it made her skin crawl.

She turned around and it was BJ.

She said, "Katie, you're up early today."

BJ looked Ingrid in the eyes and smiled at her, and Ingrid smiled too,

and BJ said, "What are us two girls to do?"

For the first time, Ingrid felt out of place,

as BJ leaned over and kissed her face.

Ingrid thought, "Maybe I should play this game,"

and kissed BJ back, gentle and tame.

BJ asked, "Have you done this before,"

just as someone else opened the door.

They both went back to taking a shower like nothing happened,

as under her breath BJ cursed the bitch and her emotions blackened.

The lady looked at Ingrid and said, "Your face looks new.

Welcome here. I'll just be here a sec, I have things to do."

The lady was quickly in and out of the shower.

BJ said, "It's still an early hour.

Most of those hags out there sleep until nine

so, if you want to fool around, we have plenty of time."

Actually, for Ingrid, this experience was all new.

Men were always on her list to do.

She looked at BJ and said, "Honestly, this is my first time..."

BJ said, "A virgin? Oh, how divine!"

She began kissing Ingrid sweetly once again

and ran a hand down her belly and slipped a finger in.

Ingrid thought to herself, "This is okay,"

as BJ got on her knees and licked away.

Ingrid thought, "I've always heard it was different if a woman did it to you,"

and from what she was getting from BJ, she found it to be true.

It was tender and compassionate and felt so divine,

and there weren't any stubbly whiskers to find.

She placed her hands gently down on BJ's head,

and thought, "If I could see a mirror, my face would be red."

She was torn between embarrassment and total desire

as BJ began to lick and suck a little higher.

Now Ingrid was in throes of ecstasy,

then she exploded, and was feeling so free.

BJ stood up and kissed her then held her close and tight,

and said, "How was it," and Ingrid said, "Out of sight."

Ingrid said, "I have a question I have to ask you:

doesn't 'BJ' refer to the men that you do?"

She said, "Well, I don't swing that way anymore,"

just as another woman walked through the door.

BJ looked at her and said, "Fuck, what is this? A parade?"

The woman was confused by the remark she had made.

They both rinsed off and went back to their beds,

as Ingrid had thoughts running through her head.

She thought, "Yes, BJ is now really my true friend,"

and let out a small giggle as she thought, "We'll do that again."

She lay back down and went back to sleep

and wondered how many more surprises this day would keep.

When she woke, the doors were unlocked and almost everyone was gone,

and wondered, "Have I slept in too long."

She went down to the office to take the tests.

Charlotte was there and said, "You look like you had a nice rest."

She thought to herself, "If you only knew...

It wasn't sleep that made me look so brand new."

"I'm kind of busy. Go have something to eat.

After your breakfast we'll have time to meet."

Ingrid got in line for coffee and the hot corned beef hash

and thought, "People eat some sad food when they don't

have any cash.

She thought, so far, it hasn't been bad and I really don't mind

but, if they make tomato soup, that's where I draw the line.

"Yuck," she thought, "tomatoes and milk? Now that's just wrong!

That's definitely two things together that don't belong."

She sat at a table to have her coffee but avoided the hash.

BJ saw her sitting there and was by her side in a flash.

She said, "Good morning, Katie, how are you today?

Did you sleep well in our little cache?"

Ingrid said, "Yes, I slept so serene.

Having my freedom is such a dream."

BJ said, "Yes, this is definitely a place to be free

and, with so many people, there's always new things to see."

She winked at Ingrid and Ingrid smiled at her.

When she smiled, BJ felt like she could purr.

BJ said, "It's nice to see a beautiful new face to come here

and with your smile you make me feel dear.

Before you got here, there were these ugly old hags

whose breasts had fallen down and their eyes blackened by bags."

Ingrid was a work of beauty as BJ did know,

and thinking what they had done made BJ's heart glow.

Ingrid said, "BJ, I have to go fill out some papers and take those tests.

After I'm through, will you guide me around? I bet you know this town best."

BJ said, "Sure, it will be a lot of fun."

Ingrid said, "Well, forgive me, but I have to run."

She went back to Charlotte's office and knocked on the door.

Charlotte said, "Come in. I'm not busy anymore."

Charlotte asked, "First, do you have any ID?

I should have asked you last night, actually..."

Ingrid said, "I have a driver's license, but it is expired."

Charlotte said, "Well something that's current is what is required."

"Well, I have my Social Security card. You can match the number to my license, can't you, please?

You should be able to look at the photo and see that its me with ease."

Charlotte thought for a second that she was bragging about the way she looked.

She reached out her hand and took the cards and Ingrid noticed she shook.

She looked at the license and said, "It only expired last week. That's not a big deal, after all."

Then she said, "For something that close, I'll make my own judgment call.

Besides, the people that I work for that make the rules here,

they don't have to put up with all the bullshit I put up with, my dear.

Oh, last night when I was telling you the rules, I left something out:

you're supposed to actively look for employment, every day, as you walk about.

There are a lot of places here to find work,

and tons of them look for a desk clerk.

Do you have any clerical or hotel skills, Katie?

If you do, employment will be easy for such a nice looking lady.

Seriously as cute as you look,

I'm sure you can find a boss that you can hook."

She said, "Yes, I can do typing, and I have some computer skills."

Charlotte said, "Interesting. It might not be long before you can live on your own will.

I love a great success story when a person leaves this place,

to know they've conquered 'rock bottom' puts a smile on my face."

Ingrid liked Charlotte, she seemed kind and sincere,

They couldn't have a better person working in a place like here.

Charlotte said, "Okay, now fill out this form the best you can,

and then we'll get to the rest of the plan.

By the way, have you ever been fingerprinted before?"

Ingrid said, "No," then looked at the floor.

She finished the form and said, "Okay, what's the next test?"

Charlotte pulled an ink pad out of her desk.

She took out the finger print form and said, "Give me your

right hand.

It will be easier for you to do this if you will stand."

She rolled all ten of her fingers on the form, then said, "You can use the sink.

Trust me, I also hate this procedure and that stupid black ink."

Ingrid washed her hands and said, "What now?"

"Well, they do the DNA and the blood tests together somehow.

So I just have to draw one vial of your blood for them.

I try my best not to make it hurt when I put the needle in."

She banded her arm and drew the vial.

Ingrid said "It didn't hurt," and gave her a smile.

"So how long does it take for the tests to come back each time?"

She said, "Actually, there's never been anyone tested that committed a crime.

It seems that the word is out on the street

about how we keep this halfway house on top of its feet."

Ingrid said, "Are we finished? Now may I go,"

then gave Charlotte a smile with a glow.

Charlotte said, "Sure, we are all done.

Just be careful in town where you go, hon.

There's some bad elements here around town,

and some that have left here have never been found."

She walked out of the office. BJ was waiting for her and said, "Are you free?

We have all day and I have so many things for you to see.

I know all the best places in town,

and where we can find some fun around."

Ingrid said, "Seriously, I'd like to look for work."

BJ said, "Come on, let's play today. Don't be a jerk.

This is only your second day in town,

there's plenty of other days for a job to be found.

Today, Katie, just sit back and let me be your guide."

Ingrid thought about how BJ had given her a warm feeling inside.

BJ said, "I know a restaurant where we can score some great food for free.

Just sit there and relax and leave everything up to me."

They walked a few blocks and she said, "This is the place."

The thought of real food put a smile on Ingrid's face.

They went inside and BJ said to the waitress, "Where is Tony?

I have a big surprise to give him from me."

She went in the back and said, "She's here again."

Tony came out to their table sporting a big, cheesy grin.

She said, "Order some coffee," and Tony said, "This one's one me,"

and BJ and Tony went to the back as she said, "See? It's all going to be free."

She came back to the table in a short while,

giggling and laughing, with a big smile.

Ingrid said, "I thought you said you didn't do men anymore?"

She responded, "For a free meal here, I don't mind being a

whore.

Besides, all Tony ever wants is a quick blow job from me,

and he cums so fast it's no effort, you see?

After all, I didn't earn this nickname,

by not being the best at that game.

So look at the menu and let's have a feast, dear,

and, maybe a little later, we can have some beer."

Ingrid said "BJ, Charlotte said no alcohol."

"Well, I always drink early so I'm clean by bed call.

Ingrid said, "BJ, it seems you've mastered this game."

She said, "Yes, I'm a little trickster that doesn't like to live lame.

I was out on the street when I was thirteen years old

and, now that I'm thirty, there's no part I've not sold.

You know, for a few bucks, I'd probably sell the devil my last breath

because, if you knew my past, at times, it was a living death.

The waitress came to the table and said, "Why the hell are you back here?"

BJ yelled out to Tony and said, "The waitress isn't being nice, dear!"

Tony said, "Just wait on their table and give them what they like,

and if you stick your nose in our business you can go take a hike.

Hell I could hire her and have the best of life here

and wouldn't have to put up with your bitching, dear."

She said, "You'd better watch it, or I'll walk out that door,

and leave this place to you and your homeless whore!"

"Okay," he said, "that was it! Now you can take your ass and hit the bricks!"

She said, "Well maybe I can find a job where I don't have to work for a prick!"

Ingrid thought to herself, "BJ is almost as good as me..."

The waitress walked out the door and said, "Fuck all you three!"

BJ said, "Tony, do you want to give me a job here?"

He said, "Do you think you can handle it, my dear?"

She said, "Sure, I've worked in many a greasy spoon,

and you can still have your benefits in the back room."

Ingrid said, "Hey, I thought you weren't looking for work, BJ."

She said, "This is an opportunity I can't turn away."

Ingrid said, "I'm happy for you," and Tony said, "When can you start?"

She said, "Well, today after breakfast, I have to depart.

I need to show my new friend around town,

but tomorrow I can be here when you want me around."

"I open at six am. Can you make it by then?"

She looked at Ingrid and said, "That's up to my friend."

Then she smiled at Ingrid and started winking.

Ingrid knew exactly what she was thinking.

Ingrid said, "I can try my best to get you up each day

if we both get jobs, we can rent a place where we can stay."

BJ said, "That would be so cool to have you as a roommate!"

Ingrid said, "Well, let's see what kind of jobs come to our fate."

Then BJ said, "How about breakfast omelets to go?

I'd like to get on with the show."

Ingrid said, "Sure, omelets would be fine."

BJ said, "Tony's cooking is so divine."

Tony said, "So, how many do you want me to make for you?"

BJ said four and Ingrid said two.

He went back to the grill and fried it up for them.

They grabbed the bag and were off like the wind.

BJ said, "We need to go down an alley to see an old friend,

but don't go here alone or it could lead to your end.

The locals here are kind of territorial at times,

even if they're homeless and don't have two dimes.

Their cardboard houses are a palace to them

and they don't want any intruders within.

Most of them here are homeless vets.

They were once brave men with no regrets.

Now their country has abandoned them,

and they live in these alleys and die each moment within.

Don't be surprised if you see a suicide

from the thoughts and emotions they have trapped inside."

Ingrid said, "I know all about PTSD,

it is an illness that's so hard to see.

But when it possesses someone's mind,

it's generally with them for their lifetime."

BJ said, "I see you're not just a regular gal,

and you're a perfect choice to be my pal.

Now let's go and find my friend Steve, he lives up ahead."

They walked through the alley, seeing people in dread.

Ingrid thought she'd never seen people like this before,

trapped in the cities and surrounded by horror.

She thought there were a few homeless in her hometown,

but not like the thousands here wandering around.

All the time that she was with BJ

she reminded herself why she was there to stay,

but the things she was seeing made her question herself

and why she needed so much wealth

when there were people dying in the street,

that for days, weeks or months had so little to eat.

She thought, "What is the difference between a Vampire taking a person's last breath,

or the rich people of the world to shun them as they starve to death?"

Already this trip had opened her eyes,

and she'd be leaving there much more wise.

That is, if she left after the Vampire she faced,

and her life was not erased.

She heard BJ say, "This is my friend, Steve. Say 'hello.'"

She said, "Hi," and he said, "What do you know?"

BJ said, "Have you ate today?

I have some food." He said, "That's okay."

She looked at Ingrid and said, "He's always like that.

He always has to be a big brat."

BJ said, "I have four omelets, and two are for you."

He said, "How can I thank you for what you do?"

She said, "Just give me a smile after you eat,

and we'll say our deal is complete."

He looked at Ingrid and said, "She does this each day

and her kindness helps me to want to stay.

For, if not for her, I would have already taken my life.

God only knows how many times I've stared at my knife."

BJ said, "Eat up, we're going to town,"

then she passed the breakfast omelets around.

Steve said, "So, where is it you want to go?"

She said, "You know my favorite place that makes my heart glow."

"No, do we have to go there again?"

She said, "Yes, we do, because you're my friend.

And you know how much it means to me,

and what we do there sets my soul free."

He said, "Okay, after we're done eating, we'll be on our way."

She said, "Oh! Guess what? I got a job today."

"A job? Really? Where is it at?"

"Working for Tony, the one that is fat."

Ingrid said, "How many Tony's do you know?"

Steve said, "Don't ask. Now let's all go."

Ingrid said, "Where are we going?" BJ said, "It's a surprise."

Steve said, "You'll know we're there when it lights up her eyes."

They walked several blocks around town and went to the end of a street,

there was a building called The Last Stop Retreat.

They went up to the front door and rang the bell.

A women greeted them and said, "Come in! It's colder than hell!"

"Katie, I'd like you to meet Ruth Ann,

she is a major part of my plan.

For months now she's let me come here and help those in need,

the ones on their last breath wishing to be freed."

Ruth Ann said, "Hello, Katie, it's nice to meet you.

BJ's a lot of help with the things she can do.

Just wait a second and I'll get you some scrubs

and, if you need, you can bathe in the tubs."

Steve said, "I could use a quick bath before we begin."

She opened the door to the shower room and said, "Go ahead and jump in."

BJ and Ingrid went in there, too.

Ingrid said, "What is it here you do?"

She said, "I bring laughter and happiness to the residents

here.

Before I came, they never had any cheer.

I tell them jokes and make them laugh,

and help some of them take a warm bath.

This is a home for the old people the world has forgot,

and their trapped in these walls and just left to rot."

Her and Ingrid showered then put on their scrubs

and waited for Steve to be done with the tub.

When they were all dressed they spent the rest of the day

going from room to room to help people laugh, eat, or play.

Ingrid thought this had taken her way off her task,

but actually, when they were though, she had such a blast.

But she said, "I have a question to ask you, BJ:

how can you be so nice to these people, yet give yourself away?"

She said, "Each one of us have different ways of dealing with sins.

I like to bury mine under these people's smiles and their grins.

For every smile they make, it takes some of my pain away.

That's why I try to come back here almost every day."

Steve looked at her and said, "I never knew

that was the reason for the things we did do.

Now that I know this, I'll never complain,

since it removes so much of your pain.

You know, actually, it relieves some of my pain, too,

now that I look at it the way that you do."

Ingrid said to herself, "I've learned something again:

to give of yourself can bury your sin."

BJ said, "Well, let's leave and get home, before it comes night."

Ingrid said, "Why did you say that? Does night give you a fright?"

BJ said, "There's some things in this town we don't talk about."

Ingrid thought to herself, "I bet there's no doubt."

They all changed back into their own things and told Ruth Ann good bye.

She said, "You all come back," and they all said they'd try.

Ruth Ann said, "If you don't, you'll truly be missed.

Your name is on top of the residents' list."

BJ said, "I'll be back as soon as I can."

Ingrid said, "Me, too. This time was so grand!"

The three of them walked out the door and headed home.

As they left Steve, BJ said, "Now don't go out walking alone."

He laughed and said, "Yes, Mother. Now go away."

She said, "I'll see you tomorrow, some time of the day.

When I get off work, I'll bring you something to eat."

Then her and Katie walked down the street.

When they got to the shelter, the sun was going down.

BJ was looking over her shoulder and all around.

Ingrid knew what she was looking for but didn't say a word,

and the word *Vampire* would never come off her lips to be heard.

They went into the cafeteria because it was dinner time

and got their plates and bowls then stood in line.

It was potato soup and BJ yelled, "What the fuck's the deal?"

She said, "It's like we have that shit every meal!"

Charlotte came up to her with a stern look on her face

and said, "If you don't want to eat what we have, you can eat some other place."

BJ said, "Well, now I can, because I've got a job now."

Charlotte tried to think of a way to praise her somehow,

but she didn't say a thing, because BJ was in one of her moods

and, no matter what she said, it would be misconstrued.

Ingrid said, "BJ, I had fun going with you to those places today.

let's don't come home and fight and ruin such a wonderful day."

"Home? Home," she yelled. "This place is for the walking dead!

In fact, it's the worst place I've ever laid my head!"

BJ ran out of the shelter and stormed off in the night,

Ingrid thought, "Will she be safe between now and daylight?"

Charlotte came up to Ingrid and said, "Hello.

I'm sorry about BJ and her show.

Sometimes she can be a real handful, but down deep she's so sweet.

I wish that she wouldn't have ran out into the night and the street.

Night time isn't a real safe place to be around here."

Ingrid looked at her face and saw notions of fear.

Then she asked, "So why is everyone here so afraid of the night?"

Charlotte said, "Oh, I'm sorry, I must run. I have reports to write."

Ingrid finished her meal and then went to her cot to sleep

and lay there wondering what adventures the next day would keep.

She wondered if BJ would survive the night,

in a town where the night time brought everyone fright.

She really wanted to live there in the shelter and be discrete,

but she also knew she'd find nothing if she wasn't on the street.

Ingrid got out of her cot and went down stairs to find Charlotte,

and told her, "If anything happens to BJ, I'll never forget it."

Charlotte said, "Out after dark here isn't a safe place to be."

Ingrid said, "I'll be okay. Can I just go have a look-see?"

Charlotte said, "I guess. I am kind of worried about BJ out in the night

but, as your searching for her, try to stay near the street lights."

Ingrid said, "Okay, but I might be out after ten.

When I get home, will anyone let me back in?"

Charlotte said, "I'll tell the attendant you'll be out

and to let you back in with out questions or doubt.

So, good luck and be safe as you're searching for BJ."

Ingrid said, "Well, we might be back in right away.

I have a pretty good idea where she might be."

Charlotte said, "Do want someone else to help you go see?

After all, you haven't been here very long in this town.

Maybe you need someone that knows their way around."

Ingrid said, "I'll be okay, I have no fear of the night."

Charlotte said, "Well, just be careful." Ingrid said, "Alright."

Then she left the shelter to go find BJ,

thinking she might know where she did stay.

She went to Tony's place and it was locked up tight,

so she continued her quest into the night.

Then she went to the alley where they had earlier met Steve,

thinking BJ went to him for the hurt she needed to relieve.

As she walked down the alley she heard someone yell, "You don't belong here!"

She called back, "I'm just looking for a friend, please don't mind me, my dear."

The voice called back and said, "The people here don't have many outside friends.

We're all castaways that the world has sent to the four winds.

We all huddle close to each other in the dark night,

And during the day we search for a little food, for a bite."

Ingrid said, "I was here earlier today,

with my friend that goes by 'BJ.'

We went though here looking for her friend, Steve, who lives down the alley a-ways."

Then several people yelled, "There's things in the night that can end your days!"

Ingrid said, "If it was one of *your* friends who was left alone in the night,

would you leave them out there or search for them with no fright?"

A woman walked up to Ingrid and said, "You have a point, dear,

and I find it interesting that you haven't any fear.

By this I can tell you haven't been in this town very long

and don't understand what lurks between sunset and dawn.

Even the everyday people that walk down the street

don't understand the misfortune us homeless ones meet.

Each day in the paper, you won't see a word about how one of us met our fate,

as we're taken in the night and used like a steak on someone's plate.

And those of us that disappear in the night,

you never find a body to be found in daylight.

The abductors secretly take ones that will never be missed by mankind,

and there's so many of us alone at night out in these alley's to find."

Ingrid said, "These abductors, what are you referring to?"

The lady replied, "The ones that suck the life out of you:

they're the ones that roam only in the night,

and send you to the grave with their horrible bite."

Ingrid said, "Vampires? Is that what you're referring to,"

pretending it wasn't something she already knew.

The woman said, "Yes, dear, they're not just a fairy tale that exists.

In these lonely alleys, at night, they're all around in our midst.

You have to believe me and be careful at night,

or you will fall prey to one of their bites."

She said, "I will go down the alley with you to find Steve and look for BJ,"

then she held Ingrid's hand and they both walked away.

As they walked past each trash barrel that burned in the night

that the homeless ones lay near waiting for daylight.

Now and then some would yell, "Who's walking our way?"

Ingrid's guide would call back, "Don't worry, it's Kay."

Eventually they made it back to Steve's makeshift home,

and Ingrid found that it was where BJ had roamed.

Ingrid said to her, "I knew this is where you'd probably be at."

BJ climbed out of Steve's home made out of cardboard, holding a cat.

The first thing BJ said is, "You shouldn't have been out in the night alone."

Ingrid said, "I was worried about you. I came to take you back home."

BJ said, "Home? That's just a place I lay my head.

I'd rather be here with Steve than with the walking dead.

All of the people at that shelter just act like a zombie,

and they don't have any real life that I can see.

After all the months I've been there, Katie, you're my best friend.

All of the of rest that live there haven't anything to give from within.

The first moment I laid my eyes on you, I knew

that there was something special about you.

It's like you have a power glowing from within,

that's why I wanted to be your friend."

Ingrid thought to herself, "If BJ only knew

all of the powers I am able to do."

Steve said, "Hello, Katie. It's so nice to see you tonight."

She said, "Well, I had to come out and make sure BJ was alright."

He said, "Well, as long as she's here with me, she'll be okay.

Come in and join us, there's room for all of us to stay."

The lady that had walked Ingrid there said, "Yes, Steve has a big home,

and he is always taking in those left out at night to roam."

BJ said, "Yeah, it's amazing what Steve has made here,"

as she took Ingrid's hand and said, "Come on in, dear."

The lady that had walked Ingrid there bid them all a good night.

As she was leaving, she called out, "It'd be best if you didn't leave before light."

Ingrid went in the makeshift home with Steve and BJ,

and said, "You're right, there's plenty of room for us to stay."

BJ sat the cat down and it ran away with a hiss,

as Ingrid laid on an old mattress with them that smelled of cat piss.

She thought that it would be good camouflage as she slept in Steve's home,

and there wouldn't be any smells to be found by those in the night that did roam.

Before she drifted off she heard a scream in the night,

and knew someone else had fallen prey to a bite.

They all held each other close and so tight

to fight the night chill and wait for daylight.

Dawn came and BJ said, "Hey, wake up, you two!

I have to be leaving, I have work to do.

If you want to come with me, I'll get both of you a plate.

Now, get up, sleepy heads; I don't want to be late."

BJ, Ingrid and Steve got up and walked out of the alley towards Tony's place,

and they all arrived at Tony's restaurant at five thirty BJ had a smile on her face.

When BJ pulled on the door, it was still locked up tight.

BJ pounded on it and said, "I need coffee! It's been a long night!"

Tony came to the door and said, "Well, look at this! You're here, BJ.

I really had my doubts that you would even show up today."

BJ looked at him and said, "I'm a reliable person, Tony.

I hope you don't mind that I brought a couple of friends with me."

Tony said, "Hey, I can't feed all your friends from the street."

She said, "I'll pay out of my wages for what they have to eat."

Steve said, "BJ, I'd rather pay my own way,"

and that was the same thing Ingrid did say.

BJ said, "It's on me. I take care of my friends."

Tony said, "Come on, BJ, let's go begin."

They went to the office and BJ said, "If you still want to be able to fuck my face,

you'd better try to be a little nicer to the people I bring in your place.

Those blow jobs I give for the eight dollar meals that I eat,

I could get fifty bucks for, out on the street.

But the reason I give them to you instead, Tony,

is—from the first time we met—you've been nice to me.

Now that I work here, I want you to give me some space,

and I'll let you know when you can wave your cock in my face."

Tony said, "Yes, we shouldn't try to mix business with pleasure, BJ."

She said, "Thanks, I'm glad we can both see it my way."

Then said, "I need to use your private shower to clean up real quick.

I smell like something that came from a cats dick."

He said, "Yes you can right away my dear

I want the customers to meet you with cheer."

She jumped in the shower and used some sweet smelling shampoo,

Then got out and dried off then dressed and thought this will do.

She walked out to Ingrid and Steve and said, "May I take your order, kind sir and ma'am?"

They both said, "We'll have the omelets. Tony makes them so grand."

Tony overheard what they both had to say,

then actually felt good about giving them away.

BJ went back with their order and Tony said, "I already know."

This set BJ's heart aglow.

Tony said, "Not many people praise the way I cook,

and those two of your friends are on top of my book."

BJ smiled and said, "Thank you, Tony.

We might have to take our break a little early."

Tony had a big smile on his face as he made the food for the friends of BJ.

They ate it all up and said thanks to Tony, then said, "We'll be on our way."

BJ said, "Steve, stay with Katie and show her around town.

Make sure to hit the best places around."

As they went out the door some customers came in

and BJ gave a warm welcome to them.

Steve said, "Katie, where do you want to go to?"

She replied, "I have some job hunting to do.

But before I start I should probably go back to the shelter and take a bath."

Steve said, "I'm sorry. My cat was angry with me and took out his wrath.

It took me almost a year to get a mattress like that,

and now it's defiled from the piss of my cat."

Ingrid said, "Yeah, I know how cats can be,

and it's so hard to get rid of the smell of their pee."

Steve asked, "So, do you want me to walk you back home,

or would you like to go there alone?"

Ingrid said, "I'll go by myself. I'll be okay.

I hope you have a wonderful day."

Steve said, "I'll go back home and tell all my friends

to not give you a hard time if you come back again.

The alley can be a gauntlet at times to a stranger.

They're protective of it because of all of the danger."

"Danger, yes. Steve, that lady last night that brought me to you and BJ

was talking about the homeless and how some of them had been taken away.

She didn't really elaborate much about the things the homeless face."

Steve said, "Well, I'll tell you they're not of our race."

Once again Ingrid acted dumb and said, "Really, do tell me more."

He said, "It's the undead that brings each night much horror."

"Undead," Ingrid said, "you mean like mummies, zombies and such?"

He said, "No, here it's the Vampires that have the homeless in their clutch."

She said, "Vampires? Steve, Vampires aren't real. You're kidding me, right?"

He took off his jacket and shirt and said, "See those scars? I escaped one, one night."

Steve's back looked like it had been torn to a shed,

From the fangs and fingernails of the undead.

He put his things back on and said, "I'm lucky I got away.

The attack happened just at the break of a new day.

A few more minutes and I wouldn't be here,"

as she watched him shake and his eyes filled with tears.

He said, "I've been in war and saw terrible things,

but there's nothing worse than the fear that they bring.

Some are vicious and kill right away,

others act like a cat and mouse play."

Ingrid said, "Isn't there anything the homeless can do?"

Steve said, with tears in his eyes, "I wish we all knew."

Ingrid said, "If you're really convinced that the Vampires are real,

there's a list of things that can put an end to their deal.

But not everything works on them the same way,

as some of them evolve with every new day.

The only sure options are fire and sunlight,

or removing their head during a fight."

Steve said, "Katie, so why do you easily believe what I have told you?"

She said, "Well, Steve, the existence of Vampires is something I already knew.

I've been around a few in my lifetime

and let's say our meetings were less than divine.

I need to take that bath. Go back to your friends and tell them what we've discussed

about how to fight and kill Vampires and turn their bodies to dust."

She went in the shelter, and Steve went back home to the alley.

and started telling everyone about the words he had heard from Katie.

A person said, "What about crosses? Or holy water and a stake to their heart?"

Steve said, "I believe what Katie said are the best options to make one depart."

He said, "Instead of us laying in alleys waiting to die and swilling on alcohol,

we can throw it on a Vampire and ignite it then watch it burn up and fall."

Then someone said, "Yes! We need to make a stand

and not lay there and be slaughtered by their hand!"

Steve said, "Yes, and we should all begin to hunt them at night,

and we'll sleep like they do: in the daylight.

It's about time the tables were turned!"

And a cheer arose, it was, "Let the Vampires be burned!"

From alley to alley, they spread the word,

"Let the Vampires burn!" was the cheer that was heard.

All of the members of each alley's homeless cliques,

pooled their money together for flammables and found sticks.

The sticks were made into torches for the Vampires they sighted,

also insuring the flammables could be easily ignited.

As all this was happening, Ingrid was going place to place,

applying for jobs with a smile on her face.

Each and every place she went,

she tried to pick up the bloods scent.

of the one Vampire she had came there to defeat,

but the smell of Brimstone Coffee was all over the street.

"Sulfur," she said to herself many times, in total disgust,

"How will I find the Vampire I wish to make dust?"

She thought if this Vampire is anything like the one before,

"If I'm am patient, it will just knock on my door.

I'm sure when he hears of his Vampires burning and being beheaded in the night,

that he will come looking for the one that organized the homeless to fight.

There were some citizens that voiced their concern

about the homeless, wandering at night, with the torches they burned.

Most of the police precincts looked the other way,

because they knew of the game that they play.

There was only one precinct that shut the homeless down,

and Ingrid knew it was where her Vampire could be found.

It was the same one that had the shelter in which she stay.

She told the homeless there to move away.

So they went to other locations where the homeless wandered all night,

which left that part of the city where she stayed a place without any homeless to bite.

Then regular citizens started to disappear

which caused the city to have an outbreak of fear.

In many miles, or directions, the Vampires couldn't feed;

and from Ingrid's help and organization, the homeless were freed.

The longer this went on, it caused the Vampires to resort to home invasions,

now that feeding on those that wouldn't be missed were no longer in their equations.

Still, they made sure there were no bodies to be found,

but all the missing people caused a panic around.

Soon there wasn't anyone that would go out at night,

and shops and businesses locked their doors up tight.

One morning Ingrid went to Tony's place.

BJ ran up to her with the look of horror on her face.

She said, "Did you hear what happened to Steve?

It's still something I can't believe.

They said right there in the light of day,

a Vampire walked up to him and took his life away.

After it killed him, it shredded him into bits,

you couldn't tell where any of the pieces fit.

The Vampire said, as he walked away,

'I will kill many of you every day.

Until you send me the one that organized you,

each day I'll multiply what I can do.

Today it was one, tomorrow it will be ten,

the next day with twenty I will begin.

I'll be in the basement of the large building I own on Howard Street.

Send me the one that believes that she cannot be beat.'

BJ said, "They say before Steve took his last breath,

he yelled 'Forgive me, Katie' as he met his death.

So, it's you, Katie, that he's looking for."

She looked at BJ then stormed out the door.

She went to Howard Street and saw the building where she was to meet

and took a good look around at all the people walking the street.

Thinking to herself, "If I fall prey to this Pure Blood with our fight,

the freedom of people here will be no longer in sight,"

she gathered herself and went in the building and took the elevator down,

and when the door opened there were once again Vampires all around.

They stepped back and made her a walkway

leading straight to the table where the Pure Blood stay.

He said, "Welcome," as she walked nearer to him,

as he smiled with such a devilish grin.

He said, "Have a seat, Lady, or do you have a name?

I'd like to know who you are before we start our game."

She said, "You can call me 'Katie,'" with a look of fear in her eyes.

He said, "I know that name's a disguise."

She said, "What does it matter if you know my name?

You won't put it on a headstone after this game."

He let a laugh out and said, "Yes, you're right."

She said, "So what kind of game do you have in your sight?"

He opened the desk drawer where he sat and pulled out a gold goblet

and said, "This is something that you left with the last Pure Blood you met."

She said, "So, what, am I supposed to be afraid or surprised?"

He said, "Mockery from you is not very wise.

I've learned several things about you,

about your powers, and the things you can do.

I know your powers cannot work underground,

or you would have used them in the basement in the last town.

I also know that drinking your blood out of this goblet of gold

was what killed the last pure blood, so wise and so old."

He pulled out a knife from his desk drawer and said, "Give

me your wrist."

He cut a deep slash in it and she said, "Ouch," and tightened her fist.

Then he held the goblet below the cut to catch her blood and said, "I have something to show you."

He asked, "Remember that blood test at the homeless shelter they had you do?

Well, every day since then, I've drank a little drop out of this goblet you left,

so that drinking your blood couldn't send me to my death."

When the goblet was full, he drank it all down,

then all of the other Vampires cheered all around.

He held up the goblet and said, "Now that was a toast!

Everyone say 'thank you' to our gracious host."

He then slammed the goblet down on the table

and said, "Any more tricks, if you think you're able?"

She just sat there and hung her head.

He said, "Don't be sad, because soon you'll be dead."

He yelled out, "Well, all of my honored guests,

she was mighty tasty, I must confess!

I don't know if I want her blood all to myself or I want to share it with you?

She is the sweetest taste and most unusual flavor I've ever knew."

He looked at her and said, "Would you like to live?

I could keep you down here and have fresh blood that you give."

She was still bleeding, so he filled the goblet again

and said, "Here, pass it around, to all of his friends.

Everyone take a sip and see if you concur

that there is a wonderful taste to her."

As they all passed it around and took a sip, they yelled "Here! Here!"

and the room was filled with the outbreak of cheer.

Ingrid just sat there and didn't say a word,

and the elder said, "Don't you want to be heard?

I've gathered a large audience for when I make this example out of you,

as you sit here powerless and helpless without anything you can do."

He said, "So, do tell, what kind of witch are you, after all?"

She said, "Witchcraft truly isn't my call.

My powers come from a whole different place."

He said, "You look pretty docile now and have fallen from grace."

She said, "Fuck you, motherfucker," and spat in his face.

There's never been a part of me that had any grace.

He said, "Now, that was very rude of you, Katie, my dear,"

then slapped her in the face and grinned ear to ear.

"I thought for a moment you were going to play nice.

Toning yourself down would be my best advice."

She spat and this time she hit his chin,

then he reared back and slapped her again.

He said, "You don't learn very fast do you?"

She said, "I don't give a fuck what you do!

Kill me or eat me, I don't really care!"

then she gave him a long, deep stare.

He said, "Well, let's take a vote on what I shall do.

How many for killing? Let me hear you!"

Almost the whole crowd said, "Yes! Yes, kill the bitch!"

He said, "We could do both. I could kill you and we could all have a sandwich."

Then she said, "You're just wasting your breath,

I don't have any fears or concerns about death.

Are you going to just sit here and babble on in this game?

If you're going to kill me, why don't you tell me your name

so I can at least know who you were, before you condemned me to death,

since you have me here helpless and alone, awaiting my last breath?"

"Well, Yarden was my name, long ago,

if you really just have to know.

But, right now, I have a more prominent name.

My birth name wouldn't work very well in my game.

I've chosen something simple that works in this modern time.

I believed that 'Charles Ray Smith' seemed plain and fine.

Do you have any more things you want to know or say before we all dine?"

She reached her hand in her pocket and said, "Yes, if I have time..."

He said, "Okay, spit it out, then." She said, "I think you need to learn your place," and pulled her hand out of her pocket and threw cremated ashes in his face.

Fighting the blindness, he said, "That wasn't very wise."

She then said, "All of your kindred have ash in their eyes!"

He said, "This can't be! Your powers don't work below ground!"

Ingrid said, "Sorry, I brought something from the surface with me on my way down.

I grabbed some ashes from your old friend I killed in the last town.

It allowed me to have something unique from above ground."

Yarden yelled out, "Grab that bitch and tear her to shreds,"

as they all clawed madly around at each other's bodies and heads.

She simply walked to the elevator as they clawed at the air,

and yelled, "It's been lots of fun," as she pushed the button without a care.

She got to the first floor and walked outside on the street,

and licked her wound and said, "Yes, I do taste very sweet."

The gash closed in where the pure blood had cut her wrist,

and she reached in her pocket and took more ash in her fist

and let it fall to the ground and said, "Building, so grand:

made of concrete, steel, and sand.

I want you to vibrate, and I want you to shake,

until you come down and a grave you do make."

As she walked away, it shook the whole street,

and buried all the Vampires that she did meet.

In the paper the next day it said a sinkhole in town,

had caused the large building to come tumbling down.

Ingrid stayed around town for a few nights and days,

to make sure that BJ would be okay.

The homeless didn't find anymore Vampires at night.

Either they were all buried, or they had taken flight.

The day Ingrid left, she told Charlotte and BJ goodbye,

and felt so sad, she began to cry.

She decided that when she got home she'd send both of them money,

for Charlotte to help the homeless and BJ's life to be sunny.

Just as before, she got back and called home.

As she sat and waited, she planned her trip to Rome.

She also thought the last pure blood she buried under ground

wasn't the one of the smartest ones around.

When he passed her blood around in the goblet, he didn't think.

If it killed the first pure blood from taking a drink,

the rest hadn't drank her blood and built up a resistance like him,

then drinking her blood should have killed all of them.

The reason the first pure blood drank her blood and died

is he believed it would, so strong, deep inside.

She kind of giggled when she thought how powerful imaginations can be,

they can let you soar like an eagle or put you somewhere you'll never get free.

Ingrid sat and thought a while about what was to come from the other six,

from their powers and their bags full of tricks.

Softly then she drifted away in her chair,

floating back in time when she hadn't a care.

Just as she'd reached that long forgotten place,

she was awoke as someone stroked her face.

It startled her and she woke with a glare,

peering at the person standing near her chair.

"Remember me," the man asked with a smile on his face.

Ingrid replied, "No, I really don't. You seem out of place.

Refresh my memory, give me a clue,

just a hint or a reminder of you."

"Rose Ann, do I really have to do that?

How about a simple smile and a tip of my hat?"

Then Ingrid said, "Ethan! My God! How long has it been?"

He replied, "Many of days, nights, and many a sin."

"Oh, Ethan, you always did like to play with the fire,

fulfilling each and every desire.

So how did you recognize me after all of these years?

Was it my nose or my big floppy ears?"

Ethan looked at her and said, "It's a secret that I won't ever tell no matter how much you scream, beg, or yell.

This is something that has protected my life, time and again, and sorry, Rose Ann, I can't ever give in."

Ingrid said, "But, Ethan, you look just as you always have to me."

He replied, "Yes, that's what I want you to see.

If I was to draw a face on a paper and say it was me,

it would also be exactly what I want you to see."

Ingrid said, "Then you're a shape shifter! Am I right?"

He said, "There isn't any shape shifting, I manipulate one's sight.

I'm more like a chameleon that blends in with one's thoughts of what they want to see.

So in actuality, Rose Ann, there are many, many images to find of me.

Even a camera cannot escape my gift.

My powers allow the lenses to shift."

Ingrid asked, "So can you look like anyone to one person or many at one time?"

"Well that depends on what the one or the many have on their mind.

I do know that each and every time I change my face,

it seems to make days, weeks, months, and even years erase.

So, Rose Ann, do tell, what have you been up to?

With the red hair and green eyes, I see a new you."

"Well, Ethan, do you want the short or long story

about where I've been from my horrors to my glory?"

"Short will work, dear, I have a plane to catch.

I must go see Deirdre, that evil wretch."

"Deirdre, wow. I haven't heard her name in years.

How is she, by the way, my dear?"

He replied, "Stubborn as ever, and still icy and cold,

and still the black widow in search of treasures and gold.

She's been married thirty-seven times in this year alone,

with husband after husband sucked dry to the bone.

The ones she didn't kill with her sly and cunning way,

gave her everything they owned as they walked away.

Many of them committed suicide later down the road,

haunted by memories of all their treasures Deirdre now beholds."

"Wow," Ingrid said, "she hasn't changed at all, has she?"

Ethan replied, "Nope, that's how she'll always be.

Well, at least until she finds that one man

that actually loves her and foils her plan.

Then as she, like the those before, begins to fall,

he'll lead her to her destiny and take it all.

Anyway, back to you, Rose Ann. You were saying what you've been up to."

"You know, Ethan, I don't want to bore you with the things that I do.

How about a hug, and we'll be on our way?

There's not a lot I want to say."

"Okay, Rose Ann, take care. Maybe again at a later date.

I'll go catch my plane, I don't want to be late."

Ingrid gave Ethan a hug goodbye

and said, "Tell Deirdre I said 'Hi.'"

Ethan bent and kissed Ingrid's hand oh, so tenderly

then he pushed a needle in it that she didn't see.

Then he ran off to catch his plane,

leaving Ingrid with a sensation of pain.

From the crowd she heard, "We're over here,"

and she looked and saw Anna and Raphael near.

Anna ran up and gave Ingrid a hug and a kiss on the cheek,

then Ingrid said, "Oh, my, I feel so weak!"

Ingrid raised her hand to her face to see what Ethan had done,

She looked at Anna and said, "I feel sick let's run."

Anna caught her before she hit the floor

and Anna and Raphael helped her to the door.

They put her in the car's back seat and laid her down,

then started the car and headed out of town.

All the way home Anna Marie

kept saying, "Mother, please talk to me."

When they got home, they took her to her bedroom and laid her on her bed.

Anna took off her street clothes and put pillows under her head.

She went to the sink and got a wet, cold washcloth for her forehead,

hopefully to revive her as she lay on her bed.

Anna put the washcloth on her forehead without any success

and decided leaving her alone would probably be best.

Just as Anna went out, closing the door to her mother's room of mirrors,

she heard her mother scream out and cry in a voice filled with tears.

Anna tried to open the door but it was locked from within.

She really began to worry as the screams began again.

She called to Raphael and he came running to Ingrid's door.

She said to him, "Mother's screaming like she's trapped in a deadly horror."

He said, "Let's gather our senses and choose the best way to act.

If we just go rushing in we don't know how she'll react.

Lets re-think the events from the airport up till now,

and hopefully we will find a clue some way, or some how."

Anna said, "Well, there was that man..."

Raphael said, "The one that kissed her hand?"

Anna replied, "The one that ran off for his plane."

Raphael thought to himself, "He's the one that brought on her pain?"

Then he thought a bit and looked at Anna Marie,

He said, "It had to be something she didn't see.

Sorceresses and sorcerers can shield themselves from almost any danger,

but sometimes their trust can leave them endangered.

That man could have drugged her, Anna Marie,

with a poison in tiny drops you almost can't see.

She must have known him to allow him so near,

because she didn't act like she had any fear.

What hand was it that he kissed?"

She said, "The one with the bracelet on her wrist."

Raphael said, "Okay, we'll have to go in her room not
knowing what we have to fight.

Now's the time for you to use your powers with all of your
might.

We can't break down her door and shatter her mirrors,

Or it might just intensify her delusions or fears.

So, Anna, this is the time for you to shine,

open your heart and control your mind.

Let your love for your mother guide you and your power,

for now you have entered a most crucial hour.

If Ingrid goes too far in this delusional stage,

it's hard to think of what she could do with her rage.

So, Anna, my dear, I believe you can handle this mess.

Now open her door so we can find out what to do best."

As Anna's heart continued to sink,

all she could say was, "Let me think."

She looked at Raphael and said, "Okay, I guess it's time
for my test.

Give me a hug and wish me the best."

Raphael wrapped his arms around Anna Marie

and then she was nowhere for him to see.

Anna had teleported herself in to her mother's domain

and found her mother lying on the floor, screaming in pain.

She was crying and digging her nails in her wrist,

trying to pump out mercury when she made a fist.

"Never," she exclaimed. "Never again

will I let my guard down, even to a friend!"

Slowly the pain started to subside,

as her blood flowed from inside.

Anna said, "Mother, you're losing a lot of blood!

It looks like the carpet was hit by a red flood!"

Ingrid said, "I'll be okay. Don't worry about me,

all of the quicksilver must go so I can be free."

Then, in a few minutes, Ingrid said, "There, that's enough.

My body has cleansed itself from all of that stuff."

Then she started running her fingers around,

touching each drop of mercury that could be found,

pushing each little drop into another

until she had one huge ball to discover.

Then she scooped it up in her hand,

and put it in her mouth with a look so grand.

Then, in one big gulp, she swallowed it down

and said, "I feel better now, let's go to town."

Anna said, "But, Mother, the mercury..."

Ingrid said, "Don't worry, I've set myself free.

Everything that I willfully ingest builds up an immunity in me.

You wouldn't believe the list of things from which I have set myself free:

free from poison, free from death,

free from taking that horrid last breath..."

Anna looked at her mother with a curious face

and said, "So when do I pick up your pace?

When can I drink poisons down

without any effects to be found?"

Ingrid put her hands to Anna's lips and said, "Patience, my child.

Don't get consumed and let your desires run wild.

Darling, back when I gave birth to you,

you were born with my defenses and all I can do.

Just take a look at you now.

You have entered my locked room somehow.

It wasn't just your powers that let you in here,

it was a combination of them and you loving me, dear.

True love is the most powerful spell on Earth.

It can take you to heaven or strip you from all that you're worth.

Speaking of love, let's get out of here.

I need a man to hold me so near."

Ingrid snapped her fingers which made a mirror panel move.

Then she said, "Let's go get on with the groove."

When they walked out of the bedroom, Anna had a sensation so strong that she yelled at the top of her lungs, "Mother! Mother! Something is wrong!"

They looked and saw muddy foot tracks all over the floor,

all of them originating at their front door.

They went into the library with none coming out.

Anna Marie got worried and, "Raphael," she did shout.

"In here," a weak voice responded to Anna's yell,

then there were many voices yelling louder than hell.

Ingrid and Anna walked up to the library doors.

Ingrid willed them open and they saw many horrors.

There were disfigured bodies and faces, too, all over the place,

as Raphael hung upside down from a rope with tears on his face.

Ingrid yelled to Raphael, "Is this what you did do?

No wonder you have so much pain inside of you."

It seemed each of his minions was tore or ripped terribly,

and left to be immortal with these injuries to see.

So, not only were they cursed with a thirst inside,

they were disfigured in ways they could never hide.

Now that Raphael was human and had no powers over them,

they have come to get vengeance and to destroy him.

Ingrid was now in a terrible place,

wondering who and if she should erase.

"Raphael, how could you have done such terrible deeds

and left these souls with curses from which they could

never be freed?"

Raphael yelled, "I'm sorry, so sorry, for what I have done!

When I was first bitten I should have faced the sun.

But I was a prisoner of pleasure and pain,

and my captor tormented my brain.

Natasha was such a tyrant and a terrible bitch

that controlled my thoughts like flipping a switch.

I've seen her do things to people before

that makes all I've done not seem like a horror."

Ingrid said, "Well, Raphael I'll take care of your mess,

but it will leave lots of clean-up, I must confess."

Ingrid threw out her arms and then drew them in

and forced her hands together and a light did begin.

Anna said, "That's brighter than anything I've seen before,"

and when Ingrid opened her hands, all the Vampires were ash on the floor.

Raphael said, "I have to thank you, I must confess."

Ingrid cut him down and said, "Clean up this mess.

Anna and I are going to town,

I want to see if there's any fun to be found."

Anna thought to herself, "Oh, no, here we go again..."

Ingrid was on the hunt for a man that can't win,

someone that she could drain to the last drop,

someone that would cry, "Please, please, stop!"

At times sexual pleasure can be such a painful thing,

when all of your nerves quiver with the sensation it brings.

Anna said, "Mother, can I just stay here and help Raphael clean?

I'm not very fond of the whole party scene."

"Sure, if you wish, Anna Marie.

I can go to town much more quickly."

In a blink of an eye Ingrid was in town,

looking for the right prey to be found.

Over the centuries she had belittled many men

whose only pride was in their organ.

From paupers to kings to soldiers or slaves,

she had screwed so many close to their graves.

Many times as her thighs were clad on a man,

she always completed her delicious plan.

Leaving most of them with an empty slate

about what had happened on their date.

But she would walk away with her clit a-throbbing

from all of the sex and the dick she'd been bobbing.

Ingrid wasn't what you'd call a nymph or a slut,

but when it did come to sex, she knew how to strut.

She would always dress in the best clothes

with her cleavage where it always shows.

She would lure men in for her attack

and it wasn't long and she was flat on her back.

At times she'd be wild and grab the man's ass cheeks and pull him in deep,

other times she would lay there so silent and meek.

No matter how the affair went, or by which name,

Ingrid was always on top of her game.

She teleported herself from home to a bar called The Place to Roam in a nearby city.

She walked in and instantly a man says, "Hell, don't you look pretty?"

She sat down with him and said, "Cowboy, what's on your mind?"

He answered, "I'm looking for the right woman to find,"

then said, "I thought you might want to sit a spell."

Ingrid looked at him and said, "Do tell."

She said, "Did you come here just for luck

or for a woman that's ready to fuck?"

He said, "Lady, you cut right to the chase."

She said, "That's why I came in this place."

She scooted close to him and put her hand on his cock.

He gave her a look and said, "You really rock."

She said, "Let's get out of this place and go have some fun."

He took her to his car and away they did run.

All the while he was driving, Ingrid's hands were all over him.

He was struck speechless but showed a huge grin.

He took her to his home but, when he opened the door,

the interior of the room filled him with horror.

Ingrid gave him a big kiss and said, "Welcome to my place, let's sit a spell."

The guy was confused and started to yell.

Anna and Raphael left the library and came out,

wanting to find out who'd made the shout.

Ingrid said, "Hey kids, I'm back for a bit.

I believe this one will be the perfect fit."

They walked out of her room and met Raphael and Anna Marie.

Ingrid said, "I've caught a live one for me.

Introduce yourself to my daughter and her friend."

Having cottonmouth from fear he uttered, "I'm Ben."

"Okay, Ben, it's nice to meet you.

Raphael and I have things we must do."

"Ingrid," said Anna, "be kind to my new friend."

Anna said, "Wow you're in for some shit Ben!"

Ben started to say, "Where am I," and Ingrid kissed his lips.

Then she took both of his hands and placed them on her hips.

"Where?" "Isn't anything that you should have any concern.

Why is the question that makes my loins burn.

Now let's retire to my warm bed,

is there anything else that needs to be said?"

Ben thought to himself, "What the hell have I got myself into?"

Ingrid said, "A sexual arena and anything I wish from you.

You can treat me rough, or treat me nice,

you can show compassion, or be cold as ice.

But no matter how you feel to treat me to suit your need,

I'm going to drain you over and over from most of your seed."

Ingrid took Ben's hand and they walked to her room.

Ben was sort of feeling sensations of doom.

Ingrid closed the door as they went back in.

Now Ingrid was sporting a really big grin.

She closed the door and now the room full of mirrors

started making Ben nervous and giving him fears.

Ingrid undressed then said, "Don't be nervous. This isn't a test."

Then she walked over and put his trembling hands on her breasts.

She slowly bent over and kissed Ben on the lips

and undid his belt and his pants fell past his hips.

She grabbed and fondled his cock through his underwear.

Now his look of fear became an intense glare.

Ingrid continued to kiss his lips and his neck gently,

and with every kiss there was a bigger erection to see.

Ben was now so hard he was in excruciating pain

and Ingrid said, "Would you like me to relieve your throbbing membrane?"

"Please, please," Ben said, "Can you relieve my hard cock?"

Ingrid pushed him to the floor and mounted him then started to rock.

"Mm," she said, "your swelling is so grand and sweet.

You're just the man I needed to meet."

Faster and faster she rocked on his cock,

loving it because he was as hard as a rock.

Ben said, "Didn't you say you'd relieve the pain?

The harder you fuck me, the more it remains."

Ingrid said, "Don't be a pussy.

I'm not letting you explode until you've pleased me.

Sex is my therapy, it removes all my pain,

but I don't let just anyone into my game.

Now Ben, start pumping and moving your ass,

or you'll never get out from behind my glass."

Ingrid had already rocked on Ben so fast

that he had rug burns covering his ass.

Now his pain was even more severe,

with his extruded cock and burning rear.

Ben looked at her and said, "I thought you said I could call the shots...

is that something that you have forgot?"

"No, honey, you can do with me what you wish,

after the first time you explode in my dish."

Ingrid looked him in the eyes and gave him a big grin

and said, "Hey, do you want to sit a spell, my friend?

I guess if you survive the night there will be a lesson to see,

especially after hitting on a woman like me."

"A woman," Ben said, "aren't you a witch?"

"No, I'm a sorceress, but many call me a bitch.

Now lets get back to the climax, my friend

and start stuffing your cock all the way in."

Most of his life, Ben had charmed many ladies and left them in pain,

now all of their torture was in his own membrane.

Ingrid always knew who to choose for her game

and would leave some with anguish they'd never tame.

Ben was just getting the first taste of Ingrid's powers

which would become more painful over the hours.

She tortured him to the point that he wanted more and more.

It's funny when your pains can become pleasure galore.

When Ingrid had enough she took him back to his place and they went inside the door,

then she wiped his memory and left him lying on the floor.

She thought just before she teleported herself back home

how Ben would awake with the worst pains he'd known.

The pain will be certainly be between his thighs

and, when it comes to future sex, he'll be a little gun shy.

Ingrid hadn't had enough to fill her desire for the night.

So, she closed her eyes and, once again, took flight.

She teleported to the slums next to a barrel full of fire,

hoping that her sexual needs could once again transpire.

She stood a while and a woman let out a scream

so she ran over to evaluate the scene.

There was a prostitute being abused by a man.

Ingrid walked up and grabbed his hand,

then said, "Why don't you try slapping me,"

but her grip was so strong he couldn't get free.

He cussed her by calling her a "stupid cunt."

She replied with, "That was a dreadful stunt."

Then she broke his hand and his wrist

and said, "You're lucky that I'm not that pissed.

Honey, does this man owe you any cash?"

She said, "No," and he was gone in a flash.

"Wow," the prostitute exclaimed. "How'd you do that?"

Ingrid said, "It's a secret," and down she sat.

The prostitute said, "I'd love to be able to do what you can,

then I won't have to get hurt by another man."

Ingrid said, "You don't need spells to set yourself free.

You just need to change your life, don't you see?"

The prostitute said, "I can't, I have to work for the man."

Ingrid said, "No, you don't," as she took her hand.

"Yes, I do, or he'll beat or kill me."

Ingrid said, "Maybe I can help set you free."

They walked to the road under a streetlight

and Ingrid waited for the pimp she wanted to fight.

Ingrid said, "What's your name," to her new found friend.

She replied, "Gwendolyn, but my friends call me Gwen."

"Gwen it is," Then, "My name is Ingrid,"

as she smiled at Gwen and winked her eyelid.

"So, tell me about your pimp, these things are new to me.

And I don't like the fact you have to sell yourself in

slavery."

Gwen said, "I met Rollo when I was about sixteen years old and had ran away from my step-dad.

I was down on my luck and feeling so sad.

He had a nice car and a beautiful home,

and said, 'Dear come with me, you're too young to roam.

These alleys and streets aren't a safe place to be,

you can stay with me at my place and feel free.'

I got in his car with a smile on my face,

little did I know it would end in disgrace.

At first he was kind and took great care of me,

but then it all changed and I couldn't get free."

Ingrid said, "Changed? How do you mean?"

She replied, "It all started when we did the drug scene.

He got me hooked on so many drugs my life was a bad dream,

that if I didn't have a fix, all I could do was scream.

I thought my step-father had been cruel and I was so abused

but, until I met this pimp, was I truly misused.

He'd put on a porn tape and get me high,'

as I sat on his lap he groped my breasts to my thighs.

Then, when it was over with a loud shout,

he said, 'My little honey, now let's act it all out.'

He made me do everything we had saw in the movie

as he moaned and groaned and looked down at me."

Ingrid said, "That bastard! He sounds like someone that

needs a lesson,

especially, Gwen, after hearing your confession."

She took Gwen's hand and said, "Come unto me,"

and out of Gwen's veins came every drug she did see.

It poured off of her skin like droplets of sweat

and all of her pains she did soon forget.

Now that Gwen had been cleansed, there was only one thing left:

to punish the man that had taken her innocence with abusive theft.

They heard a horn honk and Gwen said, "Oh, no, that's him!"

The thought of this ensuing battle made Ingrid grin.

Rollo pulled up under the streetlight and said, "What do we have here?"

as he looked at Ingrid and said, "Hello there, my dear!"

He said, "So, my beauty, are you looking for a good time?"

Ingrid replied, "That's exactly what I had in mind!"

He looked at Gwen and said, "Aren't you supposed to be fucking someone?"

Ingrid said, "She goes where I go, two will be much more fun."

Rollo chuckled and said, "I've had her so many times, she means nothing to me."

Ingrid said, "She goes where I go, or there won't be a party to see."

Rollo got out of his car and said, "If it has to be this way,

let's hit the road so we can all play."

Ingrid saw that Rollo was a huge man, over six hundred pounds.

He wasn't real tall but, boy, he was round.

He waddled to the passenger door and opened it and said, "Get in.

You're in the front and the back seat's for Gwen."

The ladies got in the car and he headed towards his home.

As sexy as Ingrid looked, all his mind did was roam.

Ingrid saw every perverted thought in his mind

as she sat back and bided her time.

It was a long ride to Rollo's home which gave Ingrid a long time to think up her plan

that she would impose on this poor excuse of a man.

He got to his home and got out of the car.

He was out of breath walking to the door which wasn't that far.

They all went inside to his living room where he did all his sexual perversions.

Ingrid thought to herself, "He's going to see some conversions."

He offered them a drink and a handful of pills.

The ladies both said, "I don't believe I will."

He said, "Let's put in a movie to set the mood for us,"

as his small penis began to rise and he filled with lust.

Ingrid said, "Sure, you just sit in your chair and I'll pick a flick."

Her words put another sensation to his little dick.

He sat back and took a swig of whiskey

and waited to watch what Ingrid picked to see.

She opened her purse and pulled out a DVD

and said, "This is one you never did see."

She popped it in the player and sat in her chair,

as Rollo did watch with demented glare.

It began with a prison and you could see the inmates.

There was a huge fat man on his knees that they'd all started to mate.

There were men in his rear and his mouth, time after time,

as he let out sounds that almost sounded divine.

Rollo said, "Wait, where the hell are the bitches?"

Ingrid said, "Sorry, I have made some switches."

Rollo tried to stand but he couldn't move an inch at all.

Ingrid said to him, "Enjoy the film, or it will be curtain call."

Rollo was confused and tried again and again to get free.

Ingrid said, "Quit struggling, you have a movie to see."

Rollo wanted another drink but he couldn't move his arm to have one.

Gwen spouted out, "Ingrid, I think I'm having fun."

Ingrid said, "Popcorn, that's what we need with such a good movie to see,"

as Rollo struggled even harder to get himself free.

Ingrid held out her hand and a bowl of popcorn did appear.

She looked at Gwen and said, "Would you like some dear?"

Gwen said, "Wow, you can really do things magically,"

as Rollo sat and couldn't believe what he did see.

Ingrid sat at Rollo's side and said, "Have some, my dear,"

as she put a handful of popcorn to his mouth, quite near.

Rollo took a big bite and chewed and then spit it in Ingrid's face.

Ingrid wiped it off and said, "I need to teach you your place."

Instantly, Rollo's chest began to beat fast and pound

and, in the room, his heart beat began to resound.

He felt like he had an avalanche in his rib cage,

growing more and more from Ingrid's rage.

He let out a scream and said, "I'm having a heart attack."

Ingrid said, "Don't worry. If you die, I'll bring you back."

"Bring me back," he uttered with a low voice.

Ingrid said, "Your death isn't my choice.

Your death will be an award earned, all by yourself,

from prostituting women for your gain and wealth.

Now, I'll stop the pain if you promise to be good and watch the movie.

There are so many great scenes to see."

He said, "I'll do anything to get rid of this pain!"

Ingrid said, "Be gone," and the sensation did drain.

"Now, let's get back to the movie, there's so many good parts to come."

She looked at Gwen and said, "Dear, are you having fun?"

Gwen said, "Oh, yes, the best time in years,"

as Rollo's eyes began to flow with tears.

Ingrid said, "Oh, does the baby need a hanky?

How does it feel to not be able to get free?"

She looked at Gwen and said, "Go slap him, or spit in his face.

Or castrate him with a dull knife to show him his place."

Gwen said, "You know, after all he has done to me,

having him helpless is all I need to see."

"Okay then, let's watch the movie; some more the best parts are coming soon.

I know there's a part that will make your heart swoon."

They went back watching the fat man in prison getting raped again and again,

worse than any man has ever got fucked in the pen.

All you could see of him was his big white pimply ass from behind,

but there was never a face that you could find.

In one scene a man stabs him over and over with a shiv,

that's the part where the fat man no longer did live.

Rollo said, "Hey, bitch, what's the point of this show?"

Ingrid said, "You bastard, watch and soon you'll know."

The movie showed the man face down on the floor, dead as could be.

Then they came and carried him off to take him to the mortuary.

The scene was cut to a crematory furnace with a wide open door,

as the mortician paced back and forth on the floor.

You could see the fat man lying on his side on a gurney.

Still, there wasn't any face that you could see.

The mortician spoke out loud to himself, "Oh, not again,"

then said, "where, oh, where will I begin?"

He walked to the wall and took down a big saw,

then Ingrid saw Rollo's eyes get wide as he dropped his jaw.

Now Rollo's mind was glued to the movie because the plot had began to grow.

The mortician said, "They made these old crematories so damn small years ago.

Buddy, there's only one way to get your fat ass in this thing."

He rolled the body over in the movie and began to sing.

Now Rollo was transfixed on the movie Ingrid played.

Then Rollo closed his eyes and silently prayed.

Because he saw his own face when the body was turned,

he was the man on the slab being chunked up to be burned.

He screamed out, "No! No, that cannot be!

That cannot be the end of me!

I have lawyers and judges that get many delights

from any of my whores that walk in the night!"

Ingrid said, "I'm sorry, you fat, ugly prick,

but those women will never see another unwanted dick.

They can all now live a life that's free from you

and walk with peace and pride until their life is through.

The money and things you amassed will be split up among them evenly,

and prison will be the last home that you'll ever see.

I hope you liked the movie, because you now know what you're in for."

With that, her and Gwen walked out the front door.

A few moments later, Rollo was able to stand

and he started plotting a revengeful plan.

He didn't believe he would end up like in that movie,

as he wondered what trickery he just did see.

A few moments later, there was a knock at his door.

He opened it up and his heart filled with horror.

There was a police officer standing in front of him

that said, "I have a warrant," with a big grin.

Rollo said, "Do you know? Do you know who I am?"

He said, "Yeah: a fat piece of shit that the law's gonna slam."

He handcuffed him and took him to a van outside,

put him in the back, and said, "Enjoy the ride."

After they booked him into the jail,

it was the first day of his oncoming hell.

He was tried and convicted then sent to the pen.

The very first day the rapes did begin.

Now the only thoughts his mind could see

was how he ended in the movie.

Walking each day, waiting to be slain,

as his blood went down a sewer drain.

After Ingrid and Gwen had left his place,

they both walked away with smiles on their face.

Ingrid said to Gwen, "You and your friends have a new life to live,

and you'll never remember all the pains your last lives did give.

Take care of yourself, Gwen. I must be on my way.

I have many things I must attend to today."

They gave each other a hug and Gwen said, "Will I see you again?"

Ingrid said, "Just close your eyes and whisper my name to the wind."

In a flash, Ingrid was back in her home with Raphael and Anna Marie.

They both said, "You're back home, we see."

She said, "Yes, I figured I'd give you time to clean up that mess in the library.

Shall we go see if it's clean enough for me?"

They walked inside and it looked nice and clean.

Ingrid said, "There's something wrong with this scene."

She reached up and took a book down from the bookcase,

then Anna Marie had a sad look on her face.

They had forgotten to take all the books down and dust them,

so their clean up would have to start all again.

Anna said, "I'll just use my powers to clean all the books."

Ingrid just smiled and gave her a look.

Anna closed her eyes and said, "All dust be gone," with all her might,

yet it was still on every book in her sight.

Ingrid said, "That was a nice try. Maybe I'll give it a spin."

Then she said, "All remains be gone and join the wind."

The books were clean and Anna Marie asked, "Why didn't it work for me?"

Ingrid said, "It wasn't dust, you see.

There's a thing in the Bible that says ashes to ashes and dust to dust. It's true.

But you have to know the difference between these two.

Dust comes from rocks and dirt and things that are only alive with energy.

Ashes come from plants, trees and bushes, animals and other living things that have burned, you see.

But, with the combination of these two,

life can always start anew,

lending new life to many of things.

Oh, it's so beautiful how nature sings.

Anyway, Raphael and Anna Marie,

this has been a long day for me.

Now, to my room, I will retire

and see what dreams will transpire.

Dearly I love some of the dreams I see.

They release some of the pain trapped in me."

"Pain," Anna said, "whatever do you mean?

I would think, with all your power, your life is serene."

Ingrid replied, "No, it's so far from that, sometimes I just want to scream

or wish for my life to be over and be released from this scene.

I know sometimes you look at me like I'm a whore,

but it puts life into me and temporarily heals my core.

For way down deep inside of me

is a passion that runs so free.

It's only reserved for my first date

with the only male being I've seen as great.

Because of a battle between the Devil, and him,

he's trapped in the underworld so deep within.

Yet I have plans to turn the tables

after I kill the ones that many call fables."

"Fables," Anna Marie asked, "what do you mean?"

Ingrid replied, "I must kill those that are unclean.

I guess it's time that you should know

where and what I do when I go.

Raphael told me of nine Vampires that the devil created,

and their demise is now the only thing I have slated.

Yeah I'll take a few minutes now and then

to sooth the urge that comes from within.

But for now the last living six Vampires?

Their death fills me with so many desires,

desires to conquer their evil seed,

the desires to annihilate the Devil's breed.

Well, it's late and if you have any other questions,

Raphael will be full of the right suggestions.

For me, before Raphael told me of the origin of the
Vampire Race,

I lived my life and let them have their place.

But when I found out Lucifer was the breed's creation,

to kill them all became my affirmation."

"But, Mother, don't you feel any fear from these Vampires?"

"Yes, I do, now and then, when I test the hour.

They've been around for such a long time,

they have a multitude of powers and brilliant minds.

But I have my share of tricks up my sleeve,

I can do more than lie and deceive.

These traits were inherited from the King of Hell

along with their secret powers that no one will tell.

It seems that each of the Vampires I've already met,

their minds seemed to be part of the same net.

So every time I must face one again,

I must have a new plan for each of them.

Just to let you know, if I don't succeed,

the earth will be covered with evil seed.

The churches will become more corrupt than they are already,

and an army of Vampires and demons will cut into man's souls like a machete,

leaving them to wander as food without any will,

falling prey to the unclean as an easy kill."

"Mother, it seems you have so much on your plate,

having to conquer and kill for humanity's fate.

Are you sure this task isn't too much for you?"

Ingrid said, "I'll just have to be careful what I do."

Anna said, "Can't Raphael and I lend you a hand?"

Ingrid said, "No, you can't match those whose powers are so grand.

Seriously, I've been trying to think of a safe place for you to be,

where you and Raphael will be content and live free.

The trouble is that these Vampires have had their hands in everything,

from the poorest ditch digger to politicians and kings.

They have so many networks and connections everywhere,

there's no place that their prying eyes and minds do not stare.

Credit cards, computers, and cameras all over the place,

ever since their introduction they have watched the human race.

Seriously I don't know why they haven't all banded together and rang my door bell,

unless their marching orders come straight from Hell.

I know the Devil has been watching me since when we first met,

but the day I bowed before him I'll never forget.

To him it was submission, like I had fell on my own sword,

but for me I was bowing for my lover who is my only one lord."

"Mother, if you love the King of the Underworld so true,

why do you let other men touch you?"

Ingrid said, "Touch, isn't that a wonderful sensation?

It can bring tears to your eyes or cause jubilation.

But, seriously, the body and it's stimulation's

can be separated from loving sensations.

Love, love, so many spout it off their lips,

and thinks it's only felt below the hips.

But seriously, if you look at the word L.O.V.E, you'll see

it stands for Luscious Omnipresent Vibrational Energy."

Anna said, "I'll have to think on that one a while."

Ingrid just replied with a big smile.

Then she said, "Okay, I have a date with my bed,

and the soft pillows where I lay my head.

Goodnight both of you. I'll see you when I wake,

and then I'll start planning for the next trip I take."

Anna said, "So, this time, will you clue us in?"

Ingrid replied, "You'd be safer if I vanished like the wind.

I'll return the vines and do other things to protect you."

Anna said, "Yes without the vines, all those Vampires got through?"

"Oh, my dear, I guess you didn't understand.

Getting them all in one place was my master plan."

Anna said, "So, you used Raphael as bait for them..."

She just winked and gave Anna a grin.

Raphael said, "You're just full of surprises."

Ingrid said, "I'm even better at my disguises."

She chuckled and said, "Would you like to play hide-and-seek sometime," with a sparkle in her eyes that looked so sublime.

"Goodnight, you two.

When I'm awake, I'll call you

and we'll take a quick trip into town

to see if any good breakfast cuisine can be found.

After that we'll all return home,

and I'll start planning my trip to Rome."

Anna said, "Rome? I always wanted to go to that place."

Raphael looked at her with a smile on his face.

He said, "Ingrid, go ahead and get your sleep in,

and I'll tell Anna all about places in Rome I have been."

They bid her goodnight and Raphael took Anna by the hand,

and led her into the living room, then he played the piano, so grand.

Once again, Anna felt a loving sensation,

and started dancing without hesitation.

She said, "I thought you were going to tell me about Rome?"

as his piano playing echoed in her home.

"Anna, let's save it for another time,

just keep dancing and try to unwind."

"Okay, I can't argue with you. Your music's so sweet,

it's like it's connected to my heart and my feet.

The best part of you playing for me now is it's free,

you don't have any alternative motives for me."

After a few more tunes Anna walked over and gave

Raphael a kiss.

He said, "That is truly something I've missed:

someone that shows emotion to me,

and because it was meant to be."

He stood and grabbed Anna around the waist

and their tongues met for the first taste.

They kissed repeatedly as they walked towards Anna's room,

where she had laid alone so many nights filled with gloom.

Gently she pulled him down to her bed.

They made passionate love without a word said.

Every movement, twist, and turn,

inside Anna's heart, the sensations did burn.

Then they collapsed after they were both spent,

and in each other's arms into the dreamland they went.

*　　　　　*　　　　　*

Made in the USA
San Bernardino, CA
12 May 2014